stained glass

FROM ITS ORIGINS TO THE PRESENT

stained glass

FROM ITS ORIGINS TO THE PRESENT

VIRGINIA CHIEFFO RAGUIN

WITH A CONTRIBUTION FROM MARY CLERKIN HIGGINS

Harry N. Abrams, Inc. Publishers

A QUINTET BOOK

Published in 2003 by Harry N. Abrams, Incorporated, New York. All rights
reserved. No part of the contents of this book may be reproduced without
written permission of the publisher.

Library of Congress Cataloging-in-Publication Data
Raguin, Virginia Chieffo, 1941-
Stained Glass : from its origins to the present / by Virginia Chieffo
Raguin
p.cm
Includes bibliographical references and index.
ISBN 0-8109-4644-0 (hc)
1. Glass painting and staining--History. I. Title

NK5306.R34 2003
748.5'028'2--dc21
2003005905

This book was conceived, designed, and produced by
Quintet Publishing
6 Blundell Street
London N7 7BH

Project Editor: Anna Kiernan
Project Manager: Corinne Masciocchi
Picture Researcher: Mirco de Cet
Designer: Ian Hunt
Creative Director: Richard Dewing
Publisher: Oliver Salzmann

Manufactured in Singapore by Pica Digital PTE Ltd
Printed and bound in China by Leefung-Asco Printers Ltd

10 9 8 7 6 5 4 3 2 1

Harry N. Abrams, Inc.
100 Fifth Avenue
New York, N.Y. 10011
www.abramsbooks.com

Abrams is a subsidiary of

FRONTISPIECE Charles Booth was a London artist working in the
United States. Known for brilliant aesthetic style designs, he also
produced highly traditional imagery, exemplified by an apostle,
about 1880, for Christ Church, Philadelphia, Pennsylvania.

Contents

111329

Introduction

Buildings are the places where the majority of us live out our lives. They also function as sites of significant public ritual, whether school, courthouse, or site of worship. All need illumination, most desirably, from our experience, natural light. The art of

RIGHT *A view of into the first bay of the north transept of the cathedral of Auxerre, constructed circa 1280, reveals the inextricable union between design in glass and in stone. Architecture and glass developed mutually, responding to change in social needs and aesthetic taste at the same pace.*

OPPOSITE *Nathaniel Hubert John Westlake wrote a seminal four-volume work,* A History of Design in Stained and Painted Glass, *1881–94, that deeply influenced both scholars and practitioners in the field. His own work as a designer with Lavers, Barraud & Westlake is represented by* The Advent of Beatrice, *1864, from Dante's* Purgatorio *now in the Victoria and Albert Museum, London.*

stained glass responds to these human needs, for it creates architectural planes that permit illumination while transforming the experience of general light to one specific and meaningful to the purpose of a building.

During the Middle Ages stained glass was associated with the massive building programs of the Church. Complex pictorial ensembles carried messages about the history of salvation and also medieval society, especially its powerful leaders. The Renaissance continued—even augmented— the cycles of windows with walls of glass that look like translucent tapestries. At the same time, on a much smaller scale, panels showing subjects of family and local interest, and roundels—drawings on a single glass sheet—brought glass into a more intimate setting with highly personalized imagery. With the Reformation and the antipathy for imagery in northern Europe and England, and with the development of the architectural style of the Baroque, stained glass no longer played a major role in architectural planning. All of this changed in the nineteenth century when the revival styles

of Gothic and Romanesque burst on the scene, with their vehement supporters dedicated to making the pictorial window once again a vital element of building.

The study of these extraordinary ensembles presents a challenge. The international organization of the Corpus Vitrearum now includes over a dozen countries dedicated to the systematic identification, evaluation, and publication of the medium of stained glass. So far, sixty-eight volumes studying specific sites have been published. I am deeply indebted to these generous colleagues, whose studies of glass of the past thousand years appear on every page of this work. The Corpus Vitrearum is also committed to developing and promulgating ethical restoration of historic buildings. This commitment reaches back through time, to the passionate William Morris and his equal love of the creative contemporary image and the context of the historic monument. By sponsoring biannual symposia that bring both historical and technical expertise to bear on the study of Medieval and Renaissance windows, the Corpus Vitrearum encourages creative exchange.

Since the beginning of the twentieth century, new directions have emerged. The patronage of art has become more secularized and the individual artist now assumes a larger role in the creation of style. Artists who had worked in other media began to work in glass. Artists working with window design are also creating architectural sculpture, bringing the material into three dimensions. Viewers are confronted with these new installations of glass in multiple public venues, sports centers, government buildings, corporate headquarters, and also in private homes. The geographic area of architectural glass has spread to become global, with windows for mosques in Saudi Arabia, shopping malls in Rio de Janeiro, and sports centers in Tokyo. The new processes developed within the last generation allow almost limitless exploration of the nature, especially the translucency, of the material. In hospital waiting room, town hall, or health club, we find kiln-formed, dichroic, laminated, and traditional leaded glass. Silkscreen, photographic transfer; painting with enamel colors, sandblasting, etching, and engraving, as well as the traditional vitreous enamel, produce images of every conceivable variety.

The very pace of architectural construction with these startling new innovations has encouraged reflection on the consequence of growth. With society's apparently limitless capacity to build up, comes an equally swift tendency to tear down. The experience of these changes in the built environment has engendered an awareness of the fragility of cultural heritage. Government-supported preservation organizations are now part of all European countries. Most individuals are loath to grant to any one individual (or even a corporate entity) the authority to judge for others which elements of our past may continue. Just as scientists monitor phenomena like global warming and air pollution from an independent standpoint, art historians labor to achieve a comprehensive and balanced overview of the past. The rarity of a specific style, the historic importance of a site, and the level of the artistic accomplishment are all factors that contribute to designating a stained glass ensemble as one of national significance.

Fashions in the appreciation of art, just like fashions in clothes, change. In Notre-Dame of Paris, Gothic windows were destroyed and replaced with nonfigural grisaille. Loss happens even when stained glass is deeply admired. The belief that a modern painter can copy old glass and produce an authentic image is now rejected. The replacing of damaged work with new copies, however, was once a standard practice and engaged in by patrons and artists committed to restoring their churches to their original splendor. It resulted in tragic over-intervention. Current attitudes advocate the retention of the original, no matter how fragmentary.

It is against the ephemeral and personal nature of taste that this study is set. The author has endeavored to characterize the

specific cultural and spiritual expectations of the many eras that produced stained glass. Each style and subject was the product of patrons with deep convictions about the value of art to society. Produced by monks, bishops, kings, and also by grieving parents, parish subscription, and a host of anonymous patrons, the windows reflect the priorities of their makers. They speak to us over time, revealing the commitment of those who have experienced and preserved them through the centuries.

ABOVE *A border of a window from Poitiers cathedral shows the reuse of segments of glass from the twelfth through the fourteenth centuries. Windows were sometimes destroyed because of offensive subject matter but they also succumbed to the march of taste. In a later effort to bring more light into Gothic interiors, deeply colored windows were sometimes destroyed and fragments reused for borders.*

LEFT *The windows designed by Bernard van Orley, 1540–47, for the Blessed Sacrament chapel of Brussels Cathedral were restored during the nineteenth century. In a practice now rejected, Jean-Baptiste Capronnier carefully copied heads that showed breakage, replacing the old with the new when the windows were reinstalled. Several of the original heads, kept in the studio, were acquired by the Royal Museum of Art, Brussels.*

Symbol and Story: The Art of Stained Glass

OPPOSITE *The choir of Cologne Cathedral, 1280–1310, is of attenuated elegance. Non-figural grisaille and ornamental pattern balance the images in order to maximize light. Honoring the presence of the relics of the Three Magi within the cathedral, the upper choir presented a series of figures of kings standing over the shields of the donors of the windows. In the central window, below a series of kings and prophets holding prophecies of the birth of the Messiah, appear the Magi before the Christ Child.*

TRANSFIGURED LIGHT: WINDOWS, PRECIOUS STONES, AND SPIRITUALITY

Stained glass, considered a precious object, was linked in the twelfth and thirteenth centuries to the aesthetics of precious stones and metalwork; it therefore received a place of honor in the building that housed it. As we look back at the history of the West, the building arts have been among the most important products of society. In the Middle Ages and the Renaissance, buildings also carried great narrative themes—on the exterior of buildings by sculpture, and on the interior by glass and wall painting. Durandus, bishop of Mende (ca. 1220–96) wrote that "the windows of the church which are made of transparent glass are the Sacred Scriptures which keep away the wind and the rain ... but allow passage of the true sun (which is God) into the church, that is, into the hearts of the faithful. The metal grilles in front of the windows represent the prophets and the doctors of the church" (Books XXIV–XXV). The emotional and intellectual effect of stained-glass programs was therefore of extraordinary importance. Indeed, the majority of buildings in this era were inconceivable without their glazing. Architects designed their elevations to house these great tapestries of colored light, which integrated the architectural space and served as planes for storytelling.

The importance of stained glass and gems may be explained by a prevailing attitude toward light as metaphor in premodern Europe. In the Old Testament light is associated with good, and darkness with God's displeasure. The very first verses of Genesis announce to the reader that "the earth was void and empty, and darkness was upon the face of the deep," when God created light and "saw the light that it was good" (Genesis 1: 2–3). Light was associated with knowledge and power, "the brightness of eternal light, and the unspotted mirror of God's majesty" (Wisdom 7: 26). Light also functioned as a symbol of God's protection. The Book of Wisdom proclaimed God's shepherding of the Israelites as they fled from Egypt, when "the whole world was enlightened with a clear light." For the impious Egyptians the opposite was true: "over

them only was spread a heavy night, an image of that darkness which was to come upon them" (Wisdom 17: 19-20). New Testament references are even more explicit and allude to the nature of God, "God is light, and in him there is no darkness" (1 John 1: 5). The Gospel of John further associated light with the nature of Christ and the means of spiritual awakening: "In him was life, and the life was the light of men. And the light shineth in the darkness, and the darkness did not comprehend it ... That was the true light, which enlighteneth every man that cometh into this world" (John 1: 4-5, 9).

To the long tradition of medieval thought, which saw the birth of stained glass, creation is a process of emanations of divine light, from the "first radiance," Christ, down to the lowliest speck of

matter. In order to ascend from the lowest to the highest, one searches for the trace of divine light in all creatures. God is not only light, but also harmony and beauty; the radiant beauty of sparkling stones and stained glass became for many of this period an intimation of God's very nature, and important as a contemplative aid. As a transparent as well as a colored material, glass resonated profoundly with the concepts of clarity and opacity that functioned as primary dichotomies for both moral and ontological systems. Light was transparent as it left the Creator, acquiring color, and thus its ability to be visible, as it penetrated the material world. Colors can therefore be seen as representing the diversity and imperfection of creatures, although they still betray the radiance of their origins.

ABOVE *Stained glass creates a kinetic environment by responding to the intensity of light, times of day, and even the passage of the seasons. The choir of the cathedral of Evreux, about 1325, shows the impression created by light from stained glass as it falls on a wall. Just as the viewer witnessed ephemeral light transforming impenetrable stone, so he or she reflected on the intangible nature of God, animating but beyond the material world.*

OPPOSITE *The rose of the west façade of the cathedral of Chartres, about 1210, shows the Last Judgment. Christ is in the center and in the outer circle angels call the dead who rise from their tombs to heaven or to hell.*

Suger, abbot of Saint-Denis in the mid-twelfth century, wrote explicitly of color, light, and brilliance, all qualities of stained glass, as essential aspects of the purpose of religious architecture. He referred to "sapphire glass," suggesting that the intense blue windows at Saint-Denis is to be understood as having the same importance as gems. He meditated:

Thus sometimes when, because of my delight in the beauty of the house of God, the multicolor loveliness of the gems has called me away from external cares, and worthy meditation, transporting me from material to immaterial things, has persuaded me to examine the diversity of holy virtues, then I seem to see myself existing on some level, as it were, beyond our earthly one, neither completely the slime of the earth nor completely in the purity of heaven. By the gift of God I can be transported in an anagogical manner from this inferior level to that superior one. (*De administratione*, XXXIII)

Suger maintained that his delight in beauty as particularly manifest in the loveliness of the many-colored gems and stained-glass windows he commissioned allowed him to redirect his thoughts from his temporal obligations to the spiritual world of divine virtues.

The cult of relics that was pervasive before the Reformation augmented the medieval fascination with precious materials. Christians characterized the dead as those who "slept in Christ" and treated

them as still members of the extended Christian community. Burial places were clustered around, in, and under places of worship, and places of worship grew up over the sites of significant graves. The custom received official sanction when the emperor Constantine built the basilica of St. Peter, 319–22, over a cemetery assumed to contain the grave of the first pope. Medieval tradition believed that subsequently St. Helena, the emperor's mother, journeyed to Jerusalem and unearthed the cross on which Christ died. Constantine supported the erection of the church of the Holy Sepulchre, 325–26, to enshrine both the place of Christ's death and his tomb.

The demand to be close to the tangible remains of heroic Christians, the great confessors and martyrs, and the tangible remains of Christ's life encouraged the distribution of relics. Fragments of bone, bits of fabric worn by a saint, or a segment of a staff, became essential talismans in Christian ritual. The enthusiasm can be seen in the 396 celebration of the arrival of relics from Rome in the French city of Rouen. A local cleric, Victricius, speaking for the Christian community, said: "Give me these temples of saints ... If a light touch of the hem of the savior's garment could cure, then there is no doubt that these dwelling places of martyrdom [the relics] carried in our arms, will cure us." Here Victricius referred to the Gospel story of Christ healing the woman with the issue of blood when she touched his robe (Luke 8: 43–48), thus stating that the saints who imitated Christ's virtues were delegated power from Christ to heal. He continues, "Let us draw down on us the favor of the saints ... Their dwelling is on high, but let us evoke them as our guests" (Hillgarth, 23).

The relics were enshrined in the most lavishly built objects, justified by reference to Scripture. Durandus (Books XII–XIII, XLVI) paraphrased a passage from Exodus (35: 4–7), "Take everything that is precious but only receive from those who are willing: gold and silver, and brass, violet and purple fabrics ... Make oil to maintain lights, and make ointment, and most sweet incense, onyx stones and precious stones to make for me a sanctuary adorned with sardonix and precious stones so that I may dwell among them." He was explicit that God had ordered that the chandelier and other ornaments of the altar be made of gold and silver. The medieval worshiper was committed to enshrining objects in the gleam of precious stones and vivid color, exactly the same qualities provided by stained glass. The design principles of reliquaries and windows were similar. The *Stavelot Triptych*, 1156–58, was believed to contain a fragment of the True Cross rescued by St. Helena. The stories of the discovery of the cross are told in circular medallions precisely like the narrative system of the windows of this era.

Scholars have associated the reliquary with the Imperial Benedictine Abbey of Stavelot and Abbot Wibald (reigned 1130–58), advisor to three successive Holy Roman Emperors, Lothair II, Conrad III, and Frederick I Barbarossa. Wibald was sent by Barbarossa on two missions to Constantinople, including one to conclude the emperor's marriage negotiations with a Byzantine princess, during which time we assume he acquired the fragment of the True Cross. The reception of so signal a relic in a monastery in what is now known as Belgium was an extraordinary event. This area, dominated by the Meuse River, was renowned as one of the most sophisticated production centers of metalwork in Europe. The precious wood was already enshrined in a small gold and enamel triptych inscribed in Greek, which when open shows Constantine and Helena on either side of the cross and four standard Byzantine

ABOVE *By decreasing realism, the medieval artist could suggest events that transcend human experience such as an angel appearing in a dream to the sleeping Emperor Constantine. Design principles were the same whether in enamel, glass, or manuscript. A stained glass medallion from the abbey of Saint-Denis of the same period shows similar bold abstractions.*

ABOVE AND OPPOSITE *The monks of Canterbury honored Thomas Becket in many storied windows, even during their 1207–13 exile when they resided in France near the cathedral of Sens. The* Sens Life of Thomas Becket *window shows twelve episodes. About 1164, Becket is reconciled with Henry II in the presence of Louis VII of France, shown above. Opposite, from the top, he sails back to England, then, rides to Canterbury with his followers. Finally, he is assassinated by Henry's knights in the presence of the monks.*

RIGHT *Becket's assassination is told in a manuscript (British Library, MS Harley 5102, fol. 32). Thomas is shown at prayer before an altar in the cathedral when the knights of Henry II enter and kill him by striking his head with a sword.*

military saints (George, Theodore, Procopius, and Demetrius) in the wings. This was placed in the center of the new reliquary commissioned by Wibald.

In the Stavelot Triptych, the central panel surrounds the Byzantine reliquary with a frame of three-dimensional cusps followed by a border set with precious stones. The wings contain three circular medallions narrating the legend of the True Cross. On the right three medallions recount Helena's journey to Jerusalem: she interviews a group of Jews to discover the location of the cross; she excavates three crosses on Golgatha; and the True Cross resurrects a dead man. The medallions on the left present Constantine: an angel reveals in a dream that he will conquer his rival and become sole emperor "by the sign of the cross"; Constantine defeats Maxentius at the battle

of the Milvian Bridge; and Constantine is baptized by Pope Sylvester. The glory of the Mosan metalworkers, these exquisite enamel panels parallel design principles in stained glass. Figures in brilliant red, blue, and green are silhouetted against a neutral ground. Bold gestures convey meaning, the angel leaning over Constantine's bed to announce, *"In Hoc Vince"* (In this you will conquer), pointing to the cross above. We have only to see contemporary stained-glass medallions in the abbeys of Saint-Denis and Canterbury to find parallel narrative structure and verbal inscriptions.

The abbeys of Canterbury and Saint-Denis, and cathedrals of the time, like Stavelot, possessed many bejeweled reliquaries. The most important were set in areas highly visible to pilgrims. The visitor to the tomb of Thomas Becket at Canterbury saw it enshrined in a raised monument fashioned by the metalworker Elias of Durham in the center of the Trinity Chapel, behind the main altar. Just as the glowing colors and radiance of jewels of the reliquary surrounded Becket's remains, so the brilliant colors and light of the twelve windows surrounded the pilgrims. Flanked by windows and shrine, pilgrims circumnavigated a multisensory environment that proclaimed Becket's exemplary life and his power.

Cologne's great reliquary of the Three Magi stands as an exemplar of the relationship of town and shrine. After the defeat of Milan by Frederick Barbarossa, the relics of the Magi were transferred from Milan to Cologne by Archbishop Reinhold von Dassel in 1164. An appropriate shrine was commissioned from the most distinguished metalworker of his time, Nicholas of Verdun, as soon as he had returned from his work on the Klosterneuburg altar in 1181. The largest and most luxurious of surviving medieval reliquaries, the shrine is still revered today—it was carried in procession through postwar

ABOVE *Cologne's Shrine of the Three Kings, 1181–1230, sculpted in gold gilt and enamel with precious stones is formed like a miniature church. On the sides, on the lowest level, appears King Solomon flanked by prophets. Above are the Apostles. On the end, the three kings offer gifts to the Christ Child, reflecting the image in the axial window of the cathedral's choir.*

OPPOSITE *Cologne honored the story of its patrons in multiple images. Early fourteenth-century paintings on the cathedral's choir screen show the discovery and transport of the relics of the Magi. St. Helena, mother of Constantine, stands before the relics, the relics are later brought to Milan, and Archbishop Reinhold von Dassel receives the relics in Cologne. In a gesture testifying to the medieval desire for continuity, the relics are shown at these three separate moments in time as if they had always been enshrined in golden reliquary houses similar to that created for them in Cologne.*

Cologne as the cathedral hovered over the devastated city like a protective angel. Set in the midst of the towering majesty of the cathedral, the golden reliquary radiates a sense of power. The often cited medieval principle of the relationship of microcosm to macrocosm is revealed as the immense building with its soaring, vaulting, and glittering windows weighs against the small house with its gables and arches of enamel, gold, and precious stones. Both structures are populated with imagery. The kings parade in long rows in the window openings that encircle the choir. Apostles, kings, and prophets appear beneath the curved arches that surround the sides of the shrine. In the Middle Ages, small objects could be as significant as monumental works; unlike in our modern era, there was then no qualitative division among categories of painting, book illustration, or the decorative arts.

The literary and theological lineage of precious stones continued throughout the Middle Ages. In the late fourteenth-century English poem *Pearl*, the author described a vision of a pearl maiden—"her priceless crown with pearls alone was set, in fashion fit and fair" (3: 3)—who leads him to the vision of the Heavenly Jerusalem. The Heavenly City as described in the Book of Revelations is the core reference for the construction and interpretation of churches. The biblical text explains: "the building of the wall thereof was of jasper stone: but the city itself pure gold, like to clear glass, and the foundations of the wall of the city adorned with all manner of precious stones" (Revelations 21: 18-19). Durandus wrote: "For the material church wherein the people assemble to praise God symbolizes that Holy Church which is built in heaven of living stones" (Durandus IX). It was a short step to link such descriptions with actual buildings and see the windows functioning as the gems that adorned the Heavenly City.

The fascination with light and the sense of its transformative power continues unabated. Steven Holl, one of the United States's most progressive architects, spoke of his selection of glass for the St. Ignatius chapel, Seattle University, 1996, by describing qualities of light: "my choice of glass corresponds to my perception of the material. A sponge can absorb several times its weight in liquid without changing its appearance. Cast glass seems to trap light within its material. Its translucency or transparency maintains a glow of reflected light, refracted light, or the light dispersed on adjacent surfaces." Indeed, with the contemporary world and the frequent use of nonfigurative pattern or abstraction, the ability of the material itself to suggest transcendence becomes even more apparent.

Stained glass was important in the Middle Ages because of its close association with religious architecture. Allied to the art of the Gothic construction, the figural window

onim̄ pꝛ martira tumulo aerata latū
er e̓ helena̅ bꝛ̄ �...no̅ ossa magoꝛ

chile rastarā nota sacra corie ꝛ̄ in
... menael da̅ ꝛ̄ ponun̄ ꝛ̄ ambꝛot n..

.. un ꝛ̄ crsar ꝛ̄ prece po̅
als tara ꝺꝛo reꝺnꝛ
ꝛ̄ uas
r̄ vn

dominated image making for four centuries, emerging again in the nineteenth century with the revival of the Gothic building. Contemporary designers, however, of distinctly nonhistoric expression now look to these great ensembles as moments when the image, space, color, light, and materials fused in a visual concord. What seizes their imaginations is the power of glass to enable the designer to sculpt interior space through light. The great artist in stained glass is always engaged with architecture, through an intimacy with the architectural plan at the origin of the building or intervening to restructure existing space into a new, expressive environment.

As lofty and speculative as thinking was concerning the ultimate meaning of light transformed by multi-hued glass, the commissioners of these windows also cherished very personal and mundane goals. Building is a reflection of community, and windows, with image as well as architectural form, could show that community in compelling ways. Since the first great architectural ensembles of stained glass in the twelfth century, patrons consistently depicted themselves, in image and in name, in the windows. Suger, abbot of the monastery of Saint-Denis, Master Gerlachus, a glass painter working at

BELOW *The Abbey of Arnstein an der Lahn installed a five window series in the choir, 1160–70. At the bottom of the image of Moses and the Burning Bush, appears the artist/patron, Master Gerlachus. He holds a pot of paint as he inscribes the surrounding inscription with his brush:* rex regu(m) clare gerlacho prop(i)ciare; *King of Kings, render favorable the acclaim of Gerlachus.*

Arnstein an der Lahn, and the rulers of England and southwestern France, Eleanor of Aquitaine and Henry II, all insured that their image was included in the windows they had commissioned. The portraits, however, are generic, presenting, in medieval fashion, not the individual but the function. Thus we see the monk, the artist, and the royal couple fulfilling their roles as patrons and believers.

As artistic tradition began to define the recognizable, individual portrait, especially since the Renaissance, donor portraits took on new meaning. Without abandoning symbolic depth, the identifiable portrait appeared in glass. During the great rebirth of the medium in the nineteenth century, modern onlookers wanted to see their own values and priorities reflected in the stories depicted in the windows. The complex theological programs of the twelfth century or the episodic stories of the saints in the thirteenth were no longer so relevant. The new windows inspire with images that present role models to viewers, especially through large, often life-size figures set in a believably "realistic" space. Donors also wished to be visibly as well as intellectually a part of the imagery of their time. Given the tradition of academic painting and of the new medium of photography, donor and family portraits often appear in virtually photographic form. The superbly drafted and executed series of portraits of the French monarchy in the royal chapel of Dreux, 1843, by Jean-Dominique Ingres exemplifies the continued use of political imagery in glass in Europe.

Churches continued the tradition of ruler portraiture, exemplified by a window installed in St. Mary's, Great Malvern, to commemorate the Diamond Jubilee of Queen Victoria, 1886. In the upper portion of the window an image of Christ is praised "King of Kings and Lord of Lords," a Biblical text made familiar by the chorus in Handel's *Messaiah*. He addresses a multinational

assembly of worshippers including a North American Indian, a Turk in a fez, an Arab in burnoose, and Asians and Africans identifiable by racial features, evocative of the dominions of the British Empire. Acts of Victoria are also depicted, associating her reign with the authority of Christ and with fulfilling his mission on earth.

Educational institutions often show site-specific representations. At University College, Cork, the Aula Maxima is a soaring medieval revival hall where the most prestigious academic exercises are conducted. A dramatic window at the balcony level represents the female personification of Wisdom enthroned surrounded by figures from the world of science. It was produced in 1866 by John Hardman & Co., Birmingham. A Latin inscription at the bottom of the window proclaims George Boole (1815–64) as the "pious and inventive" professor of mathematics at the University, whose development of algebraic computation "Boolean Algebra" forms the basis of modern computer logic.

Wisdom distributes laurel wreaths of truth and fame. She is flanked by explorers, inventors, and scientists through the ages. Among the navigators and explorers is Christopher Columbus. In the lancet of physicians and chemists whose background shows glass jars and laboratory equipment is Hippocrates, the father of medicine whose Hippocratic oath is still pronounced today. In the lancet dedicated to engineers and physicists is Archimedes, with pulleys and other manifestations of applied physics.

On the level below, directly under Wisdom, George Boole writes at his desk while behind him stand Euclid, founder of the science of geometry, and the philosopher Aristotle. Each one of the four flanking lancets shows a similarly seated scientist with two others standing behind. To the far left is Galileo, the Italian

Renaissance astronomer. He discovered sunspots, the satellites of Jupiter, and further refined Copernicus's heliocentric model for what was then believed to be the universe. In the background is Copernicus himself, like Galileo looking upwards toward the heavens. Galileo's propositions, like those of Copernicus, met with resistance from religious authorities, and the scientist was even tried before the Catholic Inquisition. The adjacent lancet shows Sir Isaac Newton in the foreground, famous for his observation of the falling apple and theories of universal attraction, inertia, and the proportionality of the forces of action and reaction. In the background are Francis Bacon and John Napier. Bacon was both statesman and scientist, serving as Lord Chancellor under James I and author of works stressing knowledge drawn from experience and inductive reasoning. Napier was a Scottish mathematician and inventor of logarithms.

In the lancet to the right of Boole is the French philosopher and scientist René Descartes, who maintained the premise that mathematical exactitude is possible in metaphysical reasoning. Behind him are Blaise Pascal, mathematician and philosopher, whose early publications set the base of probability theory and Gottfried Wilhelm Leibnitz whose work in physics

broke with Cartesian principles. On the far right, Ptolomy sits looking at the globe of the world. A second century astronomer and geographer, Ptolomy constructed a model of the universe where the planets and sun revolve around the earth. The inclusion of outmoded theories from the Middle Ages and the Renaissance demonstrates the modern ideal of science. The essential condition is freedom of inquiry, leaving to subsequent investigation by other scientists the task to disprove, modify, or confirm.

Harvard University's Memorial Hall, 1876, commemorates alumni who gave their lives in the struggle to preserve the Union. An inscription calls to the present: "Those institutions which they by dying preserved, you cultivate while you live so that men among us may be more free, happy, united." The entire program shows a mingling of classical, Early Christian, and Renaissance imagery memorializing not only Harvard's student-soldiers but also the pictorial language of an entire generation.

The transept window, 1898, honoring Martin Brimmer (1829–96), alumnus and longtime Fellow of the Harvard Corporation, is the largest and most complex of all the windows of the site. It was designed by Sarah Wyman Whitman (1842–1904) who was also an artist of landscapes, portraits, and work in the decorative arts. The window's signature element appears in the first lancet: the Chevalier Bayard standing in classical contrapposto pose, wearing steel-blue armor with a scarlet cape draped behind him. He is without helmet, as is Hector in the famous farewell to Andromache, the subject of a window by Frederic Crowninshield (1845–1918) in the Hall. The window also included St. Martin of Tours dividing his cloak with a beggar, the scene of the mortally wounded poet and soldier, Sir Philip Sidney (1544–86) tending to a wounded soldier, and Sidney as a youthful scholar. The figures of both soldier and scholar are idealized portraits of Martin Brimmer, who was of French Huguenot descent. The French hero Pierre Terrail, seigneur de Bayard (ca. 1473–1524), is depicted with fair coloring, prominent cheekbones, broad forehead, and full drooping mustache that corresponds to published images of Brimmer.

The glazing program of the dining hall itself, between 1879 and 1904, presents paired figures that embody the virtues for scholar and soldier. Typical of nineteenth-century thinking that saw all of the past—selectively chosen—available as models for the present, the subjects show a wide range. Classical and biblical quotations, personal letters of the young soldiers, images of Greek, Roman, medieval, Renaissance, and even early American history all fuse to testify to the meaning of the sacrifice made by the young men fallen in the War between the States. Figures from history that range from rulers such as Pericles of Athens and Charlemagne of medieval Europe, the inventor/artist Leonardo da Vinci, and the poet Dante, to the explorers La Salle and Marquette all fused to testify to the meaning of the sacrifice made by the young men who lost their lives. It is indeed an epic statement, as phrased by John La Farge's *Battle Window*, 1881, showing classically garbed soldiers where the American conflict becomes the stuff of Homeric legend.

A window by Edward Peck Sperry (1850–1925) shows the Rev. Phillips Brooks (1835–93) of Trinity Church, Boston, under the guise of Bernard of Clairvaux, the twelfth-century Cistercian monk and preacher of the Second Crusade. General Francis Channing Barlow (1834–96), the highest-ranking Harvard soldier, appears under the guise of Godfrey of Bouillon, the military commander most emblematic of the First Crusade which captured Jerusalem in 1099 and founded the Kingdom of Jerusalem. Both were members of Harvard's class of 1855 and deceased by 1901, the date of the window. The breadth of sources is impressive, as well as the freedom of a late nineteenth-century American Protestant patron—or set of patrons—to appropriate crusader, monk, knight, and French history as part of their own personal tradition.

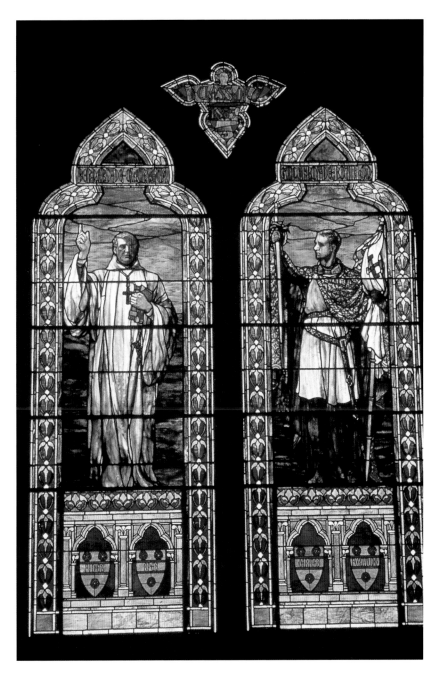

THE POPULAR IMAGE

At all times windows depicted "popular" images. That is, the patron commissioned stained glass, a project of considerable expense, clearly convinced of the need for such expenditure and in the belief that the imagery was important and relevant. It suffices only that a subsequent viewer be removed from the framing culture to render the image esoteric. In the Middle Ages a shared culture of biblical lore, saints' legends, and liturgical ritual was the base for much imagery often difficult to understand today. In the nineteenth and early twentieth centuries, framers of imagery looked to the current standards of value for sources. They found them in the public museums, a new phenomenon of the nineteenth century, invariably formed with the paintings of the Renaissance and baroque at their core. Travel became easier so that no cultivated individual's education was deemed complete without a tour of the great cities of Europe, in particular, London, Paris, Florence, and Rome. Popular journals and newspapers carried travel literature and descriptions of the cities and their art treasures, bringing awareness to the entire reading public.

With the development of cheaper forms of printing in the nineteenth century, in particular the steel and wood engraving, and the advent of photography, images of the art found a new audience. Great Masters of the past could be seen by all, presented in schools and staple elements of religious or morally instructional popular literature. The illustrated book and framed print also played a major role in the development of the canon of great art propagated across a broad spectrum from the Newport millionaire's mansion to village Sunday school. Raphael's *Sistine Madonna*, 1513, Dresden, Gemäldegalerie, for example, was carried as the frontispiece for Salomon Reinach's *Apollo*, Paris, 1907,

a seminal survey of art text; the exact same image is the frontispiece for Rev. Henri Didon's *Jesus Christ, The Savior's Person, Mission, and Spirit*, New York, 1891. These same works were the inspiration of the monumental arts of altarpieces, wall paintings, and stained glass for houses of worship. For the church-going public, the private experience of reading and viewing was repeated in community experience as these same book illustrations inspired the monumental arts of stained glass, mural painting and framed reproduction. In this era which strove to forge a common culture that would solidify all levels of society, these images on glass, canvas, or paper were important means expressing shared values.

The importance of the replica is exemplified in the Victoria and Albert Museum. The institution was founded after the Great Exhibition of 1851 in London. This was the first of the Universal Expositions that characterized the last half of the nineteenth century. Housed in the great Crystal Palace, a vast hall of glass and steel designed by Sir Joseph Paxton, the enterprise displayed manufactured goods from around the word. In 1852, with surplus funds from the Exposition, twelve acres of land was purchased in Kensington to house the collection under what was then called the Department of Practical Art. The guiding principle was art applied to industry with the expectation that contemporary artisans and the public could find inspiration for the present from the art of the past.

Not only original works of furniture, textiles, metalwork, and tableware as well as monumental sculpture, but replicas of unique objects from other sites were acquired. "Beauty and decorative attraction is perhaps the chief characteristic of the exhibits... With this object in view, the museum possesses numerous reproductions of famous art treasures: casts, facsimiles, and electrotypes, some of them so well contrived as to be almost indistinguishable from the originals" (*Encyclopedia Britannica*, 1911, vol. 19, p. 62). Today the Victoria and Albert Museum is one of the rare institutions still displaying its great hall of casts, where Trajan's column, Celtic crosses, and the Portal of Glory from St. James of Compostela cluster within easy proximity.

The United States emulated English practices. The Museum of Fine Arts, Boston, contemplated as its first acquisition a collection of casts and photographic copies. When Wellesley College, a prestigious women's college near Boston, dedicated its Farnsworth Building of Fine Arts, October 23, 1889, the walls were hung with nineteenth-century landscape paintings and the floor populated with replicas of classical sculpture. After a trip to the United States,

H. G. Wells wrote in *The Future in America* (New York, 1906, p. 233) that he retained of Wellesley a vivid memory of "a sunlit room in which girls were copying the details in the photographs of masterpieces."

The most renowned of studios and the most respected artists constructed windows after received imagery. John La Farge, for example, designed the window of the *Presentation of the Virgin in the Temple*, 1888, honoring Julia Appleton McKim for Trinity Church, Boston, donated by her husband, Charles Follen McKim and her sister Alice. McKim was a partner of McKim, Mead, and White, the prestigious firm of architects responsible for major works in the late nineteenth century, including the Boston Public Library. The window's central image reproduces the painting by Titian, 1535–38, now in the Accademia, Venice, and a Latin inscription

BELOW *Titian's* Presentation of the Virgin in the Temple, *1534–38, exemplifies the type of imagery most admired by nineteenth-century patrons. The huge painting takes up a wall in the Galleria dell'Accademia of Venice and is the subject of countless prints and photographs. A window by John La Farge in opalescent glass, Trinity Church, Boston, reproduces the central figure of the Virgin.*

RIGHT *The great painter of the Italian High Renaissance, Raphael, was arguably the most admired artist of the nineteenth century. His frescoes and oil paintings were widely disseminated through engravings, even during his lifetime.* St. Michael Conquering Satan, *1518, from the Louvre collection, inspired innumerable images and even sculptures.*

BELOW *Raphael's image was the basis for the Tiffany Studio's* St. Michael, *placed in the renovated chancel of St. Michael's Church, Charleston, South Carolina, 1893. The importance of stained glass during the opalescent era can be seen by the numerous historic buildings of the time that were altered to receive similar lavish windows.*

cites this source. The Tiffany Studios consistently showed flexibility in its sources. Raphael, along with Michelangelo and Leonardo da Vinci, were considered the three great masters of the Italian High Renaissance. Raphael's painting *St. Michael Conquering Satan*, 1518, Paris, Louvre, is the basis for the chancel window of 1893 in St. Michael's Episcopal Church, Charleston, South Carolina. Built 1752/6, the church has long been considered one of the most elegant buildings of the American Colonies. Tiffany exhibited the window in New York during the summer of 1893.

Aiding in the communication of models were the books published by the Düsseldorf Society for the Propagation of Good Religious Pictures. The books enjoyed wide dissemination and even England-language editions with reproductive steel engravings often the size of holy picture cards used for place markers in devotional books and personalized as souvenirs of First Communions or printed with prayers for the dead at funerals. Great Master paintings appeared in full and detail such as Raphael's *St. Cecilia and Four Saints*, 1515, Bologna, Pinacoteca. The German Nazarene painters furnished contemporary work such as Philipp Veit's (1793–1877) image of St. Ann teaching the Virgin to read, a theme popular since the fifteenth century. Around 1865 Emile Thibaud reproduced the engraving with slight alterations for a window in Saint-Saturnin (Puy-du-Dome), central France.

Julius Schnorr von Carolsfeld (1794–1872), in Germany, and Gustave Doré (1832–83) in France were widely known as illustrators of Bibles, a process that mirrored the publication of Illustrated Bibles of the early years of the sixteenth century. For Schnorr, a Leipzig edition of the Bible illustrated with 240 of his images was published in 1860. One Bible published in German in Cincinnati, Ohio, 1883, the *Illustrierte Prachte-Bible für das*

LEFT *Julius Schnorr von Carolsfeld, a member of the German Nazarene School, was one of the most influential of the illustrators of religious literature in the nineteenth century. His inspiration was drawn from Renaissance and Baroque Old Masters for dramatic focus, as exemplified in his* Return of the Prodigal Son *from his Bible of 1860.*

BELOW *The Studio of Félix Gaudin produced a window containing the* Return of the Prodigal Son, 1887, *for the church of Saint-Joseph, Clermont-Ferrand. Relying on the print as a compositional source, the window uses traditional glass segments in different colors of that are leaded together to form the design.*

THE GOOD SHEPHERD.
"I am the Good Shepherd; and I know mine, and mine
know me."—John 10. 14.

ABOVE *A window in opalescent glass is more simplified but shows strong colors. Even as varying degrees of artistic originality of these windows confront the viewer, the universal importance of shared subject matter is unmistakable.*

ABOVE RIGHT *Bernhard Plockhorst's* The Good Shepherd *was one of the most reproduced images of the nineteenth century and found in popular literature such as Mother Mary Loyola's* Jesus of Nazareth: the Story of His Life Written for Children *(New York: Benziger Brothers, 1906).*

OPPOSITE *In a window executed in traditional paint, the artist felt free to include all the details of the print source, with the precise arrangement of trees in the distance and the exact count of sheep.*

deutsche Volk, lists "pictures by J. Schnorr von Carolsfeld, Doré, and others, and enhanced with steel engravings after Raphael, Rubens, and others." The dramatic image of the return of the Prodigal Son by Schnorr was the basis for a Gothic-Revival window presumably executed by the studio of Félix Gaudin, 1887, in the church of Saint-Joseph in Clermond-Ferrand. Doré was copied innumerable times, even in the most prestigious commissions such as the Stanford University Chapel, California, by J. & R. Lamb.

Replications, for example, of the *Boy Jesus Disputing with the Doctors* (Heinrich Hofmann, German, 1824–1911), the *Good Shepherd* (Bernhard Plockhorst, German, 1825–1907), or *The Light of the World* of 1856 also known as *Christ Knocking at the Door* (William Holman-Hunt, English, 1827–1910), crowd religious edifices as well as illustrated literature of this time. These images were more than religious in

the narrow sense. Rather, they established and propagated social values such as the virtues of compassion, the dutiful child, the solicitous parent, and the value of the individual.

The donors of medieval windows, reflecting the economic structure of their time, had been of high social rank. Donors of the nineteenth century, while still including the elite such as Harvard's Whitman and Brimmer, were far more varied in class and social diversity. With the passing of clerical independence once enjoyed through landholdings by churches in the Middle Ages, parishioners became crucial elements of economic survival for religious institutions. In a pluralistic situation such as that of the United States, it was especially necessary to link the parishioner with both the abstract and the physical organization of the church. Confraternities, new devotional practices, and the emphasis on individual donors for building campaigns all contributed to an active relationship between the clergy and laity. Individuals and church societies were responsible for funding windows, and they used inspiration from their prayer books and manuals of art. The priorities of these groups were reflected in the themes of a glazing program, ineluctably transforming the received canon of confessional imagery. The decoration of these buildings tells us personalized values.

Stained glass windows are both beautiful and informative. They convey commitment to an aesthetic and an explicit statement of the political and religious tenets of their time period. As we look back at the history of stained glass, both its beauty and its social importance resonate through the choice of image and placement within the building. A precious material in the Middle Ages, a valued commission in the modern world, the window is a source of contemporary delight even as it retains an ability to make present the past.

2

Origins, Materials, and the Glazier's Art

Traditionally, stained glass is used as an architectural medium and, as such, it is integral to the fabric of a building; not only, or always, a work of art, but also a screen letting in and modifying the light and keeping out the elements. Its development as a major art form in the Middle Ages was dependent on the needs of a powerful client, the Christian Church, and the evolution of architectural forms that allowed for ever larger openings in the walls of both humble churches and great cathedrals, producing awe-inspiring walls of colored light.

Its exact origins are uncertain. Sheets of glass, both blown and cast, had been used architecturally since Roman times. Writers as early as the fifth century mention colored glass in windows. Ancient glass was set in patterns into wooden frames or molded and carved stucco or plaster, but each network had to be self-supporting, which limited the kinds of shapes that could be used. When or where strips of lead were first employed to hold glass pieces together is not recorded, but lead's malleability and strength greatly increased the variety of shapes available to artists,

giving them greater creative freedom. Excavations at Jarrow, in northern England, have yielded strips of lead and unpainted glass cut to specific shapes, dating from the seventh to the ninth centuries.

The process of making stained glass has changed very little over the centuries. We can still look to a treatise written late in the twelfth century by a monk using the pseudonym Theophilus for a basic understanding of the steps required both to make sheets of transparent colored glass and to fabricate a window. Over the centuries, innovations have refined techniques and expanded certain ideas, yet the basic concepts as outlined by Theophilus have not changed. In his time, the understanding of glass chemistry was limited to anecdotal observation, producing a circumscribed body of knowledge of what did and did not work. Modern stained-glass artists and artisans have at their disposal centuries of further research and therefore a more complete scientific understanding of their materials.

Stained glass is usually designed for a particular setting, with a specific light and

RIGHT *A head of Christ from the 1230s from Notre-Dame of Dijon shows the typical simplicity of the French Early Gothic. The artist uses limited shading, stressing instead the graphic of the trace line in the sweeping lines of the drapery and the hair.*

OPPOSITE *The panel* Housing the Stranger, *1560–70, is based on one of seven prints of the Corporal Works of Mercy after designs by artist Maerten van Heemskerk (1498–1574). Such small-scale works painted on a single pane of glass display superb Renaissance techniques in the application of vitreous paint. The glass painter has modeled the form by both washes of tone and by removing paint through delicate line. The lower right corner shows stopgap restoration taken from another similar panel.*

BELOW *A miracle window from Canterbury Cathedral, 1213–20, depicts the monk Hugh of Jervaulx cured by an effusion of blood. The execution shows expressive, gestural painting of the Gothic style. Indeed the development of painting styles in manuscripts and stained glass is linked, not because artists slavishly copied each other, but because they shared common artistic training and goals.*

an expected audience. That setting and audience can change radically over time. New buildings may block the original light; corrosion and dirt may obscure the details; vandalism and poor maintenance may cause loss of glass. In addition, stained glass has always been an expensive medium; the materials are costly and the fabrication of a window is time-intensive. It is the intrinsic beauty of the materials and the exceptional skill of its practitioners that have ensured its secure place in our artistic heritage.

RIGHT *Theophilus paid particular attention to techniques of applying paint, telling the glass painter to take the pigment and "smear it around in such a way that the glass is made transparent in the part where you normally make highlights in a painting," such as for faces around the eyes, nostrils, and chin and on bare feet and hands. That such practice was standard is demonstrated by a twelfth-century segment of glass from the cathedral of Poitiers showing the dead rising from the tomb.*

BELOW *In the crown method of spinning glass sheets, the central point is thicker and also shows a circular pontil mark. As the appearance of handmade glass became desirable in the nineteenth century, decorative roundels imitating blown glass were often cast. The cast bull's-eye roundels in this opalescent window show varying density of color and also refract light in changing patterns.*

The three basic glassmaking ingredients are silica, an alkali, and an alkaline earth. Silica, usually in the form of sand, forms the vitreous network of glass. By itself, silica requires a very high heat to melt, so a "network modifier" is introduced in the form of an alkali to break up the strong silica bonds, allowing the glassmaking to be done at a lower temperature and making the glass "metal" more workable. A "network stabilizer," usually in the form of lime, an alkaline earth, is added to rebuild the network, producing a stable glass. Various metallic oxides may be used to color the glass batch.

The two alkalis generally used for sheet glass are soda and potash. We know today that soda forms a much more stable glass, but potash was used extensively in the Middle Ages and is the method described by Theophilus. The materials used in the making of potash glass were readily available to medieval glassmakers, who

located their workshops in woodlands to satisfy their requirements for sand and for fuel to fire their furnaces. They found that they could produce a usable range of colors with just sand and the potash obtained from the ashes of beech trees, which already contained the balance of metallic oxides, such as iron and manganese, necessary as colorants. Even so, proportions differed somewhat from batch to batch, as the soil and other conditions changed from tree to tree. A skilled glassblower could observe what color glass the materials yielded as sheets were being blown and then manipulate the oxidation and reduction conditions in the furnace to obtain other colors from the batch.

Specific colorants were also added, such as cobalt for blue, and copper for red. Sometimes the colorants were already in glass form and might contain soda as the alkali or lead oxide, which performs both network-modifying and network-building functions in the glass matrix. In an early example of recycling, ancient vessels and opaque glass tesserae used in mosaics were added to the melt to color the glass batch. The composition of specific medieval glasses can be very complex due to impurities of the raw materials, the colorants used, and other additives, all of which affect the glass's working and aging characteristics.

These vitreous colors are permanent, but their exposure to the sun can cause manganese, a common ingredient in glass batches, to shift, resulting in a slight change of color. The purple tint created by the shift is noticeable by its absence at the glass edges that had been covered by the lead cames, and helps to account for some of the problems nineteenth-century glassmakers encountered when recreating medieval glasses from compositional analysis.

Although Theophilus discussed both the manufacture of sheet glass and its use in the making of windows, stained-glass artists rarely made their own glass. While obviously connected, these are two very different and highly specialized disciplines. Some stained-glass workshops did have glassmaking facilities on site, but glassmakers were usually located near the raw materials they needed for their work, and many medieval accounts detail the cost of transporting finished sheets of glass to workshops. Modern workshops have the same separation. Tiffany Studios stands

BELOW *Glass has been known since the second millennium BCE when recipes for its making were recorded in cuneiform writing on clay tablets. Early blown glass was produced very much as it is today. The glassblower gathers a swirl of molten glass at the end of a hollow metal blowpipe. As the glass bubble is formed it is supported in a wooden trough while being rolled from side to side as depicted in an early fourteenth-century manuscript (British Museum MS Add. 24189, fol. 16).*

out as one of the few modern stained-glass firms, though certainly not the only one, with the means and will to meld the two.

Transparent glass that is colored throughout, while still molten in the "pot" of the furnace, is known as pot-metal glass. However, not all glass is colored throughout. Red, often called ruby, can be difficult to make. The colorants used to create it must be present in such intense concentrations that the glass will appear black once it attains the thickness necessary for architectural glass, normally about ⅛".

Additionally, red glass must usually be reheated in order for the color to appear. In the twelfth and thirteenth centuries streaky reds were used, which had interspersed lines of red and clear. By the fourteenth century this method had been abandoned in favor of flashed glass, using a technique employed much earlier for vessels, called "casing." A molten gather (a glob of glass adhering to a blowpipe) of one color is coated with a thicker gather of a different color, usually clear, or a tint of green, yellow, and so forth. This layered gather is then blown into a sheet. After cooling, areas of the thin flash could be removed by abrasion, revealing the color of the base glass. One could then have two colors side by side on one piece of glass without needing a lead line, so more intricate designs could be executed with fewer leads. Later, hydrofluoric acid was used to dissolve the flash in a chemical reaction, and abrasion was abandoned. Abrasion removes all of the flash, but with acid etching it is possible to have gradations of removal, allowing shadings and various densities of color. However, it is highly dangerous to the user and must be handled with great care.

GLASS FORMING

Glass can be made into sheets in several ways. Early sheets were cast onto a flat surface, such as sand or wet wood. With the invention of the blowpipe in the first century BCE, glass could be formed much more quickly. Two methods have been used for blowing sheets: the cylinder/muff and the crown. In the first, a bladderlike shape is blown. First one end is opened up and then the other end is removed, forming a cylinder (or muff). This is then split down one side and flattened into a sheet in a re-heating process. For the crown method, a bubble is blown, transferred to a metal rod

Although enamels provided a less intense color than pot metal, they were highly useful in smaller scale work. In the Virgin Clothed with the Sun, *Bergheim, St. Remigius Church, ca. 1600, only the red of the Virgin's robe and gray of her mantel are pot metal. Several shades of silver stain and a range of shades of blue enamel define the moon, clouds, and streaming rays of the sun.*

ABOVE *Glass production is shown in a painting* Glashutte in Schwartzland, *by the eighteenth-century artist M. Dilger. Two "glory holes," or open furnaces, appear in the background while artisans are engaged in various stages of producing glass vessels.*

RIGHT *Tiffany Studios, that was not alone in the practice, frequently used drapery glass. It was produced by manipulating glass with a roller and tongs while it cooled on the steel tabletop. The deep folds are selected for the garments, such as these in Arlington Street Church, Boston, about 1905.*

OPPOSITE *In the twelfth century, the author Theophilus described making an exact size drawing on a whitewashed table as a basis for cutting and assembling a window. A table with a glazing pattern discovered by Joán Vila-Grau in the cathedral of Gerona dates from the fourteenth century. In the fifteenth century the Italian Cennino Cennini documented the use of paper cartoons, urging the gluing together of "as many sheets as you need." The artist then drew first in charcoal, then in ink to fix the exact image that would serve as a pattern for the glass master.*

called a punty (or pontil), pierced, and spun out, yielding a round sheet with no need for flattening, but with a pontil mark remaining in the center. A third, less commonly used technique called "Norman slab" was developed in the nineteenth century and involves blowing the bubble into a mold to form a hollow block that is later separated into small sheets. Modern handblown glass is referred to as mouth-blown or antique glass.

All glass must undergo a controlled cooling period, known as annealing. The glass is placed in a special annealing oven, called a lehr, and the temperature is reduced gradually. If cooled too quickly, the molecules cannot move into a stable configuration. If cooled too slowly, the glass can start to form crystals and devitrify. Badly annealed glass has interior stresses, which makes it hard to cut and can cause it to spring apart as it is scored.

Opalescent glass is a rolled translucent to semi-translucent milky glass. It is often streaky, with a mixture of different colors. Glass objects were made for centuries using milk-white glass, but it was not made into flat sheets for stained glass until the mid-1870s when artists John La Farge and Louis Comfort Tiffany began exploring its possibilities. Its development gave birth to the American Opalescent Style.

For rolled sheets of glass, the molten glass passes between rollers set about $\frac{1}{8}$"

apart, thereby determining the thickness of the glass. Textures can be imprinted on one of the rollers and pressed into the molten glass as it passes through. Tugging or pulling the glass also affects the surface, producing a rippling effect. Machines began to be used in the nineteenth century to make both machine-blown and rolled glass in a variety of textures and colors. In some factories the glass is a continuous ribbon from the batch melting in the furnace through the rollers and then onto a long annealing lehr. At the end of the lehr, when it is sufficiently cooled, it is finally cut into sheets.

For unusual or one-of-a kind effects, hand-rolled sheets are sometimes preferred. For this, a ladle of one or more colors is poured onto a steel table, mixed to a desired integration, and pushed under rollers. For drapery glass, the puddle of glass is first rolled and then manipulated to produce three-dimensional folds. It is finished through a roller, but, after manipulation to produce folds, is left in three-dimensional relief. This must be done quickly, while the glass is still malleable.

Over the centuries, technological advances allowed hotter glass furnaces and greater control over raw materials, yielding more homogeneous, thinner glass, with fewer bubbles and impurities. This glass lacked the richness earlier glass had possessed—partly as a result of its "imperfections"—and the rebirth of stained glass in the nineteenth century led directly to a similar rebirth of the art of medieval glassmaking. No matter how useful machine-made glass may be, nothing can rival the inherent beauty and versatility of mouth-blown antique glass. Although it is the most expensive of all the types available to the artist, it is most often his or her first choice.

SKETCH AND CARTOON

The process of making a stained glass window begins with the artist's sketch, known in medieval times as the "vidimus" (Latin for "we have seen"). This can come from either the studio or the client, and represents an understanding of how the final window will look. The sketch is drawn to scale and from it a full-size rendering, or cartoon, is made, which may be done by

RIGHT *Paper cartoons have been standard since the Renaissance as exemplified by the full-scale drawing of* Truth and/or Correction *for the ceiling of the Palace of Fine Arts of Rio de Janeiro, Brazil. Fabricated between 1906 and 1911 in the Gaudin Studio, France, the careful drawing of face, body, and clouds will aid the glass painter. The sharp dark line around the image indicates the division of the segments of glass. The glasscutter will cut each to the appropriate size and color.*

OPPOSITE *A detail of the* Virgin Mary *from an Annunciation about 1520 was executed by the Hirsvogel workshop after designs by Albrecht Dürer. This window in the Chapel of St. Roch is one of the many works of the German Renaissance in the city of Nuremberg. The importance of woodcut printing, one of the glories of the city, appears in the artist's choice of parallel lines to mold contour in face, hands, and folds of drapery.*

hand or, as is often the practice today, blown up mechanically. Some design adjustments often are necessary with the change in scale. A cartoon can be very detailed, with painting worked out and the basic color selection indicated.

Before paper was readily available, the full-size drawing was made on a whitewashed table that was used for cutting and painting the glass, as well as for putting the finished window together. Remarkably, one such medieval table has survived, if only because it was later used to make the door of a cabinet. Two

fourteenth-century windows made on it also survive in Gerona Cathedral in Spain. Examination under ultraviolet light has revealed several layers of drawings on the board, which contains lead lines, symbols indicating colors, and some of the dark trace lines that were to be painted on the glass. There are also nail holes from the glazing, or leading-up, of the panels.

Sketchbooks and copybooks were often passed down from glazier to glazier. With the increasing use of paper in the fifteenth century, full-size cartoons could be saved, handed down, and reused. Artists who

worked in a variety of media could also make them outside the glazier's shop. Albrecht Dürer and Hans Holbein the Younger drew many designs for stained-glass panels, which others then interpreted. Stained glass is often a collaborative art, and the careful choice of collaborators has always been crucial for the success of the final artwork.

CUTTING

After the layout and patterns are made the glass is cut. The craft part of the medium demands that the various steps be performed with great accuracy, so that the result will be a strong and stable window. For instance, if the glass pieces are cut too large or too small, the window will logically be too large or small, a wholly unacceptable result. Usually just ¼ to ½" of the panel edge sits in the frame, so small discrepancies have real consequences. At the very least, bad cutting means adjustments will be necessary during leading, and assembly will be difficult.

In the Middle Ages sheets of glass were first split into smaller pieces using a hot iron. Heat, aided by water or spit, was used to initiate a break, and the sheet was split in two. This rough shape was then refined using a grozing iron, which was a metal slot or hook into which the edge of the glass was slipped. By pulling the iron down and away, the glass edge was nibbled into shape. Skilled craftsmen could make difficult and intricate shapes.

At some point in the history of the craft, an observant artisan realized that a deep scratch or score made on the glass surface would give better control of the breaking. One can sometimes see these scratches coming off grozed edges on medieval pieces and even find, on occasion, ungrozed edges from the period. Diamonds set in handles are known to have been used for scoring by the fourteenth century, and were probably used earlier, though edges were normally still grozed, and diamonds are still used to score glass today, mainly in Europe. The steel wheel cutter was developed in the 1860s. As the wheel is rolled across the glass it focuses a tremendous amount of pressure just at the point where the wheel meets the glass, creating a surface fissure. The scored glass is then snapped apart, using the hands, or a pair of pliers as a fulcrum.

Early scores were somewhat haphazard. To be a success, a score must travel from one edge of the glass to the other in an unbroken line. If the wheel has a nick in it, there will be skips in the score, and the break will go awry at the skip. Glass is an amorphous material; it has no grain to guide a break. The score is the starting point, but the artisan must decide where else to place scores in order to break away extraneous glass without putting too much stress on the pieces that are to be kept, for the glass will break at the point of least resistance. Some shapes, such as inside curves, are difficult to cut and require some skill to make. Different types of glass cut differently. Even with relatively simple shapes, one always needs extra glass that will end up as cut-off, even more so when shapes are difficult.

The lead lines are painted onto a large piece of plate glass for the color selection. As each piece of glass for the panel is selected and cut, it is attached to the plate glass with small globules of wax (a process called waxing-up), allowing the artist to study color relationships in the light and make changes as needed. This step is

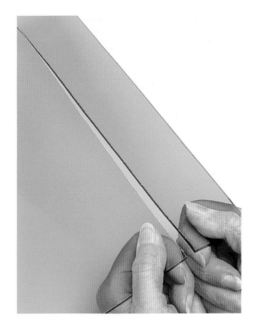

critical, since color relationships change depending on the size of the pieces and the colors that surround them. Color relationships also change depending on the light in which they are viewed. Daylight differs significantly from fluorescent or incandescent light, and when selecting glass one must mimic the eventual light source. The cut segments of glass stay on the plate for painting.

LEFT *By holding the glass with both hands, the glass cutter forces a break along the line scored on the surface.*

BELOW *A panel during restoration from the cathedral of the Holy Cross, Boston, shows the use of glazing nails holding the panels in place. The glass was installed about 1880 and by the 1990s the thin lead had substantially deteriorated. The restoration replaced the old lead with conservation grade came but mended cracks with copper foil edge repair.*

OPPOSITE *Throughout the Middle Ages, windows were often enriched by the application of a damascene background behind the figures, a technique also common to panel paintings. The brilliance of the red and the delicacy of the trefoil pattern act as a foil for the brutality of the torturer swinging the lash in the* Flagellation, *about 1390, St. Erhard church, Austria.*

PAINTING

The German term *Glasmalerei*, or glass painting, most aptly captures what enabled stained glass to move beyond its obvious decorative and practical functions to develop into a powerfully expressive medium. Painting on glass gave artists the opportunity to construct large-scale imagery using light, color, and line. With stained glass, unlike other graphic media, the artist must be sensitive to translucency as well as line and form. The modulation of light animates the image.

Paint is used both to control light and to provide details. It can be applied in washes, mats, and dark trace lines to both the front and the back of the glass. The trace lines provide the main outlines. Crosshatching, using thick or thin trace lines, and mats provide the shading. The same paint mixture can be used for both, diluted in different amounts or mixed with different media. Glass-painting styles have changed

RIGHT *The ability to modulate contour with a tonal wash, as in a drawing, clearly inspired the artist rendering the head of St. Ursula for St. Roch, Nuremberg, in the 1520s. The city's rich production was designed by artists also producing oil paintings, prints, and drawings. Ursula's halo shows the technique of applying the mat as a medium wash and then removing it with a stick to reveal the clear color.*

over the years, especially in the application of mats, which have ranged from a thin wash with visible brush strokes, to a smoothed or "badgered" (referring to the bristles used to smooth the paint) mat. The badger can also be used to apply texture to the wet or dry mat through a striking action, called stippling.

The vitreous paint for stained glass is composed of a low-firing, essentially clear, glass-flux and opaque metallic oxides, generally iron or copper. It comes in powdered form, allowing the artist to mix it with water, vinegar, or oil, and layer it, depending on the desired effect. A binder, such as gum Arabic with water or Venetian turpentine with oil, is used to temporarily hold the paint to the glass. The paint must be built up in a series of thin coats, either using different binders or firing between applications. A variety of brushes, sticks, and other tools are used to apply and remove the paint before it is adhered permanently. The glass is fired in a kiln to approximately 1,250° F, at which point the glass-flux fuses to the base glass, which is beginning to soften, holding the opaque metallic oxides in place.

A highly important innovation appeared in architectural glass around the beginning of the fourteenth century: silver stain, the only true "stain" in stained glass. Since the eighth century, Islamic glass vessels, prized imported luxuries during the Middle Ages, had used silver stain as a colorant in painting designs on predominantly clear glass. With increased contact with Islamic artistry in Spain as the Christian kings of Aragon and Castile conquered Muslim territories, the innovation was eventually adopted by French artisans. In coloring the glass, a silver oxide in an opaque medium is applied, usually to the back of the glass, and fired. During the firing, silver ions migrate into the glass. They are suspended within the glass network, rather than fused onto the surface, as are glass paints and

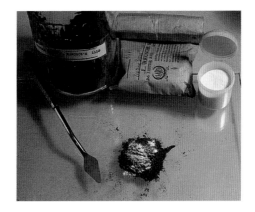

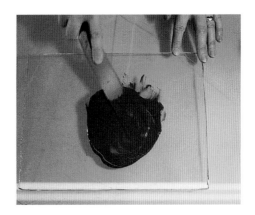

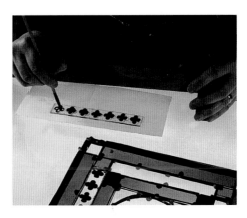

enamels. After firing, the opaque medium is removed from the glass, revealing the transparent yellow. Glass can be stained a pale yellow to a deep red, depending on the composition of the glass and stain, the number of applications, and the temperature of the kiln, and the stain can read as green when fired onto blue glass. Silver stain thus enables the painter to add various shades of yellow to a piece of glass without using a separating lead. It also

TOP LEFT *The vitreous paint comes in powdered form in a limited range of opaque colors, from brick red, to brown, to black. The artist can mix together compatible colors. Gum Arabic, which temporarily binds the paint to the glass before firing, is seen sprinkled over brown vitreous paint.*

MIDDLE LEFT *The paint is mixed with water, vinegar, oil, or alcohol. The artist decides how much liquid and binder to add, depending on the desired effect.*

BOTTOM LEFT *An armrest can be used to steady the hand. When painting is complete the glass is fired in a kiln at approximately 1,200° F.*

RIGHT *Silver stain, once introduced in the early fourteenth century, became one of the most valuable techniques for window design. It was used in broad applications, such as the triumphal banner against a golden sky from a Brussels window of the 1530s.*

BELOW LEFT *Various shades of neutral paint can also be seen in the figure of an angel about 1300 from the cathedral of Gerona. A dense paint outlines the curls of the hair and facial contours. A lighter wash models the neck and hands and also the depth of the folds of the angel's robes.*

BELOW RIGHT *Plating, the setting of layers of segments of glass one behind the other, can be seen in a detail of the Tiffany Studio's Personification of Spring, about 1900, from a private collection. On one level are several sections of different colors; on the next a single translucent layer. By plating, the dark copper-foiled lines can be muted, enabling designers to accent or tone down the graphic as if they were manipulating a pencil or brush.*

OPPOSITE *Impact and viewer reaction was always a consideration in stained glass. Meticulous realism as in the painted head of St. Otto of Bamburg for Regensburg Cathedral, 1857, by the German Max E. Ainmiller could give a sense of actuality to the spectator.*

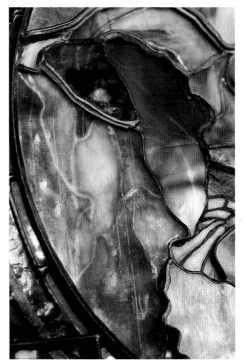

helped to solve the centuries-old problem of producing a readily available and reliable yellow glass.

Due both to a dwindling source of pot-metal glass sheets and to changes in scale and taste, by the mid-seventeenth century many glass painters were increasingly turning to colored glass enamels instead of pot-metal glasses. Enamels are intensely colored ground-up glasses that are painted onto the base glass, which is often a light tint for best effect. They fire at lower temperatures than opaque vitreous paints. Enamels are fused onto the glass surface, and, while they are not opaque, they lack the transparency of pot-metal sheet glass. The revival of stained glass in the nineteenth century was very much a

reaction against the extensive use of these paints, but they remain useful and are still employed today. The flesh painting (heads, hands, and feet) found in Tiffany windows was usually done in colored enamels. As a rule, enamels are not as durable as vitreous paints, though vitreous paints can also fail, due to poor composition of the paint or the base glass, or to under-firing, as well as to environmental factors.

LEAD CAME

The advantages of lead in window glazing are several and significant: it is malleable; it can be formed to almost any shape; it solders well and easily; it can survive for

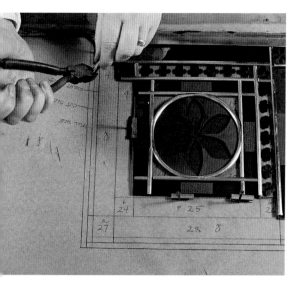

centuries with little or no maintenance. The earliest lead cames were cast. Molten lead was poured into a heated mold and planed to shape after cooling. By the end of the sixteenth century, almost all lead came was milled, which took less time than casting but yielded a thinner, less substantial came. Lead today is made in a variety of sizes and shapes: round, flat, high or low heart, wide, narrow, and so on.

The alloy used is important. Pure lead, while technically possible today, is not a good choice, since it is more susceptible to fatiguing and attack by acids than an alloy containing trace amounts of antimony, tin, and silver or copper. Old leads and cut-offs from new cames are recycled. Cames may also be made from other metals, such as brass and zinc, though their lack of malleability makes them much less useful.

When the glass is ready to be leaded together, or "glazed," the glazing guide is placed flat on the bench, and strips of wood are nailed down to hold the assembled pieces. The outer piece of lead is cut, placed on the guide, and glass is slipped into place. The next strip is cut and placed, and the next piece of glass inserted, and so on. During the process the glass and lead are held in place using glazing nails. Nailing can cause chipping of the glass edges, so they are protected using small pieces of lead. The guide ensures that the panel's size remains correct and constant. Once all the glass and leads are in place the panel is ready to be soldered at the joints, both front and back. The space between the glass and leads must be filled in order to give the panel additional strength and to make it waterproof. Linseed oil putty is either brushed or thumbed under the leads on both the back and the front of the panel. Finally, excess putty and oils are cleaned off the glass and leads.

TOP LEFT *Cutting pliers and lead knives are used to cut the lead came to the correct length. Glazing nails prevent the glass from moving during glazing.*

MIDDLE LEFT *Once all the lead is cut and brought to the correct size, the joints are soldered on the front and back of the panel.*

BOTTOM LEFT *Putty is forced under the leads on both sides to waterproof and strengthen the panel.*

BARRING

In an architectural setting, windows are subjected to extremes of weather—to wind pushing in and pulling out, to rain, sleet, hail, snow, and so forth. The malleability that makes lead ideal for the freedom the artist needs also makes windows vulnerable to gravity and wind, so support bars must be anchored into the frame and attached to the stained glass. Often, panels are set individually on T-bars set into the frame, in order to support the weight of glass and lead.

RIGHT *The axial window of the cathedral of Poitiers, about 1175, contains in an upper segment, the Ascension, in the center, the Crucifixion, and in the quatrefoil shape at the bottom, the Three Marys at the Tomb, martyrdoms of St. Peter and St. Paul, the Resurrection of the Dead, and donors Eleanor of Aquitain and King Henry II of England. The window is actually made up of many different independent sections supported by iron frames. In addition, horizontal support bars are placed into the interior molding frames to help to stabilize the window under wind stress.*

CONSERVATION

Stained glass has been repaired and restored since its earliest days. Complete windows survive that date back at least 900 years, and some individual panes are even older still, but this cannot change the fact that glass is a highly vulnerable medium. Glass loss occurs due to random vandalism, weather, political and/or religious upheavals (organized or otherwise), and simple changes in taste. Their function as an essential part of a building's fabric has helped save many windows, since window openings have to be filled with something, and stained glass is an expensive material that is usually replaced only with great difficulty. Still, there are many accounts of windows being removed and sometimes destroyed because of what was seen as offensive subject matter or to make way for new windows more in tune with current fashion. This is how many works of stained glass art have come into museum and private collections.

GLASS DETERIORATION

Glass is itself vulnerable to decay. Seemingly innocuous water is the first to attack. Its presence, in liquid or vapor form, promotes the leaching of the alkalis from the glass, weakening the network and building up corrosion products on the glass surface, although rainwater can actually be beneficial to a window, as it can wash away leached alkalis before they become concentrated on the glass surface. The way each glass ages depends on its composition and its environment. Certain glasses can develop an opaque surface crust that retains moisture and becomes highly alkaline. As the leaching solution becomes more alkaline (above pH 9), the silica network itself is attacked. Air pollution is thought to exacerbate the process. However, not all corrosion is due to weathering. It was observed that windows removed for storage and kept in damp conditions, notably during World War II, showed marked deterioration, while those kept in dry conditions fared much better. At the time, it was not realized that damp conditions would negatively affect the glass and paint.

Protective glazing, an external layer on the exterior of a window, is now a conservation possibility and, in Europe, has been one of the most effective ways to protect medieval glass. Such treatment is valid only if the space between the stained-glass window and its protective glazing is vented to allow a moving column of air. Otherwise, the window traps moisture, which actually accelerates deterioration of the historic glass. Nineteenth- and twentieth-century glass is less vulnerable than medieval glass, owing to its different composition, and rarely needs such protection. In modern buildings with climate control, an architectural choice may be to station the artistic glass on the interior, almost as a screen in front

of the functioning window. This solution has also been used for conservation of historic windows, thus removing them from the stress of functioning as a weight-bearing element.

CLEANING

Just as glass paint is a film on the surface of the glass, so too are dirt and corrosion, which obscure the painted details and cut down significantly on the light passing through the glass. Since stained glass relies on transmitted light, these foreign materials often must be removed so that light may shine through. However, such cleaning is not always easy, nor is it simple to do under even the best of circumstances. It must be approached with great care. Glass paint can be fragile and hard to distinguish from the film of dirt. Opalescent windows are often several layers thick. The soot, dirt, and old putty trapped between the layers can be very difficult to reach and they diminish a window's effect considerably.

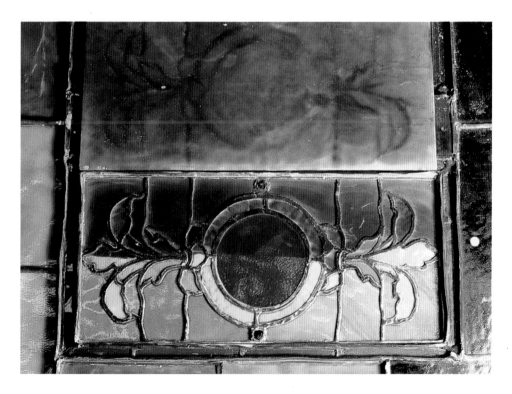

LEFT *Films of dirt build up on each glass surface. In* The Helping Hand, *1890, by John La Farge (The Detroit Institute of Arts, Detroit Michigan, Accession 59.168), a plate of glass has been removed and flipped over. The pattern of the lead that was directly in front of the plate can be seen clearly in the film of dirt, showing how some of the dirt entered the interspace. The bottom base layer has been half cleaned, showing how much dirt was sitting on the glass surface.*

Traditionally, there were only two reliable, waterproof methods of repairing breaks or losses in architectural glass: the replacement of the broken glass with a new piece—sometimes a good match, sometimes not—or the insertion of repair leads. The former means that original material is completely removed. The latter is unsightly, compromises the panel's legibility, and usually results in partial removal of original material, as the break line is grozed to make room for the heart of the repair lead.

Today, broken glass can be repaired using a variety of methods, depending on the setting. In a museum, exposure to weathering, ultraviolet light, humidity, temperature fluctuations, and the like is stringently controlled. The same is not true in an architectural setting, where the term "museum conditions" is often used to denote the presence of some form of protective glazing, though actual conditions vary widely. The protection is not just for the stained glass, but also for the material used to repair it. Traditional materials have been used in the field for a number of years, being both well known and well understood. Accelerated aging tests must be performed on newer materials to give an indication of how they will react over time—though, in the end, only time itself will actually tell.

Epoxies have proven very effective for bonding broken glass. They adhere well to glass, and their refractive index, which is the amount that a ray of light is bent when traveling from air into a solid, can be close to that of the various glasses, so they significantly reduce the reflection of light off a break edge as they hold the glass together. However, they do not hold up well against the weather, so their use in architectural settings is limited to areas where they can be protected, either with overall protective glazing or with a plate of glass placed directly behind the glued repair.

RTV silicones and neutral cure silicones are useful where the repair will be exposed to the elements, since they have tested better than epoxies under those conditions. Their biggest drawback is that their refractive index is not a good match for much glass, so light reflects noticeably off the cracks. With opalescent glass this is not a problem because it is so dense, but with transparent glass it can be unsightly. Silicones have some "give," which is good for simple breaks when the glass is under wind load, but they are not a good choice for a compound break, since they may allow too much movement.

Copper foil is another alternative, though it reads as an opaque black line, albeit a narrow one. It consists of a thin copper strip with adhesive on one side, which is wrapped around and pressed onto the edge of the glass. The pieces are then soldered together, so the glass being repaired must be able to withstand heat. It has the advantage of being a mechanical, reversible repair.

Lead came should never be used to repair new breaks in glass. The heart of the lead joining the upper and lower flanges pushes the pieces of glass apart, so they invariably must be grozed in order to realign the painting; in addition, the upper and lower lead flanges cover painted details, bringing them into contact with the waterproofing putty and moisture. Even flanges used to hide a break on the front and back without actually inserting a lead can affect the paint and the readability of the graphic. With old breaks mended with lead came, the restorer and client usually discuss the advisability of removing the old came and replacing it with copper foil or edge bonding in order to restore greater legibility.

LEAD

Lead cames perform the very important function of supporting the glass, but in addition to that they provide a rhythm and scale to the composition. Deciding where the lead lines should be placed is an important step in the realization of any sketch. When releading, it is important to establish the location of the original lead lines so that the conservator or artisan does not end up reinterpreting the composition according to his or her own preferences, since the choices were made by the work's original creators. Put another way, who are we to argue with the choices made by the work's original creators?

Over time, the cycle of expansion and contraction due to heating and cooling can cause cracking and metal fatigue, especially in milled and extruded leads. While the lead itself is an artifact, when it has lost the ability to hold the glass securely, one must consider replacing it. Early cast leads are occasionally found on panels from the sixteenth century (and earlier). Every attempt must be made to keep these rare leads. Later milled leads will have milling marks on the hearts. Usually these are a series of slanted and perpendicular lines, but occasionally one finds names, dates, or symbols. These should be recorded, since they can tell us something about the history of the piece.

There is no absolute dated time failure for leads. Decisions about releading need to be made case by case. If releading is warranted, it is important to duplicate the original leads in width and height. It is not uncommon to find medieval pieces releaded in the nineteenth century with wide flat leads, which cover important painted details. Leading is not just a mechanical operation; it requires skill and attention. A plodding or sloppy releading destroys the energy of the original line.

The modern world has brought many new ways of working with glass, as discussed in the final chapter. Dalle-de-verre, a technique that embeds chunks of glass in concrete or epoxy, was popular in the 1950s. In the last twenty years, new techniques, such as fused, acid-etched, molded, or photo-screened treatments have been used in many modern glass installations. Inexpensive commercial glass is now often combined with other glass and glazing processes, especially in large-scale installations. Stained glass, however, still largely follows the general guidelines set down by Theophilus, testimony of the power of the material and the lasting relevance of historic windows for inspiration in the present. Although we may solve problems in new ways or make use of new technologies, the artist is still using glass to transform the light of interior space.

BELOW *The severe cracking seen on these milled leads necessitated releading this window produced by the Tiffany Studios, 1897, for Congregation Shearith Israel, The Spanish and Portuguese Synagogue, New York. When the lead can no longer perform its intended function it needs to be replaced.*

The Revival of Monumental Architecture and the Place of Glass

3

OPPOSITE *Strong frontality is characteristic of a seated emperor, traditionally referred to as Charlemagne, from Strasbourg Cathedral of the late twelfth century. The heads of servants at the side of the throne are fourteenth-century stopgaps.*

BELOW LEFT AND RIGHT *Imagery was pervasive, whether a tenth-century Byzantine wall painting of the Birth of Christ from Göreme, Turkey, or an Anglo-Saxon manuscript, such as the Benedictionale of St. Aethelwold (British Library MS Add. 49598, fol. 24v).*

Stained glass achieved its dominance as an art form in the Middle Ages because of its ability to include images, essential criteria of Christianity in western Europe. After a tentative beginning in the first centuries, as the new religion tried to distance itself from the conflicting image tradition of the classical past, Christianity developed customs of representing God and his saints, individuals who became revered for exemplary lives in imitation of Christ. Stories from Holy Scripture also furnished the basis for image cycles. A core element of the Christian belief was that within a triune God, consisting of Father, Son, and Holy Spirit, the second person, the Son, became man through his birth from the Virgin Mary. Thus, the depiction of the human form of Christ did not diminish his dignity as God.

The tradition was expanded through wall paintings and illuminated books from

the eighth through the tenth centuries under the reign of Carolingian and Ottonian rulers. In the eleventh century, Europe witnessed a great rise of building construction. The very splendor of the churches was justified by allusion to Solomon's Temple (for example, Suger of Saint-Denis, *De consecratione*, II). The buildings were seen to create images of the Heavenly Jerusalem, where Christ will welcome the faithful in a heavenly realm. The earliest extant program, the series of prophets of Augsburg Cathedral, which assuredly were complemented by apostles, stood as witnesses to the story of salvation. These great iconic figures ablaze with light must have framed an image of Christ or the Virgin set in the eastern part of the church. Significantly, the color harmonies of red, green, and yellow, with blue as an accent, set the tone for subsequent German glass. A wide border of foliate design, similar to the metalwork and stone carving of the time, would have originally surrounded the figures.

Such a disposition of wide border can be seen in the standing figures in the church of St. Kunibert in Cologne, 1220–30. The figure of St. John the Baptist floats upon a background of geometric pattern, at his feet a donor with name (modern restoration) on the banderole. John carries his greeting to Christ: "Behold the Lamb of God, behold him who takes away [the sins of the world]" (John 1: 29). The lush border growth of white fronds around a central blue leaf is a vital part of the majesty of the window. Such fascination with ornament may extend to the figure itself, as in the image of an emperor, traditionally called Charlemagne, from Strasbourg Cathedral. The importance of pattern for this era transcends any notion of simple decoration. To medieval minds, pattern lifted the specific from its temporal restrictions, linking it to unchanging patterns in the mind of God. A king was

not simply a man of a certain height, length of nose, or color of hair, in power between specific dates, but an image of eternal rulership whose power flowed from divine decree.

The medieval designer produced both the iconic (image-rich) and aniconic (image-absent) window. Within each church, sculpted or painted images enunciated the creed of the makers while designating the hierarchy of space, most vividly demonstrated in the High Gothic

ABOVE *Decorative borders were as important as the image in early medieval glass. Glass from St. Patroclus, Soest, Germany, shows the abstracted floral ornament and beaded borders typical of the twelfth century.*

BELOW *Abstraction and ornament of early medieval design continues well into the thirteenth century, as in the windows of St. Kunibert, Cologne. The donor, who is located outside the sacred space created by the border around the saint, addresses his patron with an ascending scroll.*

OPPOSITE *Augsburg Cathedral, about 1110, retains the earliest extant stained glass program. Imaged here, Osee (Hosea) is on the left and David on the right. Abstract and dignified, the prophets were most probably juxtaposed with the Apostles to proclaim the unity of the Old and New Testaments.*

ABOVE LEFT *Biblical stories were often depicted in sculptural programs of churches. The angel Gabriel from the west façade of the cathedral of Amiens gestures in greeting to the Virgin Mary as he announces God's plan of salvation.*

ABOVE RIGHT *The organization of imagery both within and without a medieval church, however varied, was always highly organized. Viewers recognized individuals because of identifying insignia but also because of the placement within a series. This trend culminated in the thirteenth-century facades such as that of the cathedral of Amiens, of the 1230s.*

programs of exterior sculpture. Windows organized the interior, filling the entire space with light and form. In the ideal building campaign, great window programs were conceived and most often under way as the building itself was nearing completion. The art historian Madeline Caviness described the reuse and alteration of cartoons (full-scale line designs on wood, vellum, or linen for stained-glass windows) in the twelfth-century glazing of the choir of Saint-Rémi, Reims, even as the architecture was in the final stages of construction: "the sequence suggested here shows artists designing in series, each modification based on a critique of completed panels viewed in their intended position in the building" (*Sumptuous Arts*, p. 116). In short, windows were designed as part of the architectural ensemble, not as an added embellishment to merely decorate the building.

Placement was a key issue. The axial window, the one close to an important altar, was seen as the place of greatest prestige. Thus the centrally located *Crucifixion/ Ascension* window of Poitiers

Cathedral was without question the most complex as well as most prestigious window within the building. A monumental cross is placed below the image of the *Ascension of Christ*. The scenes actually intersect; the apostles and the Virgin witnessing Christ's ascent into heaven stand in the space just above the arms of the cross. Below is a quatrefoil of narrative scenes: the *Three Marys at the Tomb*, the *Judgment and Martyrdom of Saints Peter and Paul*, and the *Resurrection of the Dead*, and donors.

The contradictions of the Christian themes that were developed in Passion dramas and meditative poetry are visualized in the window. Christ is dead, but also alive; he is king, but also a felon; he is naked, but clothed in regal purple. The points of view shift, as do representations of space and the proportions of figures. Multiple events are conflated into a single spatial plane. The richness of the treatment of the cross and the royal purple cloth worn by Christ transcend generic images to evoke the presence of the piece of the wood from

Christ's cross in the Holy Cross Abbey adjacent to the cathedral. Hymns written, like the *Vexilla Regis* by the late-sixth-century Venantius Fortunatus, to honor the reception of the relic in Poitiers were sung throughout the Middle Ages: "Hail Cross! On which the Life Himself / Died and by death our life restor'd." One of the verses describes the cross as "arbor decora et fulgida / ornatus Regis purpura" (shining tree adorned with splendor, decorated with royal purple).

Keenly aware of the prestige of place, donors vied for the most visible areas in churches to place their portraits. Eleanor of Aquitaine and King Henry II of England, as donors of Poitiers Cathedral, could have themselves depicted at the bottom of the central window above the high altar.

The laity, within cathedral or monastic programs, manipulated their presence to be adjacent to sacred space and to be recognized as participants. Often such portrayal included the works of art—the illuminated book, church, or window. For example, Emperor Henry II holds a model of Basle Minster in the cloister of Wettingen, Switzerland. The image augments the importance of the city of Basle, which sponsored the window, even as it makes a statement that rulers have obligations to support great building campaigns.

Married in Poitiers in 1154, Eleanor of Aquitaine and King Henry II of England were believed to have financed the initial building of the new cathedral. Eleanor was one of the most fascinating individuals of the twelfth century. She had inherited Aquitaine, directly to the south of Poitiers, a richly productive area that included the vineyards of Bordeaux, and married Louis VII of France in 1137. The court that surrounded the queen was renowned for its support of the arts and of music, as attested in the troubadour compositions celebrating poetry and the art of love. Divorced from Louis in 1152, Eleanor retained her dowry of Aquitaine and married Henry Plantagenet, the future king of England. Honored by her son Richard

the Lionheart, who reigned from 1189 to 1199, she ruled as regent of England while he was in the Holy Land on crusade. After Richard's death she saw her youngest son, John Lackland, the signer of the Magna Carta, succeed to the throne. It has been suggested that Eleanor's exposure to cutting-edge compositions in glass such as the *Jesse Tree* window of Saint-Denis influenced stained glass in England, specifically the *Jesse Tree* window of York Minster (ca. 1180–90). Eleanor and Henry had themselves depicted offering the window in the lowest medallion of the *Crucifixion/Ascension* window of the cathedral probably about 1175.

Windows were made of glass, iron, and lead, which were costly materials in the Middle Ages; indeed, their value was frequently described in terms of precious stones. Windows were essential to the fabric of a church for the medieval thinker and viewer. Their colored glass modulated light within the interior space while illustrating the sacred narrative that defined the faith. Images and scenes leaded together into windows literally and symbolically shed light on the central drama of salvation enacted daily in the ritual consecration of the eucharist during mass, when Christ's presence became present to worshipers.

MONASTIC PROGRAMS

The new building activity in the eleventh century and the subsequent development of stained glass were closely linked to the social and religious structure called monasticism. Benedict of Nursia (ca. 480–544) had transformed early Christian movements of withdrawal for spiritual purity into a system whereby groups of individuals came together for communal prayer (the divine office), study, work, and social support. His foundation of Monte Cassino, about halfway between Rome and Naples, became a model for a system that soon dominated European intellectual and religious life. The monks—male or female—did not marry, but formed single-sex communities that were an economic and political counterbalance to the control of wealth through landed families and their descendents. As the centers of education in the seventh and eight centuries, monasteries sent forth emissaries who converted the tribes of northern Europe. With Christianity came education and links to the civilization of the Mediterranean.

Formal orders of monks such as those of Cluny, founded in 910, rose to extraordinary power and influence by the twelfth century through protection by the nobility. With wealth and prestige came the establishment of great churches to serve the liturgical needs of the monks. Monastic churches were not parish churches. As they evolved over time, and towns often grew around them, accommodations were made for the laity. Sometimes a separate church was established for townsfolk: at Bury St. Edmunds (Suffolk), for example, the church of St. Mary was built adjacent to the monastic walls. Frequently the nave areas of monastic churches were given over to parish functions, exemplified by Boppard-am-Rhine, or the Benedictine abbeys of Tewkesbury and Wymondham (Norfolk);

the latter's north aisle for the town came to dominate the profile of the building by the end of the fifteenth century.

In the twelfth century, however, the monks were the elite class, the most highly educated. The windows they commissioned reflected not only their erudition but also their method of prayer: gathering several times a day in the choir area of the church to pray communally, primarily by singing psalms. The monks would remain in the presence of the works of art they set in these spaces. With the construction of his abbey's new choir, Abbot Suger (1081–1155) of Saint-Denis installed a series of windows exemplary of monastic spirituality and twelfth-century visual thinking.

Suger, a man of unusual determination and management skills, was a trusted advisor of Louis VII, who reigned from 1137 to 1180. Responding to the call of Bernard of Clairvaux, Louis embarked on the unsuccessful Second Crusade, 1147–49, leaving Suger to act as regent of France in his absence. The abbot's influence with the monarchy consolidated Saint-Denis's place as the site of burial for French kings and repository of the regalia— crown, scepter, spurs, and other ceremonial objects—of coronation (coronations themselves, however, were held in the cathedral of Reims). Suger rebuilt the eastern and western ends of the church around 1141–44, using revolutionary vaulting and construction techniques that proclaimed the new Gothic style. In a gesture unusual in medieval history, he left explicit writings (named *De administratione* and *De consecratione*) detailing his construction and embellishment of the church. For the windows he stated that "we also had painted, by the hands of many masters sought out in various nations, a splendid variety of new windows." These included, in the central chapel, a *Tree of Jesse*, and to the sides, windows of the *New*

ABOVE *Often cited as the first Gothic construction, the choir of the Abbey of Saint-Denis, 1140–44, gives an important place to stained glass. Each radiating chapel has two stained-glass windows, some showing ornamental design, demonstrating that aesthetics as well as imagery was accepted as a spiritual need.*

ABOVE *In the image of the Brazen Serpent from the Moses window, twelfth-century viewers recalled an episode from the story of Moses but saw it as prefiguring Christ who saved his followers just as Moses rescued the Israelites.*

OPPOSITE *The Moses window of Saint-Denis, 1140–44, was one of several for which Abbot Suger provided complex descriptions. From the bottom we see: Pharoah's daughter finding Moses, Moses and the Burning Bush, and the Israelites crossing the Red Sea. The side panels are modern restorations. The medallion pattern parallels illuminated manuscripts of the time.*

Alliance, Infancy of Christ, Anagogical Themes, and the *Story of Moses,* as well as decorative patterns with griffins, historical themes, and lives of the saints.

The most complex windows, such as the *Story of Moses,* Suger described, recording the Latin verses he prepared to explain the meaning of the scenes.

In the window where Pharaoh's daughter finds Moses in the basket,
    Moses in the basket is that child
    Whom the Church, the royal maiden,
        nurses with holy mind.

Where the Lord appears to Moses in the burning bush,
    Just as the bush is seen to burn yet is not
        consumed,
    So he who is full of the divine fire burns yet
        is not consumed.

Where Pharaoh and his horsemen are submerged in the Red Sea,
    What baptism does to the good,
    A like form but an unlike cause does to the
        pharaoh's army.

Where Moses raises the bronze serpent,
    Just as the bronze serpent slays all
        serpents,
    So Christ raised on the cross slays his
        enemies.

Where Moses receives the Ten Commandments on Mount Sinai,
    The law having been given to Moses,
    The grace of Christ comes to its aid.
    Grace gives life, the letter kills.

The scenes might at first appear to construct a straightforward account of the story of Moses (Exodus 2: 20): Moses is found by Pharaoh's daughter; he is called to lead his people out of Egypt, crosses the Red Sea, cures the Israelites of snakebites, and receives the Commandments. Suger's inscriptions, however, demonstrate that the Old Testament story is seen as prefiguring the actions of Christ and his Church, so that the Crossing of the Red Sea becomes a reference to the sacrament of baptism and the purification of sin. The image of the brazen serpent (Numbers 21: 8–9) lifted up in the desert after the fleeing Israelites were attacked by serpents is seen as prefiguring Christ lifted up on the cross. The Israelites had become weary of the journey and "began to speak against God and Moses," whereupon God sent fiery serpents that bit and killed many of them. Repenting, the Israelites asked Moses to pray to God, who instructed him to make an image of a serpent in brass and raise it up. As Suger presents the analogy, just as all who looked on the image made by Moses were cured of bodily affliction, in looking toward Christ humanity is cured of spiritual ills. In the window, the brazen

ABOVE *The* Magi before Herod, *1179–80, was part of a complicated window comparing the Gospel events foretold by the Scripture. The Benedictine monks of Canterbury Cathedral were learned patrons of the arts who engaged highly trained artists to construct windows for their meditation. The Methuselah Master, so called because of his work on the image of the patriarch, also designed this medallion window.*

serpent on the column becomes a dragon from which emerges a green (living) cross, inscribed with the body of Christ against vine scrolls.

The richness of ornament in the windows was as important as the image. Within medieval social structure, continuity was the ideal, with objects being used over centuries. Suger, for example, wrote about the altarpieces, furniture, and vessels used for mass dating from the time of King Dagobert I five centuries earlier. What was constructed was meant to be permanent, and the most exquisite materials and skill were lavished on the making. Stained glass was seen as an adorment of significant value and in the twelfth century linked to metalwork for both its cost and its forms. Bronze casting, the mark of excellence in antiquity, had been revived with the great doors of Abbot Bernward of Hildesheim, 1014, and those

of Saint-Denis, 1140, which Suger inscribed with the injunction "marvel not at the gold and the expense but at the craftsmanship of the work" (XXIV). So popular were these works that the monk Bernard of Clairvaux was moved to question them: "the church is adorned with gemmed crowns of light—nay with lusters like cart wheels, girt all round with lamps, but no less brilliant with the precious stones that stud them." He saw candelabra "like massive trees of bronze" also studded with gems (*Apologia*). Wheel-shaped candelabra representing the Heavenly Jerusalem have survived, notably at the abbey at Hildesheim. That of the abbey of Saint-Rémi of Reims, installed in the 1120s, was restored or replaced in the eighteenth century and later in modern times, but its celebrated candelabrum of eighteen feet in height was lost during the French Revolution. Suger describes a pedestal for a cross incorporating 80 marks of refined gold on which goldsmiths from Lorraine "sometimes five, sometimes seven," labored for two years.

The windows and the metalwork Suger commissioned were of such importance that he took special care to ensure their upkeep. "Since their marvelous workmanship and the cost of the sapphire [colored] and painted glass makes these windows very valuable, we appointed a master craftsman for their protection and maintenance, just as we also appointed a skilled goldsmith for the gold and silver ornaments. These would receive their allowances and whatever was apportioned to them in addition, such as coins from the altar and flour from the common storehouse of the brethren, and they were never to neglect their duties." To the medieval user, the work of art was not a superfluous luxury but an essential part of the expression of the body politic.

Equally erudite and valued were the windows in the monks' choir at Canterbury

Cathedral. A coherent series of twelve typological windows was installed with the rebuilding of the church, the most extensive of any in the period. Typology, the juxtaposition of Christian events with Old Testament prototypes, had been at the core of Suger's thinking. Christ himself had cited these parallels, for example, the image of Jonah and the whale and Christ's entombment: "For as Jonah was in the whale's belly three days and three nights: so shall the Son of man be in the heart of the earth three days and three nights" (Matthew 12: 40). The Gospels explain that the Crucifixion was prefigured in the exodus from Egypt: "And as Moses lifted up the serpent in the desert, so must the Son of man be lifted up" (John 3: 14). From such statements, an entire system of resonances was developed. Isaac walking with Abraham to be sacrificed (Genesis 22) formed a prototype for Christ carrying his cross to Golgatha. Samson escaping from Gaza by tearing down the gates (Judges 16: 3) was likened to Christ entering the gates of Hell to redeem those waiting in Limbo—often with Adam and Eve in the front row. By the later Middle Ages these concepts were codified in the *Biblia pauperum*, inspiring programs as vast as King's College Chapel, Cambridge, and the multiple openings of cloister walks.

The monks often employed verbal as well as visual embellishment, with sophisticated, rhymed Latin inscriptions as in both Suger's program at Saint-Denis and the Canterbury series. Although much of the typological glass at Canterbury was destroyed by religious iconoclasts, the original program can be reconstructed through examination of medieval records and a study of the extant window armatures that show the medallion patterns. The series contained numerous typological juxtapositions that later became standard references, exemplified by a window that has survived substantially intact.

At the top center is the New Testament scene of the Three Kings riding to Judea and to left and right are Old Testament prototypes—the prophet Balaam riding on his ass (Numbers 22: 21–35) and Isaiah, who prophesied, "Behold a virgin shall conceive, and bear a son, and his name shall be called Emmanuel" (Isaiah 7: 14). In the register below, the three kings speak with King Herod, who endeavors to learn the location of the Messiah's birth so that he can kill the child. To the left, Moses leads the Israelites out of Egypt. Pharaoh, appropriately labeled, is seated in his palace while Moses moves away, the waters of the Red Sea at his feet and the pillar of fire that led him through the desert of Sinai in the background. On the right, is a highly unusual scene

LEFT Moses Leading the Israelites Out of Egypt, *Canterbury Cathedral, 1179–80, reflects the Magi who are warned not to report back to Herod about the location of the Christ Child. Moses strides forward and away from the seated Pharoah, who is therefore associated with the seated king Herod as a person to be shunned.*

BELOW LEFT *In* Christ Leading the Gentiles Away from Pagan Gods, *Canterbury Cathedral, 1179–80, the pagan temple frames an image of a nude male statue mounted on a classical capital that evokes with extraordinary sensitivity the musculature of late-Hellenistic bronzes. The structure of the two scenes establishes the relationships: the Red Sea is like the baptismal font, the pillar of fire is the church, Pharaoh is like the pagan idol, Moses like Christ, and the Israelites the equivalent of the Christian gentiles.*

of Christ, identifiable by the red cruciform halo, leading the faithful away from idolatry.

The ordinance of large-scale figures in the upper windows of the church and small-scale narrative compositions on the lower level is firmly established with Canterbury. On the upper level, the ancestors of Christ appear as massive, single, seated figures with their feet resting on arched bases reminiscent of the curving drapery signifying the vaulted heavens under the feet of Christ in early Christian sarcophagi. The power of the large-scale exposition can be seen in the manner of drafting of the heads. The relationship to the viewer was taken into account by the designer, even to the shifts of painterly decisions for artists when they produced large-scale images or when they were planning the narrative composition of typological windows. For example, the typological window showing Moses leading the Israelites out of Egypt, and Christ leading the people away from paganism, was designed by the same artist who was responsible for the great figure of Methuselah. This strategy of representation became standard in the Gothic style— common to the cathedrals of Chartres, Bourges, Auxerre, Clermont-Ferrand, and other sites.

In the lands of the Holy Roman Empire—essentially German-speaking Europe—similar systems prevailed. The abbey of Arnstein an der Lahn, part of the Premonstratensian order, installed a five-window series in the choir, 1170/80. The two outermost windows contained scenes from the Story of Moses, and the two inner windows depicted the Life of Christ, beginning with the Annunciation and ending with the Crucifixion. The central window contained a *Tree of Jesse*, a theme Durandus (Book X) later mentioned explicitly as an example of allegory. The image corresponds to Isaiah's prophecy describing the reign of peace and justice with the coming of the Messiah. The text begins with the Messiah's origins and gifts: "And there shall come forth a rod out of the root of Jesse and a flower shall rise up of this root. And the spirit of the Lord shall rest upon him: the spirit of wisdom, and of understanding, the spirit of counsel, and of fortitude, the spirit of knowledge, and of godliness. And he shall be filled with the spirit of the fear of the Lord" (Isaiah 11: 1–3).

From this image, the Middle Ages developed a construction of a tree with the recumbent figure of the patriarch Jesse asleep at the bottom, his position as progenitor imaged by the vine coming from his loins. Within the vine are kings, often identifiable as David and Solomon, followed by the Virgin, the "flower" in Isaiah's text, with Christ seated above her. Depending on the placement of the theme, the schema could be expanded or contracted. A manuscript page may show two or three segments of the vine, while a sculptural program such as the north portal of Chartres Cathedral could spin out the vine into a series of arches framing the portal.

In the lands of the Holy Roman Empire, the Jesse Tree developed internal typological systems with depictions of the events in the Life of Christ, as in the parish church of St. Kunibert in Cologne.

Surrounding Christ are seven doves, each representing one of the gifts of the Holy Spirit. At the top, central to human understanding, is *timor Domini*, the fear of the awesome majesty of God and the acknowledgment of human frailty. Beginning from the left and reading clockwise are wisdom *(sapientia)*, intelligence *(intelligentia)*, counsel *(consilium)*, fortitude *(fortitudo)*, knowledge *(scientia)*, and piety *(pietas)*. The order repeats Isaiah's text, the subject of which also formed the focus of the daily masses following the feast of Pentecost, the descent of the Holy Spirit

upon the Apostles after Christ's Ascension. In the later Middle Ages, the Jesse Tree became an extraordinary vision of kings and prophets entwined on complex branches showing tour-de-force delineation of exotic costume.

The *Life of Moses* includes a self-portrait of the glass painter, Master Gerlachus, shown holding a pot of paint as he inscribes the surrounding inscription with his brush: "Rex regu[m] clare gerlacho prop[i]ciare" (King of Kings, render favorable the acclaim

of Gerlachus). Clearly an artist of great power and honor within his community, Gerlachus takes the position usually filled by the donor. Although all other documented glass painters in the twelfth century were either monks or priests, Gerlachus is dressed in secular clothes and not as a member of the Premonstratensian community. Whoever he was, he was keenly attuned to the style of his time. Similar lavish borders, schematized figures with draperies defined by the sharp outline of

ABOVE *The* Tree of Jesse, *1170/80, here from the Premonstratensian Abbey of Arnstein an der Lahn, was a widely used reference to speak of the coming of the reign of Christ, the Messiah prophesied by Isaiah.*

folds, and marvelously intricate tendril designs in the backgrounds appear in contemporaneous manuscripts. The prestigious commission of the *Psalter of Henry the Lion*, ca. 1167, for example, also includes typological images such as the *Annunciation* and *Moses* and *Gideon*. The reference compared Mary's virginity to Moses's vision of the Burning Bush (Exodus 3), which burned but was not consumed, and Gideon's fleece, which alone received dew while the rest of the ground was dry (Judges 6: 37–40).

Medieval Christian art in Europe presupposed a culture shared by the maker, the patron, and other viewers. In this system, an artist was perceived as an agent expressing visually the culture's beliefs. Judgments of quality therefore focused primarily on the evaluation of the usefulness of the artist's work, not on the artist himself. Gerlachus's image and signature are unusual; in almost all instances, if a work of art bore a representation or a name, it was of the patron, not the artist. Abbot Suger, for example, inscribed his name on the lintel of the bronze doors to Saint-Denis and also had his image placed worshiping at the feet of the Virgin Mary in the scene of the Annunciation in one of his windows.

Suger's writing followed the prevailing belief that the importance of the object was determined by the value of the materials used and the creator's skill in manipulating them. He frequently alluded to a medieval formula of praise: the workmanship surpassed the materials (*De Administratione* XXXIII). Yet the ultimate use of the work of art—or building—was to offer the viewer a locus of transcendence.

The new preaching orders of the thirteenth century continued such erudite depictions. The Dominicans, or Order of Preachers, were founded in 1205 (papal confirmation of the rule 1216) and the Franciscans in 1209 (rule confirmed 1223). Although these orders were committed to interaction with lay communities, especially those in the burgeoning cities of the thirteenth century, they retained monastic discipline of communal recitation of the office in their churches and the intellectual investment in art. The windows of the Franciscan church in Erfurt, 1230–35, show the life of Christ and the life of the order's founder, including Francis's reception of the stigmata.

The depiction may seem simple but is in reality a highly complex exposition of the new accessibility of Christ to individual believers heralded by the saint's actions. Francis, in an ecstatic vision, received the signs of Christ's wounds in his body, identifying him as someone empathetically united to Christ. The system of typology, demonstrated at Saint-Denis, Canterbury, and Arnstein, was used by the friars as a way of explaining the new piety exemplified by their founder. Christ's life represented the lives of the prophets, Francis's life represented the life of Christ. As Francis's biographer Thomas of Celano wrote, "For in truth, the venerable father was marked in five parts of his body with the marks of the passion and of the cross as though he had hung upon the cross with the Son of God."

Rhymed Latin couplets like those at Saint-Denis surround the Erfurt panels. The stigmata panel reads: "He sees on the cross a distinct seraphim anointed with wounds" and "from this event, those signs [in Latin, *stigmata*] of Christ are soon to be known." Text and images both make clear the importance of the seraphic vision: in the future these signs or marks—the marks in his hands, the marks of these words, and also the mark of the image depicted in the glass—will allow this singular event to become known. Compositionally simple, to the extent that the viewer recognizes Francis, his wounds, and the seraphim, the details in the composition and the inscription convey a deeper meaning about the event and the believer's ability to become closer to Christ through empathy with suffering.

Soon after Erfurt, the basilica of San Francesco at Assisi was built to honor the saint's tomb. The upper church houses the oldest stained glass in Italy. Produced by northern craftsmen around 1255, making the windows contemporary with Cologne Cathedral's Bible window, the double-lancet windows of the axial chapel present a typological theme. In a left-to-right correspondence, the *Burning Bush* is set next to the *Nativity*; *Joab embracing Amasa* (2 Samuel 20: 9–10), whom he then stabs, is set across from the *Kiss of Judas*. Later in the century, the Assisi Franciscans mirrored the Gothic in both form and content. Images of the saints, and scenes from their lives, were installed throughout the basilica's windows. A typical example is the window of *St. Francis and St. Anthony of Padua*. Dress and attributes differentiate the saints, and scenes such as the miraculous vision of the cross speaking to Francis at St. Damiano are pictured in Gothic medallions above.

ARTISTIC DECISIONS

In all of this work, stylistic affinities link the artists' approach to imagery and to pattern. The twelfth-century aesthetic concentrated on rich effects of surface, emphatically two-dimensional images, and a sense of stern power. Close to metalwork of the time, the twelfth-century window

delighted in multiple textures achieved by juxtaposition of color and pattern to achieve a voluptuous sense of ornament. In these early windows, the border patterns, frames for individual scenes, and designs filling the interstices between medallions are as important as the flat schematized images they frame. Scholars have explored the richness of such motifs that cross over in metal work, manuscript illuminations, and glass.

The image and decorative embellishment are conceived similarly. The border of the *Crucifixion* window at Poitiers, 1175, presents elongated heart-shaped motifs linked by white bands of interlace. These red segments against a blue ground profile an internal grouping of five symmetrically arranged fronds of blue and gold. The same kinds of color harmonies and framing appear in a figural motif from the former chapel of the château of Gargilesse. The image of Christ in majesty, like the border

motif, is framed by a curving white banding. Essentially, no priority is given to the figure over the background; all elements of the design are on the same plane. The colors, like a modern abstract "color-field" work, pulsate within the viewer's perception, making all aspects of the window appear of equal importance. The crosshatch over the blue ground behind the body of Christ is activated with the same energy as the lines delineating Christ's features. Geometric patterns control the parallel strokes of Christ's beard and hair just as they inspire the pearled border of the halo.

The windows of Canterbury contain some of the richest and most complex ornament of all medieval programs. A single motif displays pairs of white fronds forming heart-shaped frames dividing red and blue grounds. They contain palmettes of green, yellow, purple, and white leaves with green shoots in between them. Border designs from the *St. Eustace* window of Sens Cathedral are analogous. Canterbury's corona's *Redemption* window displays acanthus foliage coiling in fluid rinceaux in the interstices between the medallions. The ground is a pulsating red against which the connecting fronds of light blue, white, and gold interplay. The wide border uses a contrasting red ground to relieve purple and white fronds sprouting alternately from the left and the right. The sides are connected by a white zigzag strap and red rosettes. Almost identical patterns are found in the French cathedrals of Troyes (in the *St. Andrew* window) and Auxerre (in the *Life of St. Nicholas* window). Scholars have hypothesized that workshops traveled from site to site, or that other means, such as the sharing of copybooks, enabled communication of common patterns, compositions, and even design habits like ways of depicting drapery.

RIGHT *Many windows terminated with an image of affirmation, often the enthroned Christ. This late twelfth-century window was created for the chapel of the château of Gargilesse, now Notre-Dame de Gargilesse (Indre). A cruciform halo marks this image as Christ, as distinguished from God the Father.*

OPPOSITE *The renowned* Ascension *window of the cathedral of Le Mans, 1140–45, is one of the earliest in France. The elongated figures and sharp, knife-like folds are typical of the region of Poitou.*

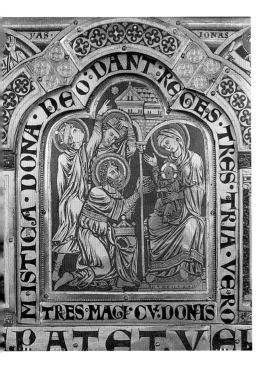

ABOVE *Often the most renowned of artists of the twelfth century were metalworkers. Nicholas of Verdun who executed the enameled altarpiece for Klosterneuburg, an Imperial abbey, was one of the rare individuals known by name and also by itinerary. After his work in Austria, he was called to Cologne. His style that evokes the weight of classical drapery and movement in the figure later appeared in stained glass and manuscript painting.*

RIGHT *A Tree of Jesse in Freiburg-en-Brisgau., before 1218, shows the vigor of Nicholas of Verdun's influence. Medieval styles were not rigidly chronological but varied from region to region and appear to reflect artistic personalities.*

Scholars have identified regional patterns in much of the work of the twelfth-century glaziers. The style of southwest France, with much early glass remaining in the cathedral of Le Mans, shows a boldness associated with manuscripts of the region around 1100. In the cathedral's *Ascension* window, 1140–45, figures are characterized by elongated proportions, and their drapery falls in sharp V-shaped folds. Animated gestures enliven the scenes.

Heads with typically long, rectangular faces are capped with short curly hair. The curls frequently extend beyond the leadlines and are painted on the surrounding halos. Artists working in the style also executed windows in the eastern part of Poitiers Cathedral, such as the *Crucifixion*. A different style, which may have been propagated though the metalwork of Nicholas of Verdun, shows a highly sculptural inspiration. His Klosterneuburg pulpit, later altar, dated 1181 is composed of multiple enamel plaques in a typological disposition. The altar actually inspired the stained glass installed in the monastery in the 1330s. Nicholas worked in Cologne after 1181, achieving the major work of the great shrine of the Three Magi. The three-dimensionality and sculptural power of the draftsmanship appear again in the *Tree of Jesse* in the cathedral of Freiburg-en-Brisgau. The nine extant panels were originally in the central window of the choir of the Romanesque church, now cathedral, and testify to the immense importance of the theme through brilliant color balance and draftsmanship.

OPPOSITION TO THE IMAGE

There was opposition to the trend to embellish monasteries with richly worked programs in glass, fresco, panel painting, and sculpture. The Cistercian movement, named after the order's first foundation at the Burgundian site of Cîteaux, advocated austerity. William of Malmesbury, who wrote an extensive chronicle of his time, called the Cistercians "a model for all monks, a mirror for the diligent, a spur to the indolent." Bernard of Clairvaux was one of the luminaries of the order, which at his death consisted of 350 monasteries across Europe. He was not an iconoclast, for in a famous letter to a fellow abbot, he did not see imagery as harmful to the "simple and devote." Bishops, he noted, are pastors for an uneducated population for whom they must "excite devotion ... by bodily adornments."

He was, however, adamantly opposed to imagery for the monk, who might be "more tempted to read in the marble than in ... books, and to spend the whole day in wondering at these things [depicted in cloisters] rather than in meditating the Law of God." The Cistercian houses were

nevertheless not without beauty. Their remarkably austere and eloquent architecture creates symphonies of abstract forms, and their windows display seemingly endless variations of patterned intersection. Scholars have argued that such patterns may very well have aided meditation, the complexities of interlace helping the mind to focus on a reality beyond the forms of this world. Cistercian glass from the Burgundian monasteries of Obazine, La Bénissons-Dieu, in the second third of the twelfth century, and Pontigny, about 1210, has survived. The Benedictine abbey of Saint-Pierre, Orbais, apparently derived inspiration for its ornament from its close association with Pontigny. Although Orbais displays a complex program of figural glass, it also installed grisaille windows within its choir. The design, dated about 1200, is constructed using only the contour of the leads.

These patterns of flat strapwork interwoven in a large variety of arrangements became enormously successful throughout all the widely flung

ABOVE *Cistercian monasticism rejected imagery. Its twelfth-century rules still insisted on the traditional pattern of housing for the monk; a separate courtyard called a cloister for private reading and meditation. In the abbey of Fontenay, Burgundy, from the mid-twelfth century, the cloister's columns avoid the elaborate carved capitals common in buildings of many other monastic orders.*

LEFT *The Cistercian monks promoted non-figural glass, such as these interlaced circles from the church at Orbais. The influential order had copybooks with such designs that helped to spread their use by many non-Cistercian sites.*

Cistercian houses and exerted much influence on the grisaille windows that appeared in almost all building programs. A pattern book from the monastery of Rein, Austria, dating from the early thirteenth century, shows thirteen pages of ornament, mostly variants of interlace used at many times, including the early fourteenth-century choir glass of Cologne Cathedral. Of this type, the Cistercian monastery of Santes Creus, Catalonia, shows windows of wonderful ornamental complexity. Four panels combine to create a large circle whose quadrants contain pointed quatrelobes. The visual dynamics that reconcile rectilinear, circular, and diagonal thrust very probably evoked for the meditating monk the seeming confusion but ultimate harmony of all creation as it emanates from the mind of God.

The strict geometric reliance that distinguished early Cistercian glazing was modified through the thirteenth century, ultimately even allowing for elaborate glazed cloister programs such as those of the abbeys of Muri and Wettingen, Switzerland, or the *Life of St. Bernard* at Altenberg, Germany. At Schulpforta, glazed 1251 to 1268, affronting dragons are integrated into the leaf patterns of the uncolored glass. Within the architectural structure of the rose, radiating triangular lobes fit the dragons' bodies. The depiction seems almost to constitute a reverse echo of the fantastic beasts that excited Bernard's condemnation. He referred to carvings in the twelfth-century cloister and questioned the value of that "marvelous and deformed comeliness, that comely deformity" *(Apologia)*.

In the Holy Roman Empire, Cistercian houses continued these great glazing traditions, none more brilliantly than the monastery of Altenberg, 1259–87, near Cologne. The elegantly attenuated architecture is patterned after that of the Cistercian monasteries of Longpont and

Royaumont in northern France. Choir, radiating chapels, transepts, and nave were all glazed with a wide variety of Cistercian floral and geometric ornament. In the tall, narrow double-lancet windows of the choir chapels, heart-shaped patterns of vines with grape clusters are relieved against a crosshatched background. Other patterns show the mugwort leaf in symmetrical ascendancy. The upper choir windows were installed later and are shorter. A variety of stylized leaf forms are arranged in geometric patterns. Altenberg's forms influenced its daughter house, Haina, 1260–70, in North Hessen, which installed similar grisailles decorated with plant motifs.

Heiligenkreuz, outside of Vienna, was a Cistercian foundation, 1290 to 1300. Between rows of grisaille ornament in the choir are depictions of apostles and prophets and of the founders, Leopold III and his wife Agnes. Just as the new order of the Franciscans followed the monastic lead, so too did their counterparts the Dominicans. In Erfurt's Dominican church, about 1280, the nave walls show traditional "Cistercian" patterns that can be traced to work almost a century earlier.

CLERICAL PATRON AND LAY SOCIETY

The educated clergy, monastic or associated with cathedrals, also designed programs to reach the laity. The parables as well as typology could serve this purpose. In the parable of the Good Samaritan (Luke 10: 30–35), Christ commands his followers to "love thy neighbor as thyself," illustrating this with the story of a wounded man who is ignored by respectable individuals, but aided by a foreigner. In the cathedral of Sens, 1220, a window depicts the parable in three key medallions,

ABOVE *The upper windows of the choir of Altenberg date to 1276–87. Grisaille windows were often executed by highly sensitive artists, showing delicate painting modulated by light through brushwork.*

LEFT *Pattern was a means of organizing thought in a primarily oral culture. A window based on the parable of the Good Samaritan in the cathedral of Sens, 1207–13, uses three scenes from the parable set in canted squares to reflect on the history of salvation. The second medallion shows the wayfarer ignored by priest and Levite surrounded by episodes from the story of Moses.*

OPPOSITE *The mid-thirteenth century windows of Schulpforta show the Cistercian preference for grisaille. Here the area surrounding the leaves and intertwined dragons was coated with a wash of paint and then the crosshatch pattern scratched out with a needle.*

setting them as the center of quatrefoils illustrating the story of salvation.

In *Before the Law* (*ante legem*), the wayfarer is set upon by robbers, beaten, and stripped. The surrounding images show the fall of Adam and Eve (Genesis 2–3), as they are set upon by Satan and stripped of grace. In the upper left, God is shown giving them paradise but forbidding them to eat of the tree of knowledge. Tricked by the serpent, Adam and Eve eat its fruit and, knowing their sin, attempt to hide. In the lower left, God appears out of a cloud as they cower in the bushes. Finally, on the lower right, an angel brandishing a burning

sword (created by using red glass) expels Adam and Eve from the gates of paradise.

In the central segment, *Under the Law* (*sub lege*), Moses receives the Commandments, yet this is insufficient to repair the breach created between God and humanity. The parable image shows the priest and Levite passing by the wayfarer, who sits naked in the center. Around this are scenes of Moses. At the upper left, Moses raises up the brazen serpent (Numbers 21: 8–9), and the Israelites who were bitten by serpents are cured by looking at it. To the right, Moses and Aaron stand before Pharaoh and demonstrate the power of God by casting down Aaron's rod, which is transformed into a serpent (Exodus 7: 10-13). In the lowest left medallion, the Israelites worship the golden calf and Moses, returned from Mount Sinai, smashes the tablets (Exodus 32:4-19). In the lower right, God speaks to Moses from the burning bush (Exodus 3).

In the final segment, the advent of Christ is depicted as creating an era *Under Grace* (*sub gracia*). In the central parable image, the Good Samaritan rescues the wayfarer, binds his wounds, sets him on his horse, takes him to the inn, and pays the innkeeper. The flanking images show Christ's Passion and Resurrection. In the upper left, Christ stands before Pilate, who is counseled by a devil whispering in his ear. Christ is then beaten, on the right. Below left, a mystical Crucifixion shows Christ on the Cross. In the medallion on the right, the angel at the tomb greets the holy women who have come to anoint Christ's body and tells them that Christ is no longer dead but has risen.

Given the vast expenditure necessary for buildings and for their windows, politics and the commemoration of important individuals were inextricably linked to decisions about imagery in stained glass. Monasteries were among the most aggressive in designing programs that reflected their own importance and the importance of their supporters. They depicted not only a sainted founder like St. Francis, but kings, abbots, and bishops connected to the site. The abbey of Saint-Rémi of Reims, 1185-1200, developed a program that became a prototype for the windows of the nave of the cathedral of Strasbourg at the beginning of the thirteenth century, and the cathedral of Reims after 1230. Saint-Rémi's program presents the first continuous use of the seated figure, a motif repeated continually during the Gothic period. Through the imagery in glass, the abbey constructed its desired relationship with the monarchy and

the history of salvation. Clerical authority is depicted as a continuous tradition from the Old Testament prophets to the present. Reims's clerical elite are shown as enthroned archbishops below the patriarchs and apostles. They appear in full episcopal regalia of chasuble (robe) and pallium (Y shaped vestment worn over the chasuble), wearing miter (hat) and holding a crosier, whose curved top refers to a shepherd's crook symbolic of the bishop's authority over his flock. In the nave, a series of kings are surmounted by patriarchs. Ancestors of Christ appear in the retrochoir tribune.

As the monasteries interacted more and more with the secular world, particularly as sites of pilgrimages, their programs reflected these purposes. The windows of Canterbury Cathedral's Trinity Chapel, to the east of the choir, depict the miracles of St. Thomas Becket (1119-70). Becket, archbishop of Canterbury, was murdered by emissaries of

BELOW *The widows of the Trinity chapel of Canterbury 1185–1220, show vivid images of the miraculous healing power of St. Thomas Becket. Petronella of Polesworth, an epileptic nun, is cured. The windows show the medieval glass painter's ability to design legible depictions of events. In elegantly manipulated curves, Petronella is framed in the center, obviously suffering, and helped by other women.*

Henry II in a dispute over clerical privilege. He was canonized two years after his death, and miracles were soon recorded at his tomb. The windows installed in 1185–1207 and 1213/15–20 promulgated his cult, a tradition that formed the basis for Chaucer's *Canterbury Tales*, in which late-fourteenth-century pilgrims journey "the hooly blisful martir for the seke / That hem hath holpen, whan that they were seeke." The shrine of Thomas Becket by Elias of Durham dominates the center of the Trinity Chapel. The resplendent colors of the twelve surrounding windows recounting Becket's life and miracles reiterate the glow of the precious stones and richly worked metals of the shrine. In an extraordinary diversity of armature designs the windows recount the different miracles from all classes of society. Scene after scene shows the martyred archbishop, who intervenes to rescue a man from drowning, to resurrect another, and to effect a wide manner of cures of madness, suffocation, hemorrhaging, or mutilation, in people as diverse as a nun from Cologne, the King of France, and a naughty child from a neighboring town. Caviness has demonstrated that the twelve windows represent a conflation of two major prose texts of Becket's miracles compiled by two monks of the cathedral, Benedict and William. The miracles are often grouped by type, such as resurrections to teach the validity of the belief in the Resurrection, rescue from secular courts (Eilward of Westoning unjustly punished with blinding and castration but healed by Becket), or the healing of the sick in mind and body. The windows make claims for the power of God through his saints. Abbot Hugh of Jervaulx is cured when a monk pushes aside a lay physician and approaches the sick bed.

The windows are an arresting display, a seemingly endless reiteration of the martyr's power to intercede on behalf of

ABOVE *Windows in the Abbey of St. Rémi, Reims, 1180–90, include images of the cathedral clergy since great families controlled both religious and secular offices. Archbishop Henry of France was the brother of the French king Louis VII.*

OPPOSITE *Twelfth-century windows are distinguished by their powerful graphic expression as in the* Dormition and Assumption of the Virgin, *about 1180, from Angers Cathedral. The Virgin was believed not to have died in a normal sense, but to have experienced a "dormition" or sleep, after which Christ came and brought her bodily into heaven.*

his petitioners. The sheer brilliance of the multiple patterns—angular petals radiating from squares, circles divided in quadrants, canted squares and half-circles, fan-shaped successions, quatrefoils within circles, alternations of circles and diamonds—reinforces the multiplicity of cures. Just as preachers developed sermons for specific purposes for a lay audience, it is probable that the monks who led the pilgrims around the Trinity Chapel explained the individual miracles. Pilgrim literature in the later Middle Ages, such as Margery Kempe's account of her visit to the Holy Sepulchre in 1416 (*The Book of Margery Kempe*, Chapters 28–29), describes activities such as the Franciscans leading pilgrims through the church and pointing out the sights.

The cathedrals and parish churches of the twelfth century followed the lead of monastic patrons but organized their programs to serve their lay constituencies. They continued the expressive aesthetics of the monks, but concentrated on the placement of image and simplicity to communicate the essential message. A telling example is found in the window of the *Dormition and Assumption of the Virgin* in Angers Cathedral, 1180. The religious message is that the Assumption of the Virgin bodily into heaven prefigures the union of body and spirit granted to Christian believers at the end of time—the "resurrection of the dead" recited in the Apostles' Creed. The window contains six circular scenes in imagery that is bold and easy to read. The scenes were repositioned in a restoration. They should read from bottom to top: the apostles miraculously transported to Jerusalem by an angel, the death of the Virgin, the funeral procession, the laying of the Virgin's body in the tomb, the Assumption of the Virgin to heaven, and, finally, the coronation of the Virgin by Christ.

Similarly, the window of *St. Catherine of Alexandria* in Angers Cathedral presents

a clearly legible narrative structure. Catherine was one of the most honored saints in the later Middle Ages, and became an archetype of heroic female virtue in the face of intellectual pride and sexual manipulation. The daughter of King Costus, Catherine was educated in the liberal arts but is determined to live her life a chaste bride of Christ, praying and reading the Scriptures. When the Roman emperor Maxentius begins to persecute Christians, she confronts him and condemns him for his idolatry and for his cruelty. He then summons philosophers and rhetoricians to convince her of her errors. She, however, filled with the power of God, confounds the arguments of these learned men, who convert to Christianity. Maxentius, enraged, kills the philosophers and rhetoricians, and proposes to take Catherine as a wife, second only to the

empress. She scorns his offer and is subjected to tortures, including being stripped and beaten by guards. Christ comes to comfort her while she is in prison, an apparition witnessed by the empress, who also converts and is executed by Maxentius. Ultimately, Catherine is condemned to be torn apart between two wheels (which become her symbol) but intervention from heaven destroys the wheels and the pagan onlookers. She is beheaded and her tomb becomes a source of healing miracles. The story of Catherine, along with those of St. Margaret and St. Barbara, was highly popular in literature as well as image. Catherine was invariably depicted as a noble person, privileged to enter into a mystic marriage with Christ. The marriage was often shown through the device of the Christ Child placing a ring on the saint's finger.

At St. Kunibert in Cologne, the choir retains its original windows and placement. In the upper level, large windows honor the church's patrons on either side of a *Tree of Jesse*. The Jesse Tree, as it developed in the Holy Roman Empire, shows scenes of the life of Christ—the Annunciation, Nativity, Crucifixion, and Resurrection—leading to Christ surrounded by the gifts of the Holy Spirit, as well as images of kings and prophets with their identifying banderoles. St. Kunibert's life is told in lobed medallions similar to the framing of the *John the Baptist* window. The upper three show: St. Kunibert named archbishop of Cologne by King Clothar; during mass in St. Ursula's Church he reveals the grave of the saint (the patron of the city); finally, Kunibert meets his death. The images are enunciated with great clarity so that lay viewers can easily read the stories.

Subsequent centuries elaborated all of the themes developed in this early phase. Monastic programs continued, adapting

to social change. Great urban cathedrals, and the cathedral schools, however, came to dominate the production of art, as they did religious intellectual life. Stained glass changed with the times and new buildings.

ABOVE *The abstraction of the human form, in this 1180 detail of* Apostles, *from Angers, creates timeless associations. In the early twentieth century the artists of the German Expressionist movement were inspired by such works.*

LEFT *Medieval tradition encouraged the honoring of local saints, very much in the tradition of regional pride. Kunibert was an early archbishop of Cologne whose life was associated with the discovery of the relics of St. Ursula. Ursula was martyred along with 10,000 maidens and, with the warrior St. Gereon, was a patron saint of the city. Kunibert is blessed by a ray of heavenly light witnessed by King Dagobert in the lowest section of a window, 1220–30, in the churched dedicated to him in Cologne.*

The Age of Great Cathedrals: The Thirteenth to Fifteenth Centuries

4

THE CATHEDRAL AND ITS SETTING

The Gothic style, which dominated stained glass in Europe between the thirteenth and fifteenth centuries, comprised enormous richness, breadth, and variety. This remarkably vigorous era was connected to the rise of cities and with them urban populations and the cathedrals that served them. A cathedral is the seat of a bishop, the central authority for all churches within his diocese. The clergy who inhabited the cathedral were not monks (with the exception of some English sites such as Canterbury, both a monastery and a cathedral). Rather, cathedral clergy were connected only to their own establishment and although celibate had a high degree of interaction with their communities. These urban centers supported not only their cathedrals and parish churches but also the preaching orders, the Dominicans and Franciscans, and additional new foundations.

Frequently members of powerful families of the region, the clerics were highly educated and keenly aware of issues of art and architecture. They built in the new Gothic style, tapping into the economic development of the thirteenth century. The only completely new style since antiquity, the Gothic developed with stained glass as a necessary construction element. The high visibility attracted sponsorship such as the multiple donors of the nave windows of York. Although the clergy still claimed its own space in cathedral choirs, the church as a whole was a corporate structure—with diverse population—and highly public. By selecting a few cathedrals to profile, and looking at their installation of windows over centuries, the crucial position of the cathedral within its community can be seen. First, however, it is important to review shared principles of building and working with glass.

GENERAL PRINCIPLES OF IMAGERY

These separate cities with their churches, wherever found in Europe, shared a belief in Christian rituals and forms (including images) that communicated both social and religious meaning. In most regions, Church and state were linked to one

OPPOSITE *English Gothic elegance is exemplified in the nave at York Minster. A complex ribbed vault frames the broad five lancet windows of the clerestory. The unified molding of the arcade arches acts as a frame for the triple lancet windows of the aisles. The gifts of many individual donors, the Minster's aisle windows, about 1325, respond primarily to the desires of the donors to honor their patron saints and to see their own representation through heraldic badge and image.*

another, and populations, although economically diverse, were ethnically monolithic. Europe shared a single common base of biblical text and saints' legends (with some local variation). Despite broad thematic unity, however, no two artistic statements were ever exactly alike. For example, the birth of Christ was an expected presence on a Gothic sculptured portal and each element of the story—the infant in the manger, the shepherds, the Magi, and King Herod—was easily recognizable. Their placement in any given artistic interpretation, however, differed to construct and express meaning in a way particularly relevant to the local audience. At the cathedral of Notre-Dame in Paris, within walking distance of the royal residence, the west portal sculpture emphasizes the Three Kings, carving in stone the belief that a divinely inspired monarch ruled France. All art of the time, be it manuscripts, wall painting, sculpture, or metalwork, employed similar systems

of framed and interrelated images. Emphasizing the power of these "seen" truths, which informed and reinforced the belief system, was the fact that the vast majority of people saw images only in church. Not until Johannes Gutenberg's exploitation of moveable type in the printing of the Bible about 1450–55, and the mechanical reproduction of images it heralded, were images available to a broader, though still limited, audience for use in their own homes.

The monastic programs of the previous century had already established a system of window placement that would hold for subsequent centuries. The windows of Chartres or Cologne placed single figures of large format in the upper windows and dense medallion narrative in the aisles. The tall, impressive figures of the upper choir, as at Bourges or Auxerre, radiate a correspondence between the Old and New Testaments and frame images of the eternal Godhead in the eastern bays. On the lower level, in shining splendor, narratives of exemplars of Christian action demonstrate the path leading to that upper realm. Narrative windows, although devoted to specific themes, frequently show striking similarities. Iconographic systems transformed specific truths into ritual manifestations of one significant truth: that the life of the Christian reflected the life of Christ.

The art of painted windows was the dominant mode of pictorial narrative of the thirteenth century, nearly eclipsing the related art of illuminated manuscripts. Within each scene the designers invariably simplified pictorial space by silhouetting dramatic actions against uniform red or blue grounds. Reflecting contemporary systems for the stories of saints, similar iconographic motifs characterize similar actions. Healing the sick, the resurrection of the dead, the curing of the possessed, and ultimate martyrdom appear with predictable and reassuring rhythms. The viewer did not approach a window as if it were an exercise in reading with a beginning, middle, and end, but saw the representation visually, as a whole. Essential to a window's success was its inclusion of a number of key images most frequently associated with the miracles or martyrdoms of specific saints or biblical characters. St. Catherine's wheel, St. Margaret's dragon, St. Andrew's X-shaped cross, or Joseph's dream immediately marked the subject of the long history.

There are generic patterns for narrative sequences, patterns that tap deeper sources than our contemporary distinctions of Old and New Testament, or religious and secular. Above all, the windows must be seen as the products of a predominantly oral culture. Their development took place at the same time as the elaboration of the romance in vernacular literature. The essential elements of medieval narrative are repetition, dialogue or altercation, and a passage through the story by means of key episodes. Star-crossed lovers are many, but we recognize Tristan and Iseult by the episode of the love potion at the head of the narrative. Similarly confessors, virgins, martyrs, and even miracle workers, are many, but the viewer notices specifically St. Nicholas, who saves the boy from drowning in the Miracle of the Cup, as distinct from the cures of demonic possession by St. Benedict.

Significantly, although the stories depicted in the windows—or other media— had written versions, there was almost never a direct correspondence between the written text and the image. Rather, there were parallels. For example, in the biblical windows of the twelfth-century monastic programs, the inscribed verses rarely reproduced Scripture. They were meditations on the meaning of the scriptural reference in the specific context that was the organizing principle of the window. Windows, briefly said, were not

constructed to illustrate words. They were designed to encourage reflection, through multiple viewings, on timeless truths in the same manner that a text could be read again and again with ever deepening—and differing—results.

Windows can be grouped by type— martyrs, confessors, virgins, penitents, miracle workers, and so forth—according to the demands of a program, a pattern reflecting medieval traditions of rank and precedence in society. Patterns of narrative were similar for each type. For example, for martyrs, Christ or his angels would appear to the saint, healing his or her wounds before the next encounter, or administering the last rites before the ultimate trial. Confessor saints were recognized by their heroic chastity and self-denial and by their ability to perform wondrous cures of the soul and of the body. Often the life of the saint was accompanied by a story of the discovery and translation of the saint's relics and subsequent miracles.

Medallion window designs and borders in deeply saturated color were common to German, French, and English art of the time. Similar ecclesiastical patrons and even royal marriage alliances meant that a panel from Soissons in northern France

ABOVE *In 1185 the monks at Canterbury engaged the French architect William of Sens to rebuild their church as a fitting memorial for the martyred archbishop, Thomas Becket. The Trinity Chapel to the east of the choir once contained his splendid gold shrine embellished with jewels. The complex medallion windows still remain.*

and a panel from Canterbury in southern England could have similar concepts of medallion structure. The Canterbury glazing is particularly revealing of the mobility of ideas in early Gothic Europe. A French architect, William of Sens, was called to supervise the rebuilding of the ruined choir. Windows in Sens Cathedral were then executed by a workshop that accompanied the Canterbury monks into French exile from 1207 to 1213 during the interdict leveled against King John. Likewise, the English artisans that constructed the windows have been traced to Saint-Yved of Braine, an international exchange noted in chronicles of the time: "Agnes [Countess of Braine] ... constructed a lavish church, scarcely second to any in the elegance of its art and decoration: and she filled the windows with glass brought from England that was amazing in its wonderful brushwork and in the unparalleled harmony and variety of its colors" (Caviness, p. 65). As one begins to read medieval documents free of the nineteenth-century bias that saw a wife's actions as simply executing her husband's intent, one finds a consistent pattern of patronage among women of means.

CHARTRES CATHEDRAL, FRANCE

To provide the necessary windows for Chartres Cathedral, workers were assembled who brought their own traditions from various regions. The glass that they cut and painted, however, was produced at the site, a situation that appears to have encouraged early cooperation among the workshops. The cathedral had experienced a devastating fire in 1194, and except for the three mid-twelfth-century lancets of the façade and a *Virgin and Child* (the Belle Verrière), no windows survived from the twelfth-century building. Arguably among the most complete examples of medieval glazing, almost all the windows at Chartres were accomplished between 1205 and 1235.

With its vast program in sculpture as well as glass, Chartres shows thematic and stylistic coherence. The rigidly frontal Virgin as "Throne of Wisdom" appears on the west portal sculpture as well as in glass. In such a format the Virgin supports Christ in his Godhead, as "pure effusion of the glory of the Almighty" (Wisdom 7: 25). In certain instances both sculpture and stained-glass programs were altered at the same time, demonstrating that they were seen as a whole. In 1205 the cathedral received a relic of the head of St. Anne, mother of the Virgin. The gift was from Catherine, Countess of Blois and Champagne, whose husband had brought it to France after the conquest of Constantinople in 1204. The relic encouraged a new devotion, which prompted the inclusion of the sculpted figure of St. Anne in the center of the north portal and also her depiction in stained glass, holding the Virgin, in the central lancet beneath the north transept rose.

The artists continued to employ all of the techniques of the craft from the twelfth century, but emphasized greater clarity, especially as the churches became larger. Concepts of large-scale work can be seen

RIGHT *Windows could be majestic in their solemnity. The enthroned Virgin and Child is from the* Belle Verrière *(beautiful window), the only window of Chartres cathedral, besides the three lancets of the façade, to survive the devastating fire of 1194.*

in the execution of the figures from Chartres's clerestory, such as the prophet Daniel. The fluidity of line delineating beard, cascading hair, and facial features demonstrates the confidence of glass painters deeply at home in the medium. Pattern continued to dominate ideas of representation, just as it structured the architectonic sculpture of the mid-twelfth-century west portal. The complexity of the natural and geometric designs on the columns continued in the very structure of the windows and the explosion of decorative motifs and patterns in their borders and medallion interstices. Throughout the windows, surface pattern interplays with the spatial push and pull of color, integrating them both.

The stylistic diversity of the windows attests to the gathering of workshops from different geographic regions. Given the scale of the task and the apparently ready patronage, Chartres supported a large number of collaborators. The nave was begun first, and study indicates that the workshops began to exchange painters and even designers, resulting in a more uniform style as the campaign progressed. Stories from the Bible, such as Noah, Joseph, the parable of the Good Samaritan, the patroness of the cathedral in the Death and Assumption of the Virgin, and saints such as Eustace, Mary Magdalene, and Charlemagne intermingle. The windows are indeed unified in their common concepts, yet the individual approach can differ. The workshop responsible for the *Joseph* window designed thin, elegant figures, with restricted gestures even when physically active, as when the Egyptians obey Joseph's order to pour chaff on the River Nile so that Jacob can see it. The *Nicholas* window designer was what a modern viewer might call a more expressive artist, more gestural and dramatic. His figures seem too large to fit within their borders and sometimes even

LEFT *From Chartres's west portal of about 1150 comes an image of the Throne of Wisdom, emphasizing the Divinity of Christ, fully manifest, even in his infancy. The sculptors and the makers of stained glass, as well as other artists of the time, shared common models so that their work formed a unified statement and communicated readily with its audience.*

LEFT *The brush work of the glass painters rivals that of the most sophisticated of artists of the modern era. The image of the prophet Daniel 1205–15, Chartres nave clerestory, bay 141, is easily recognized, yet the graphic sweeps of the hair and beard show the artist transcending momentary likeness to create timeless pattern.*

appear to push beyond them. Their large heads are powerfully delineated and their drapery falls in deep and animated folds.

There has been much debate over the means of financing these great windows of the early thirteenth century. At that time money was not the dominant means of exchange; barter was, and the trade associations, called guilds, common in the later Middle Ages did not yet exist. At Chartres, craftsmen such as sculptors, shoemakers, and textile workers appear at the bottom of windows, but were these windows actually "given" by the trades depicted? Does the presence of specific armorials such as those of the Counts

ABOVE *Accustomed to designing in medallion form, the medieval artist could adapt compositions such as a seated and standing man to fit within equal spaces in the Nicholas window, 1205–15. So engaged by the dynamic drapery patterns and the complementary gestures, the viewer does not notice the size disparity.*

RIGHT *The Joseph window at Chartres, 1205–15, brings the eye through a complex story by repetition. Joseph appears below, asleep, paralleled by the sleeping Pharaoh in the medallion above.*

of Dreux-Bretagne in the south transept, prove that that family actually donated the window? There is little data to prove that the small town of Chartres could support such trade associations. Rather, a study of the economics of the time suggests that the clerical owners of the building, the chapter, operated as a powerful corporation, constructing a message to create a vision of social harmony. In such a world, powerful lords acted with pious affection for the Church, and laborers selflessly donated their time both to haul cartloads of stone when the oxen were exhausted and to fund images of the saints in glass.

The *Charlemagne* window contains an epic retelling of the battle of Roncevaux of 778. A battle against local Basques has been transformed into a chapter in the marvelous exploits of Charlemagne, the sacred emperor, defending Christendom against pagan invasion. Roland, the emperor's nephew, shows supernatural strength and courage. Fearing to be labeled weak, Roland blows too late his horn to signal that his rearguard has been ambushed. Finally, as the late eleventh-century-poem recounts

> Roland has set Olifant to his lips,
> Firmly he holds it and blows it with a will
> High are the Mountains, the blast is long
>   and shrill,
> Thirty great leagues the sound went
>   echoing.
> King Carlon (Charlemagne) heard it and
>   all who rode with him.
> "Lo, now, our men are fighting," quoth
>   the King.
> (*The Song of Roland*, stanza 133, trans.
>   Dorothy L. Sayers)

And they do fight, dying to a man. Roland is last, and tries to destroy his sword, which is weighted with sacred relics, to prevent its falling into unworthy hands.

Count Roland smites upon the marble
   stone;
I cannot tell you how he hewed it and
   smote;
Yet the blade breaks not nor splinters,
   though it groans;
Upward to heaven it rebounds from the
   blow.
When the Count sees it never will be broke,
Then to himself right softly he makes
   moan:
"Ah Durendal, fair, hallowed, and devote,
What store of relics lies in thy hilt of gold!"
(*The Song of Roland*, stanza 173, trans.
   Dorothy L. Sayers)

All across France, cathedrals were
being expanded and reconstructed in the
new Gothic style. Notre-Dame of Paris
was begun earlier than Chartres but the
medieval glass that remains in the west rose
of about 1210 continues the twelfth-
century tradition of representing the virtues
and vices and signs of the zodiac. These
themes emphasized the concept of God as
creator of both the moral and the physical
universe. The wondrous walls of glass that
are the north and south transepts show
the mid-thirteenth-century fusion of lacy
Gothic structure with kaleidoscopic color.
Bourges parallels Chartres in date and
complexity, with large-scale figures in the
clerestory and with a variety of armature
designs in the choir. Rouen in Normandy,
Soissons in Champagne, and Sens and
Troyes in Burgundy, retain programs of
early Gothic as well as windows installed
in later campaigns of construction.

ABOVE *Details of the windows at
Chartres reveal different glass painters
at work. All of the artists, however,
shared a deep conviction in clarity of
design, single color backgrounds, and
an absence of any kind of perspective.
Here, in the Joseph window, 1205–15,
the waving brown, white, and green
bands at the bottom represent the shore
and the river Nile.*

REIMS CATHEDRAL, FRANCE

The imagery of Notre-Dame of Reims was constructed not only to depict the story of salvation but to refer to the cathedral's place as the site of the coronation of French kings. The archbishop of Reims began to claim this privilege with particular insistence in the twelfth century with the consecration of Louis VI in 1131. The legitimacy of the monarchy was seen to rest on the *sacre*, the ritual anointing of the king with oil that had been produced by a dove from heaven at the moment when St. Rémi baptized Clovis, the king of the Franks, in 498. Imagery in sculpture, especially on the interior of the west façade, developed this theme with kings and priests from the Old Testament, showing the Church as blessing and legitimizing secular power. Inspired by the earlier window of Saint-Rémi of Reims, the cycle of clerestory windows in transept and nave of the cathedral arranges kings in the upper section and bishops below. The choir, 1235–45, augments this format through a program showing the dioceses dependent on Reims, in double-lancet windows: to the left the cathedral church is surmounted by an angel, and to the right the respective bishop appears below an apostle. The axial window presents Reims Cathedral with Archbishop Henri de Braine, its builder, then in the remaining windows the cathedrals of Laon, Soissons, Châlons, Beauvais, Senlis, Noyons, Thérouanne, and Tournai with their bishops.

ABOVE *Themes from medieval literature also appear in windows. Chartres' Charlemagne window, about 1225, includes scenes also described in the* Song of Roland: *the French combat the Saracens; Charlemagne speaks to Ganelon; Roland duels with the enemy; and Roland breaks his sword Durendal and sounds his horn.*

RIGHT *For the site of coronations, the archbishops of Reims Cathedral commissioned both glass and sculpture to emphasize their privileges. The interior of the west façade dates from 1255–99.*

NAUMBURG CATHEDRAL, GERMANY

Like Reims Cathedral, Naumburg shows the close relationship of secular and ecclesiastic power in the Middle Ages. Family alliances are as vividly represented as religious piety in the remarkable choir program of sculpture and glass. Begun in the first half of the thirteenth century, the cathedral was completed under Bishop Dietrich II von Wettin (1243–72). The western choir honored the local nobility of which Dietrich was a member. The choir screen has been celebrated as a masterwork of expressive naturalism and on either side presents sculpted reliefs narrating Christ's Passion, including the Kiss of Judas and Christ before Pilate. At the entrance door, a life-size sculpture of Christ Crucified flanked by the Virgin and St. John confronts the viewer with heartbreaking realism. Within the chapel, over the seats of the canons, are sculpted figures of the donor's extended family, which included counts and countesses and two abbesses. Best known, because of their remarkable realism, may be Eckhard of Meissen and his wife Uta. Uta, especially, with dramatic collar accenting her face, has impressed viewers. The interrelationship of architecture, sculpture, and stained glass is one of the most telling demonstrations of medieval artistic integration extant. The living bodies of the canons and nobility witnessing services, juxtaposed with the stone bodies of the recently deceased family members, are set against the bodies depicted in the

LEFT *Architecture, sculpture, and stained glass are exceptionally unified in Naumburg Cathedral. After passing beyond the west choir screen with its heartrending image of the Crucifixion, the worshipper sees a series of tall windows of saints juxtaposed with the sculpted images of noble donors and family members.*

stained glass—a heavenly, transparent choir, glowing with the brightness of the reflected Godhead.

The window program continues the understanding of earthly social hierarchy into the heavenly realm. To the south are bishops and deacon saints. In the central three windows, the twelve apostles appear over their adversaries—St. Peter, for example, over Simon Magus, and James the Great over Herod. In the companion lancet are personifications of twelve virtues and vices, a program with a long lineage. The virtues appear as formidable women, crowned and carrying spears with which they pierce the enemies they trample underfoot. Patience conquers Wrath, Charity bests Avarice, Peace triumphs over Discord, and Hope defeats Despair. In the lancet to the north are Saints Catherine, Agnes, Mary Magdalene, and Elizabeth, complementing the warrior saints Mauritius, George, Demitrius, Sebastian, and Pancras. As they appear in a left and right alignment, their male and female relationship mirrors the stances of the donor couples in sculpture. The multilobed frame is common to glazing practices in

the Holy Roman Empire, such as Austria's Heiligenkreuz, Cologne's St. Kunibert, and St. Elizabeth at Marburg. In circular medallions in the lowest section of the widows appear the bust-length representations of the cathedral's bishops, with Dietrich II in the central lancet.

SAINTE-CHAPELLE, PARIS, AND MID-CENTURY FRANCE

Like Naumburg's choir program, France's Sainte-Chapelle honors its donor. The edifice was built to emphasize the possession of the relic of the Crown of Thorns given in 1239 to Louis IX by Emperor Baldwin II of Constantinople in gratitude for French assistance against Muslim invaders. The church evokes the form of a metal reliquary, the lower chapel a wide and stable base, and the upper chapel a vision of attenuated space and brilliant light. A veritable cage of glass, the upper chapel has fifteen multi-lancet windows almost fifteen meters high. They show a coherent theme—continuity of kingship—that of the Old Testament

patriarchs, reign of Christ and of the Capetian kings of France. In the charter granted Louis by Innocent IV, the pope stated that "the Lord has crowned you with his crown of thorns." Executed within six years, the glass is stylistically homologous, although different "hands" or types of execution can be distinguished. Frequently royal insignia appear, the fleur-de-lis for France or the castles for Castile, the Spanish principality, the heritage of the king's influential mother, Eleanor of Castile.

The Sainte-Chapelle exerted considerable influence over glazing programs at other sites, notably the cathedrals of Soissons, Le Mans, Tours, and Clermont-Ferrand. The stained glass of the choir of the cathedral of Tours, about 1260, has been considered a pivotal installation. Artists adopted the Parisian style and developed it to suit

different spaces and distances from the viewer. The church of Saint-Julien of Tours was glazed by the same workshops, producing panels of *Cain and Abel*, and *Adam and Eve*, now in the chapel of the Pomfret School, Pomfret, Connecticut. Swift execution and economical brushstrokes characterize the windows. The simplified designs depend on bold silhouettes with few figures per scene. In the elaboration of the windows by the Tours glaziers, stock figural compositions are often repeated. The Pomfret images include Adam delving and Eve spinning as a consequence of the expulsion from paradise. Similar labor is imposed on Cain and Abel as they sow grain and then reap the harvest—a juxtaposition that appears again in a window by the nineteenth-century artist Daniel Cottier. An unusual

ABOVE LEFT *After their disobedience, Adam and Eve were driven out of Paradise and forced to labor for their livelihood. This panel from the Abbey Church of Saint-Julien, Tours, 1265–70, shows the universal image depicting the aftermath of the fall. The old verse states: "Adam delved and Eve span—tell me who then was the happy man?"*

ABOVE RIGHT *At Saint-Julien, Cain and Abel, the sons of Adams and Eve also labor. They form a beginning and ending sequence of the concept of sower and reaper.*

window in the cathedral's choir, that displaying the canons of Loches (1255–70), however, announced a new style of window interspersing grisaille (uncolored glass) and image. The success of this new format made the color-saturated program of the Sainte-Chapelle a style of the past.

GRISAILLE TRANSFORMATION

Grisaille systems were to dominate glazing throughout the next century and a half in cathedral churches and elsewhere. The first complete manifestation of the building change was a smaller building, Saint-Urbain in Troyes. Built swiftly, in 1262–77, Saint-Urbain was the result of the largess of Jacques Pantaléon, a native of Troyes who became Pope Urban IV (1261–64). Gone is the sober, balanced interplay of architectural divisions of arcade, triforium, and clerestory or the articulation of support, decoration, and wall. In its place

is architecture conceived of as a supporting cage in which tapestries of light shimmer instead of walls. The delicacy of the stonework encouraged the increased transparence of the windows. In Saint-Urbain, the shimmer of grisaille-filtered light floats the colored panels in an atmosphere of transcendence. The figural work is reduced to simple silhouetted shapes to facilitate legibility. Narrative panels in the lower windows, such as the image of the miracle of the Cup of St. Nicholas, tell their stories vividly, with energetic stocky figures set against unmodulated blue backdrops.

Many other buildings espoused this new aesthetic. At Saint-Pierre of Chartres the entire program displays various approaches to the intermingling of grisaille and figure. In the nave, windows of fully saturated figural glass alternate with vertical shafts of grisaille and standing figures under architectural canopies. The figures of apostles, abbots, bishops, and popes begin to show the hip-shot position that characterized figures in the fourteenth century. Holding a knife, the instrument of his martyrdom, the apostle Bartholomew sways gracefully against a blue background.

As with all of medieval art, correspondences in the manner of presentation extended across media. The standing figures framed by decorative banding appear in the interior of the west façade of Reims Cathedral. Although isolated within their niches the figures are part of a narrative of the Life of the Virgin. In programs of glazing as installed in the cathedral of Evreux, the isolated panels can also construct a narrative such as the Crucifixion, with the central lancet carrying an image of Christ, and the Virgin and St. John in the flanking lancets. Designers began to simplify the work of cutting and assembling the windows by employing a quarry format, sections of glass cut in straight lines to form a trellis pattern, rather than the irregular cuts of interlace

RIGHT *The church of Saint-Urbain in Troyes was built between 1262 and 1277 giving a far greater place to the window opening and to the use of uncolored glass throughout.*

OPPOSITE *At Saint-Urbain in Troyes, stories in the windows were simplified and told in square compartments. The miracle of the golden cup, also present at Chartres, is a well-known episode from the Legend of St. Nicholas. A boy falls overboard carrying the cup which his parents had vowed to give to St. Nicholas but then decided to keep. When the distraught parents arrive at the saint's shrine, they find their son and the cup, which they immediately place on the altar. The panel is now at Portsmouth Abbey, Portsmouth, Rhode Island.*

or medallions. The interiors from this era create integrated ensembles with multiple vistas of framing by real and by fictive architecture. The abbey of Saint-Ouen of Rouen is another building of this type. Narratives of saints' lives play out in a series of richly painted vignettes enhanced with the newly introduced technique of silver stain. Terminated by towering architectural canopies, the scenes evoke the application of lacy architectural forms that were becoming elements of wall embellishment.

In England, the east wall of Gloucester Cathedral, about 1350, established the benchmark for the integration of glass and architecture in the new form. The earlier Norman choir had been renovated, with a new multi-segmented vault in the English Decorated style. Cluster shafts extending from the vaults overlay the walls as a screen and opened up the east wall into a stunning reredos of light. Evoking a gigantic triptych, the tiers of niches begin at the base with the shields of the leading nobles of the time, then abbots and bishops, then saints, then apostles with the crowned Christ and the Virgin in the center and, above them, angels.

BELOW *The band window, interspersing full color figural images and grisaille, gained great popularity by 1300. At the church of Saint-Pierre of Chartres, a standing figure might be isolated in a vertical panel in a simplified format. St. Bartholomew is recognized by the knife that recalls his martyrdom by flaying.*

YORK MINSTER, ENGLAND

York Minster is a prime example of how building phases of these vast edifices reflected up-to-date architectural practices, such as the use of grisaille. York was one of the most ancient cities in England and was once the chief Roman military post of the British Isles. In the fifteenth century, York also supported fifty parish churches, twenty of which survive today. Combined, the minster and the parish churches contain the largest deposit of stained glass in England. Some glass remains from glazing programs from the earlier cathedral, destroyed in the rebuilding in the late thirteenth and fourteenth centuries. Remnants include a panel of a *Tree of Jesse*, one of Daniel, and a number from saints' lives. The windows appear to have been influenced by traditions of northern France, including Saint-Denis's *Jesse Tree* window.

Nonfigural glass was a part of York's glazing program from the beginning. The grisaille windows in the nave clerestory use patterns copied from windows of the twelfth and early thirteenth centuries or may be the reused panels themselves.

The glass shows interlace achieved through leadline contours without surface paint, similar to the windows of Orbais, France. Like the extensive use of grisaille in the cathedrals of Salisbury, Lincoln, and Westminster, the minster's grisaille appears throughout the edifice, alone and in various combinations with figural panels. Most impressive for the visitor may be the five great lancets of the north transept executed entirely in grisaille about 1250, known as the "Five Sisters." The glass, although its clarity has been damaged by corrosion and repair, exhibits highly sophisticated internal leading patterns and painted foliage.

Grisaille windows embellish the minster's chapter house, about 1285–90, renowned for its architectural elegance. Rows of scenes are interspersed with large areas of grisaille between. Even the tracery does not use fully saturated glass but isolates heraldic shields on grisaille ground. The borders show climbing trellises of leaves, and naturalistic oak leaves and acorns are painted on the uncolored glass. Likewise, the nave windows were designed for a system that interspersed grisaille and colored glass. Windows carry in the upper band identifying scenes of a saint, such as the martyrdom of St. Peter crucified upside down, or St. Stephen kneeling as he is stoned to death. In the lower band are the identifying arms of the donor families, very much like the glass in the chapter house, instantly recognizable to a local audience. A window showing the story of St. Catherine (nXXIII), 1307–12, makes references to the royalty and peerages of Europe: the Holy Roman Empire, England, France, Provence, King of Rome, Castile and León, Jerusalem, Navarre, Earls of Lancaster, Gloucester, Surrey, and Warwick, and Barons Rose, Mowbray, Clifford, and Percy. It is also the earliest extant use of silver stain noted in the British Isles. Donors are depicted as kneeling

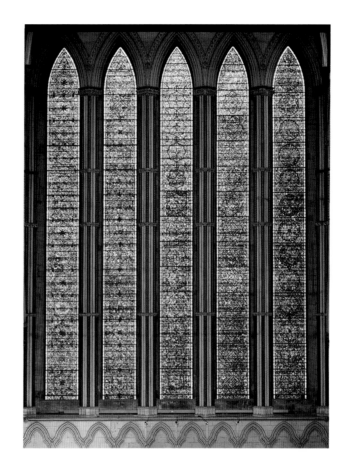

ABOVE *At York, the five narrow lancets of the north transept were glazed entirely in grisaille about 1250. The decision reflects the important place of non-figural glass within these buildings, allowing light into the interior to reveal complex carving and wall painting.*

LEFT *The York master glaziers were renowned for their sensitive of draftsmanship. By using uncolored glass and the yellow color of silver stain, they created windows, such at this image of Gabriel of 1450, that looks very much like a drawing and announced the style of the roundels.*

figures, often holding an image of the window that their largess has provided. Such customs repeat time-honored patterns seen in the twelfth-century donation of Eleanor of Aquitaine and Henry II to the cathedral of Poitiers. Sophisticated models, such as the marginalia of manuscripts appeared in the glass. York's north nave shows a monkey's funeral in the bottom border of one window, a fox preaching from a lectern in another, and various hybrid forms of griffins and centaurs common to illuminators of the time.

Images of saints were often presented as single figures with characteristic gestures or attributes. St. Christopher, one of the most cherished figures in the late Middle Ages, was the patron saint of travelers. The legend describes him as a man of ordinary intellect but unusual strength. In service to Christ, he ferried travelers over streams. One day a child asked to be carried, and in midstream an intolerable weight pressed on the saint's shoulders. Christopher, as his name indicates, then understood that he was carrying Christ, who carried the sins of the world. Large-scale images of the saint set adjacent to portals were frequent aspects of parish wall painting.

York's glass, through the centuries and subsequent period styles, continually evidenced exquisite levels of execution. The celebrated east window of the *Creation and the End of the World* was given in 1405 by Bishop Skirlow of Durham, who aspired to be archbishop of York. He had himself depicted in the center of the lowest register, with historic figures of York (ancient kings, mythical kings, etc.) on either side. The *St. William* window, 1415, narrates events in successive rectangles, similar to systems in York's parish churches. The window's clear purpose was to promote William's shrine as a place of cures. The glass painter exhibits a refined sensitivity of brushwork, detailing faces with small, rounded eyes, narrow noses, and rounded chins, a style that also appears in the windows of All Saints, North Street. The delicate use of silver stain reflects its integration by English artists for almost a century. Work from the midcentury shows the use of quarry (tile-like) background to silhouette a light-color figure. Windows were often comprised entirely of uncolored glass with neutral vitreous paint and silver stain creating different tints of yellow and value.

COLOGNE CATHEDRAL, GERMANY

Cologne enjoyed similar national stature to York. A great and ancient commercial site situated on the Rhine river, Cologne was the seat of the archbishop, one of the seven electors of the Holy Roman Emperor. The cathedral claimed as its patron saints the Three Kings who had visited Jesus. Honored as well as precious, the great shrine of the Magi crafted by Nicholas of Verdun reflects the cathedral as a whole. The cathedral's glazing responds to two equally important criteria: permitting the maximum amount of light into the interior, and elaborating a program of imagery connected to ideals of its heritage, protecting saints, and power. The developing trend toward a combination of grisaille and figural glass was ideally suited to these needs.

In 1250–60 the windows of the choir chapels were set with ornamental glass— only the central chapel contained a Bible window setting images of the Gospel story against prototypes from the Old Testament. The upper levels followed almost a half-century later with a series of forty-eight figures of kings under grisaille strapwork. The axial window shows the *Adoration of the Magi* below bust-length figures of kings and prophets reminiscent of the *Jesse Tree* format. To either side, kings proceed in a dignified row, alternating youthful and mature figures and red and blue backgrounds. Below their feet are the shields of the donors of the windows. Above the kings, pot-metal banding enhances the design of the grisaille, which is carried through leadline alone.

In the early fourteenth century, new figural glass honoring saints with special ties to the archdiocese was substituted for the grisaille in the lower windows. Although executed in dense pot-metal colors, the emphasis on architectural frame and on pattern echoes the format of the grisaille and figural window. Individual events taking place at different times and places are presented as if they were sculptural elements of an elaborate tabernacle. The emphasis on gold in the glass, and the red and green checkerboard background enhance the dynamics of the surface.

Construction continued into the sixteenth century, when the north nave aisle was glazed by workshops associated with two important panel painters known as the Master of the Holy Kinship and the Master of St. Severin. Highly prized for their brilliance, the five windows were described a century later by a chronicler of Cologne, Aegidius Gelenius, as "greatly celebrated marvels." The windows demonstrate the commitment of Cologne's archbishops to the building campaigns and their understanding of quality commissions. Philip von Daun, archbishop in 1508, appears twice, first in the *Passion* window, attired as cathedral deacon, and then in the *Life of St. Peter/Tree of Jesse* window as archbishop presented by St. Peter, who wears the papal crown. Other saints associated with the cathedral, such as St. George, St. Gereon, and St. Lawrence appear above the donors. The later Middle Ages and Renaissance saw a resurgence of interest in twelfth-century themes such as typology and the *Tree of Jesse*. Two of the nave windows show the *Adoration of the Shepherds* preceded by *Moses and the Burning Bush*, and the *Adoration of the Magi* preceded by the *Visit of the Queen of Sheba to Solomon*. The *Coronation of the Virgin* completes the series. Still framed by architectural motifs, the figures are now three-dimensional. Silver stain is now a part of the important golden tonality of the windows. The cathedral's glazing continued in the nineteenth century when the nave and façade were finally completed, adding spectacular windows in the south aisle.

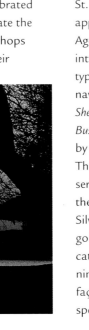

FLORENCE CATHEDRAL, ITALY

ABOVE *The cathedral of Florence, Santa Maria del Fiore, became not only a symbol of Florence but of the Renaissance. The great dome that still soars above the city was the largest vaulted space since antiquity and established the reputation of Brunelleschi as Italy's premier architect.*

RIGHT *Lorenzo Ghiberti designed many windows for the cathedral. His* Presentation in the Temple, 1445, *for the dome skillfully adapted the round oculus form to the vertical arrangement of the figures. Simeon holds the child in his arms and declares: "Now thou dost dismiss thy servant, Oh Lord, according to thy word in peace; because my eyes have seen thy salvation." (Luke 2:29-30)*

In Florence, the artists who executed panel painting and sculpture were also responsible for window design. Although painters such as Agnolo Gaddi (fl. 1369–96) installed stained glass in Florence during the fourteenth century at Santa Croce and other sites, it is the cathedral that exhibits the most comprehensive glazing program. Santa Maria del Fiore was a source of enormous civic pride for Florence's citizens. Begun around 1300, the work proceeded sporadically in an Italian Gothic style until the early fifteenth century. Indeed, stained glass, rather than wall painting or sculpture, was planned at the outset to carry the religious themes of the cathedral. Competition and public debate marked many of the commissions, similar to the public contest before awarding the bronze doors of the baptistery to Lorenzo Ghiberti (1378–1455), a goldsmith. The first door, whose scenes were set in Gothic quatrefoil medallions, was begun in 1403. In 1404 Ghiberti completed his first stained-glass window, an oculus (round window) for the center of the west façade in a Gothic-influenced *Assumption of the Virgin*. Ten years later he designed the flanking oculi, *St. Lawrence* and *St. Stephen*, creating compositions with more substantial weight and Renaissance balance. The earliest four windows of the nave had been installed in 1394 by Antonio da Pisa. Ghiberti designed the remaining four following the tradition of three levels of standing pairs of saints. He also designed eleven or possibly seventeen of the thirty lancet windows in the apse and

chapels. The program most frequently shows two levels of paired saints, remarkable for their brilliant color carried by exotic costume and architectural frame.

With the construction of the cupola by Filippo Brunelleschi (1377-1446), the issue of prestige reached a new height. Placement of windows in the most significant vaulted space since classical Rome was highly competitive. Ghiberti, despite his success in other windows, had his design for the eastern oculus rejected. The sculptor Donatello (1386-1466) was given the commission for the *Coronation of the Virgin*. Despite some loss of surface paint and repairs, the monumental composition is an arresting presence. As the Virgin bows her head, worshiping her son, he crowns her "queen taken up into heaven" and "queen of angels," as recited in the litany of the Blessed Virgin.

There are eight oculi in the dome, seven glazed in the 1440s shortly after construction was completed. Andrea del Castagno's (1423-57) *Deposition* on the north is a highly moving image of Mary at the foot of the cross with her son's body stretched across her lap. Christ's head falls dramatically, his hair cascading toward the Virgin's feet. Paolo Uccello (1386-1466), a painter of portraits and history scenes, designed the *Nativity* and the *Resurrection* on either side. Ghiberti designed the three windows on the south, the *Presentation in the Temple*, the *Agony in the Garden*, and the *Ascension*.

Other painters of renown designed stained glass for churches in Florence. Domenico Ghirlandaio (1449-94), for example, created in 1491 superbly organized compositions of the *Circumcision*, the *Miracle of the Foundation of Santa Maria Maggiore in Rome*, and the *Miracle of the Virgin Giving her Girdle to St. Thomas* in the apse windows of Santa Maria Novella, where he had also painted frescoes. Perugino (1445-1523), the teacher of Raphael, created the oculus of the *Pentecost*

for the church of Santo Spiritu, designed by Brunelleschi.

The great cathedrals have long been viewed by the public as the quintessential place for the art of stained glass. Large, corporate enterprises, invariably constructed and modified over time, they often contain a wide variety of styles and subjects. Within them the viewer sees shifts in sensibilities concerning religion and changes in the social status of the commissioners of the windows. The success of these windows has often been attributed to the cooperation between the arts of image making and of architecture in a manner lost today. Every decision was made with an understanding of purpose and audience and with the skill to accomplish the vision. This was no mere decoration, but an expression vital to its society

ABOVE *The honor of designing windows for Brunelleschi's dome excited the interest of Florence's greatest artists. Donatello, a sculptor, designed the* Coronation of the Virgin *in 1440, using a considerable amount of crown glass. This axial window honored the Virgin, to whom the cathedral was dedicated. Unlike the image in Cologne's cathedral, Christ alone crowns his mother, who bends her head demurely. The encircling blue and red angels form a border that plays on the relationship of image to architecture.*

ARTISTIC DECISIONS

The changes evident in the installations of windows in these great cathedrals are reflective of general trends. Change did not follow a rigid chronology, but developed through the variable intersection of patronage and artistic exchange. Did the commissioning of artists such as the Master of St. Severin for the north nave windows of Cologne Cathedral reside with a patron's (the archbishop's) discernment? Were artists eager pioneers in absorbing progressive styles such as the three-dimensionality of the Italian Renaissance? Perhaps we should also look to the core issues of stained glass—and question the interplay between the real architecture of the building and the fictive architecture of the painted format—to assess the sequence of styles.

A transitional moment is found in the eleven windows of the double monastery of Königsfelden, Switzerland (1325–50). After erecting a chapel on the site where Emperor Albert I was assassinated in 1308, Queen Elisabeth and her daughter, Agnes of Hungary, founded a Franciscan monastery. It became a mausoleum for the Habsburgs after 1316. The church serviced a community of both men and women, as attested by the windows dedicated to both male (Francis) and female (Clare) founders. A complex program began with the axial lancets that focused on Christ: *Infancy*, *Passion*, and *Posthumous Miracles*. The subsequent windows included the *Life of St. Paul*, the *Death of the Virgin*, *John the Baptist*, and *Martyrdom of St. Catherine*, two windows portraying six apostles each, *St. Nicholas*, *St. Francis*, *St. Clare*, and *St. Anne* (the mother of the Virgin). All were offered by descendants of Albert I and provided with images of the Habsburg donors in the lower portions of the windows.

The Königsfelden program is a brilliant installation, which demonstrates that glaziers were as concerned with spatial innovation as their counterparts in fresco or panel design. Each window is highly legible, clearly commissioned from skilled glass painters. The ensemble shows a precocious engagement with the issues of real and represented space. Italianate ideas of ocular perspective had been visible only since the work of Giotto at sites such as the Arena Chapel of Padua in 1305–06. The earliest windows, those of the apse,

BELOW *Königsfelden, Switzerland, was a memorial to an assassinated king, a double cloister of Franciscans and Poor Clares. The windows of the apse were dedicated to the Passion of Christ. Here, in perfect symmetry, Christ is taken down from the Cross and placed in the lap of his mother.*

show more two-dimensional formats, although with complex schemas that appear to question the meaning of the frame. The later windows, such as those of the *Life of St. Francis*, incorporate perspective recession in the framing devices and also elements of the setting.

It would be inappropriate, however, to see interest in representing three-dimensionality as originating from a single geographic source. In Tewkesbury Abbey, western England, the choir clerestory of about 1340 presents a *Last Judgment* in the apse, and prophets, kings, and the principal secular benefactors of the abbey over time at the sides. In two facing windows, eight figures of knights with their heraldic surcoats appear in full armor. Demonstrating the power of donor association, the windows also show incipient attempts to render what appears to be a hexagonal tower set above the decorated framing arch.

Often smaller foundations retain the glazing that once dominated great metropolitan centers. The parish church of St. Erhard, constructed about 1390, contains seventy-four windows of highly sophisticated execution that exemplify what the Austrian capital once enjoyed. They are the results of the largess of Duke Albrecht III and his wives, first Elisabeth of Bohemia and then Beatrice of Hohenzollern. The windows are associated with the Court School workshop that also glazed the cathedral of St. Stephen in Vienna. A panel of the *Flagellation* demonstrates the hallmarks of an accomplished artistic cooperation. The body of Christ is isolated as a central object of mediation. Patiently, as the texts describe, he undergoes painful humiliation in order to redeem the human race from sin. The stances of the torturers are more animated, one facing forward and the other backward, one raising a whip, the other preparing to strike the sufferer.

TOP *The noble secular donors to the abbey of Tewskesbury appear in choir clerestory windows, about 1338–40. They wear armor over which their heraldic surcoats identify them as specific individuals. Hugh Dispencer, third from the left, was married to Eleanor de Clare, donor of the window.*

ABOVE *Installed shortly after 1340, the Köngisfelden windows show the influence of early Italian perspective. Here, St. Francis leaves his father who tries to restrain him. Stripping off even his clothes, Francis takes refuge in the Church, symbolically represented by the enfolding cloak of the seated bishop.*

RIGHT *The* Annunciation *window, about 1450, in the cathedral of Bourges achieves exquisite detail. The archangel Gabriel wears a cope, the mantle used by the priests in the most elaborate church ceremonies. Above, Gothic vaults are painted blue with gold fleurs-de-lis, the symbol of the French monarchy.*

This confrontation of the innocent and the aggressor is accentuated by the silhouetting of the figures against a brilliant red ground, rendered all the more abstract through the exquisite pattern of trefoil foliage. The Court School also produced windows for the abbey church of Viktring.

As Gothic architecture became more attenuated and open, the medallion window with its interplay of episodes was replaced by a sequential format reading like a book. Playing to a public with access to private imagery in illuminated prayer books, large volumetric figures in three-dimensional settings appeared under increasingly realistic architectural canopies. A window in the cathedral of Evreux of Bishop Guillaume de Cantier before the Virgin shows a perspective interior of vaults of a chapel posed over both individuals.

The cathedral of Bourges installed a series of side windows in the fifteenth century all emphasizing figures under three-dimensional architecture. As in the north aisle of Cologne, the installations evoke contemporaneous panel painting. In the 1430s the Flemish painter Jan van Eyck demonstrated extraordinary spatial sensibility and ability to depict materials such as the reflected light of gold, crystal, and jewels and elaborate textiles as seen behind the enthroned Deity of the *Ghent Altarpiece* (1432, cathedral of St. Bavo, Ghent). A similar fascination with systems of depth and tactile resonances in yellow-haired saints, damask robes, jeweled hems, gold-trimmed sculpture, and painted vaults appears in the *Annunciation* window installed in Bourges by Jacques Coeur, Master of the King's Mint.

ABOVE LEFT *Standing to the right of the Virgin Annunciate in Bourges, St. Barbara wears a green velvet cloak with gold applique. Behind her is her tower, where her father kept her in a vain attempt to prevent her from learning about Christianity. The gold decoration painted on the architecture reveals how many buildings were actually treated in the mid-fifteenth century.*

ABOVE *In Viktring, Austria, as all over Europe, window narratives were organized as self-contained entities in consecutive sequences. The energetic action of the* Flagellation, *about 1390, is frozen to form a timeless symbol of Christ's suffering.*

5

Fifteenth- and Sixteenth-Century Transformation of the Narrative

Artists do not work in a vacuum but are influenced by intellectual, economic, religious, and political forces. Changes in European society in the later Middle Ages, therefore, profoundly influenced the development of stained glass. The changes happened most rapidly in England and in the lands of the Holy Roman Empire, an area encompassing the modern nations of the Low Countries (Belgium and Holland), Switzerland, Austria, and Germany. Economically and politically, the rise of a merchant class transformed artistic patronage. No longer were church buildings and their decoration determined by ecclesiastical taste. Indeed, the Reformation, which challenged the hegemony of the papacy, also challenged the very meaning and usefulness of the image. The age of great cathedrals was past, and building concentrated on parish churches, many of impressive size. Influential families added private chapels to already established buildings to commemorate their own members. Even private houses received windows that were new both in technique and in subject matter.

Imagery was influenced by the development of the printing press, affecting both the working habits of the stained-glass workshops and the expectations of the patron. Johannes Gutenberg's moveable type appeared in 1450, but the use of the woodblock to print image and text had gained great popularity by the 1430s. The influence of the printed book appears in the reiteration of widely disseminated phrases and images often quite removed in time and place from their original manifestation. Images and texts were frequently borrowed in part, altered, and intermingled with texts and images from other sources, as in the Swiss stained-glass panel based on the *Passionale Christi und Antichristi* discussed below. Just as the woodblocks in the printers' shops constituted a great pool of material for various editions, so did printed material as well as drawings accumulated by the glass-painters' studios constitute a pool of images and themes. Biblical picture books, or *Bilderbibeln*, which were produced in a number of versions, many in the Protestant city of Basle, were one of the most common sources for images. Hans Holbein's *Icones* of the Old Testament was

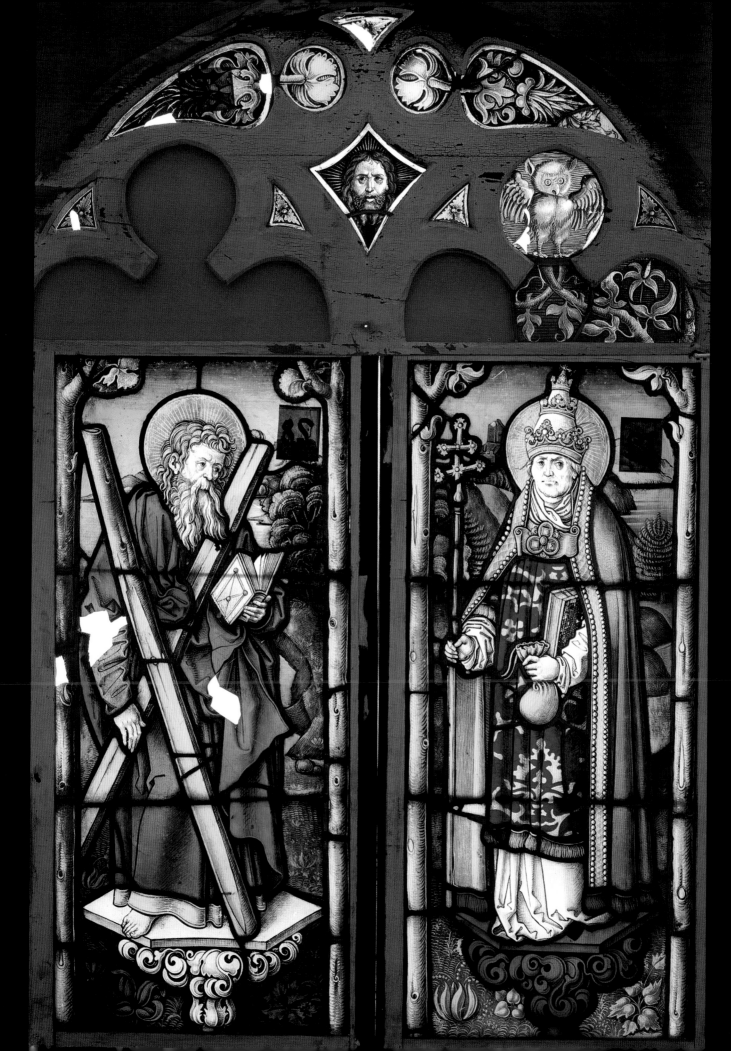

ABOVE LEFT *Given the division of labor between the designer and the fabricator that developed around 1500 in many major cities, the artist's designs for the window became more finished, and also more highly prized by collectors. Hans Sebald Beham's drawing for glass of 1522 is now in the British Museum, London.*

ABOVE RIGHT *In Beham's stained glass panel, now in the Metropolitan Museum, New York, the glazier leaded according to color. Green would demand a segment to itself. The cross was simply painted on the segment of blue used for the sky. Red, however, employed a layered segment of glass with red only on one side. Areas were abraded where the red was not wanted.*

published in 1538. Hans Baldung Grien's *Laien Bibel* of 1540 contained both Old and New Testament scenes. Hans Sebald Beham published a *Bibliae historiae* in Frankfurt in 1533, and Tobias Stimmer supplied the images and Johann Fischart the rhymed verses for an enormously popular publication of 1576 containing 135 Old Testament and thirty-four New Testament scenes.

The printed book and the single sheet or series radically altered the relationship of the glazing workshop to a master designer. Major artists like those named above still received specific commissions and produced one-of-a-kind designs for a designated site. Hans Süss von Kulmbach, for example, designed the huge window for the Margrave Friedrich von Brandenburg in St. Sebald's Church, Nuremberg, 1514. In great cities such as Nuremberg, Cologne, Brussels, Bruges, or Antwerp, a sophisticated clientele could demand high-quality and original work from well-established workshops. By using print sources, however, any workshop could produce windows resonating with commonly understood models. For example, in Switzerland, in the small town of Brugg, Jakob Brunner exercised the profession of innkeeper as well as being a painter of stained-glass panels, frescoes, and other architectural designs. Such admittedly part-time artists were still connected to a broad world of artistic models.

In the 1460s and 1480s, designers were generally integrated within stained-glass workshops and took an active part in painting and in supervising the fabrication of windows. By the turn of the century, however, work had become more subdivided, with many individuals producing designs only, and important dynasties of glass painters, such as the Hirsvogels of Nuremberg, fabricating windows for other artists. By the early sixteenth century, for example, the production of stained glass in Nuremberg involved major artists whose designs were used also for prints, panel paintings, and the decorative arts. They included Albrecht Dürer, Hans Baldung Grien, Hans Süss von Kulmbach, H. L. Schäufelein, and Hans Sebald Beham. We see this division codified half a century later in the illustrations of Jost Amman for his survey of mechanical and sedentary occupations (*Panoplia illiberalium mechanicarum aut sedentariarum artium*, 1568). His woodcuts show three separate craftsmen involved with the production of stained glass, the designer or draftsman *(der Reisser)*, the glazier *(der Glaser)*, and the glass painter *(der Glasmaler)*.

Dürer was the dominant artistic personality and his prints were among the most commonly used iconographic and stylistic models of the era. His fifteen-woodcut series of 1497–98 depicting the *Apocalypse* was particularly influential. These dramatic images of the end of the world and the Second Coming of Christ served as the design source for the Apocalypse windows in the French parish churches of Saint-Florentin (Yonne) about 1529 and Chavanges (Aube) about 1550. Dürer's print of St. Eustace about 1501 appeared in a highly sophisticated, but altered 1543 version by a follower of Engrand Le Prince in the church of Saint-Patrice, Rouen. A superbly designed window in the parish church of Gisors, France, about 1550, used Dürer's *Marriage of the Virgin* from the woodcut series of the *Life of the Virgin*. His woodcut of the *Coronation of the Virgin by the Holy Trinity* from the same series became the standard treatment for this subject in innumerable instances of Renaissance glazing.

Dürer also designed specifically for glass, most of this work fabricated by the workshop of Veit Hirsvogel the Elder. For the chapel of the house of Dr. Sixtus Tucher, Dürer designed a series of windows, including the *Annunciation* and *St. Andrew and Pope Sixtus II*. Two years previously, for the study in Tucher's house, Dürer had executed trefoil windows of Tucher standing at his open grave complemented by Death on Horseback taking aim at Tucher. The chapel windows were installed about 1504–05 and demonstrate brilliant

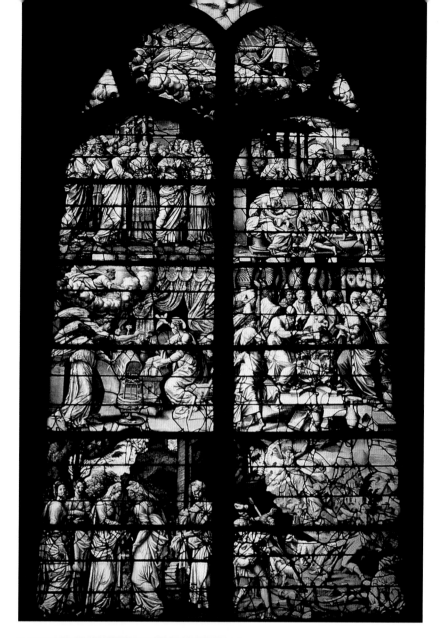

technical expertise as well as consummate design. Hirsvogel employed various shades of purple, blue, green, and silver stain on blue to create green tonalities in the landscape. The red flashed and abraded glass creates the damascene pattern of Pope Sixtus's garments. Dürer also designed the Bamberg Window, 1501–02, in St. Sebald's Church, Nuremberg, a

ABOVE *The appeal of large-scale compositions in uncolored glass, such as the* Life of the Virgin, *1545, Parish Church of Saint-Gervais-Saint-Protais, Gisors, reflects the popularity of the Renaissance roundel. Here, the school of Fontainbleau influenced the style.*

LEFT *A detail of the* Circumcision *demonstrates how the uncolored glass allows the viewer to perceive the sophistication of the painting. Dürer's lingering influence is seen in the placement of the man holding the tall candle on the left, an echo of Dürer's 1505 woodcut on the theme from* The Life of the Virgin *series.*

large-scale work. The traditional design presents donor bishops with patron saints, Saints Peter and Paul with the sainted Holy Roman Emperor and Empress Henry II and Kunigonde.

The major artistic innovation concerned the small-scale work and its relationship to a new kind of viewer, one standing in an intimate, personal relationship with the window. About 1522, Hans Selbald Beham made a series of more than twenty circular drawings of the Life of Christ and Life of the Virgin for stained glass. The drawings are 9 inches in diameter, the finished panel

with border, 12 inches. The composition of several of the designs, the Descent from the Cross, the Entombment, and Christ in Limbo, echoes Dürer's *Small Passion*. The drawing for the scenes where Pontius Pilate presents Christ to the people outside the judgment hall (John 19: 4–6) shows the clarity of the composition and the sure strokes of hatch and crosshatch shading to define volume. The stained-glass panel made after the drawing includes an inscription that in translation says, "Pontius came forth and led with him Jesus. Behold, he said to the crowds, a just man without sin." For the stained glass, the panel is divided into segments to allow the artist to use green and red flashed glass.

A popular structure of the quatrefoil received a new kind of treatment prioritizing drawing. Hans Schäufelein, for example, designed *Quatrefoil with the Coat of Arms of Heinrich IV von Lichtenau, Bishop of Augsburg, and Deeds of Hercules* in 1510, now in Berlin's Kunstgewerbemuseum. The quatrefoil was part of a series in honor of the Holy Roman Emperor's stay at the residence of the bishop of Augsburg, which took place after a meeting of the Imperial Council. The image of the classical hero Hercules is associated with the tradition of the chivalric Order of the Golden Fleece, founded by Philip, Duke of Burgundy, in 1429. Clockwise, from the top, Hercules captures the oxen of Geryon, he wrestles Antaeus by lifting him off the earth to break his relationship with his mother Earth, he destroys the lethal Stymphalian birds, and kills the Nemean lion, whose skin he wears as his distinguishing garment. Schäufelein's *Scenes from the Life of John the Baptist*, in the Uffizi, Florence, is also associated with the sophisticated atmosphere of Augsburg. The finished window, now in Berlin's Kunstgewerbemuseum, shows in the center the arms of the bishopric of Augsburg; at the bottom, John is led to his execution; at the left, Salome receives his head; at the top, the head is placed on the table between Herod and Herodias, who had been criticized by John for an incestuous marriage. To the right, Emperor Julian the Apostate orders the burning of John's bones.

The commanding power of imagery in glass, even during an age when panel painting was highly developed, is testified by the work of Hans Baldung Grien. Baldung, as he is referred to, produced intensely personal and expressive images in prints, painting, and glass. *Christ as Man of Sorrows and the Mater Dolorosa* was made for the charterhouse (Carthusian monastery) of Freiburg. Mary, suffering as she witnesses her son beaten, mocked, and finally put to death, becomes the Mother of Sorrows, the female complement to the suffering Savior, Christ as the Man of Sorrows. The Virgin is shown with a sword piercing her heart, a reference to the moment when she presented her son in the temple (Luke 2: 35). Simeon, a priest of the temple, who received the child, predicted her suffering: "And thy own soul a sword shall pierce."

LATE-MEDIEVAL CLOISTER WINDOWS

The fifteenth century supported great programs of stained glass, both as installations in new churches and as embellishment to the old. In German cities such as Cologne and Nuremberg, or Lowlands cities such as Louvain and Antwerp, cloister glazing opened a rich new field for the glass painter. Each of the four sides of a late-medieval cloister could have numerous multilight windows, and the panels were most often arranged in registers, as many as three to a light. Narrative systems, placing one scene after another sequentially, reached a peak of popularity at this time. Traditional images showing honored saints, sometimes standing, sometimes in a narrative

sequence, continued to be used. The multilight windows were exploited to great effect for the extensive and often thematically complex glazed cloisters at the monasteries of St. Cecilia in Cologne, Altenberg, Mariawald, and Steinfeld, in the Rhineland, and the charterhouse of Louvain, Belgium.

These new programs were often connected to printed illustrated concordances, such as the *Biblia pauperum* and the *Speculum humanae salvationis*, popular spiritual guides that encouraged an understanding of Christ's message through juxtaposition with precedents from Old Testament tradition. The glass painters did not copy the printed illustrations, but rather used the pattern of juxtapositions and the images themselves as a basis for further elaboration. Bust-length images of the prophets with scrolls carrying their texts (as in the printed books) were often set in the tracery lights. Larger panels might also repeat the formula. In a Lowlands panel measuring about 4 feet in height and 3 feet in width, God the Father sits in glory, blessing the word of his prophets Solomon and David. They hold scrolls whose Latin texts note verses associated with each. Solomon, believed to have written the Song

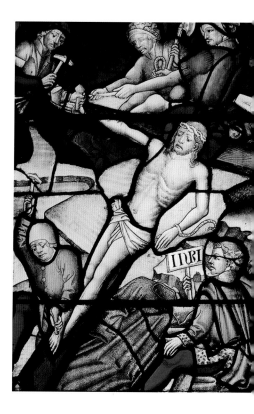

ABOVE *The representation of Christ being nailed to the cross follows popular devotional texts. Listeners would be asked to imagine the actions of the soldiers pulling Christ's limbs with ropes and his calm acceptance for love of the sinner. The above panel and the one on the next page from a destroyed cloister are now in Trinity Cathedral, Cleveland, Ohio.*

LEFT *Narrative images of the Passion of Christ were often juxtaposed with symbolic representations, such as prophets foretelling the events. In a panel showing* God Flanked by David and Solomon, *about 1520, Southern Lowlands, the Old Testament figures carry huge banderoles with inscriptions of their prophecies.*

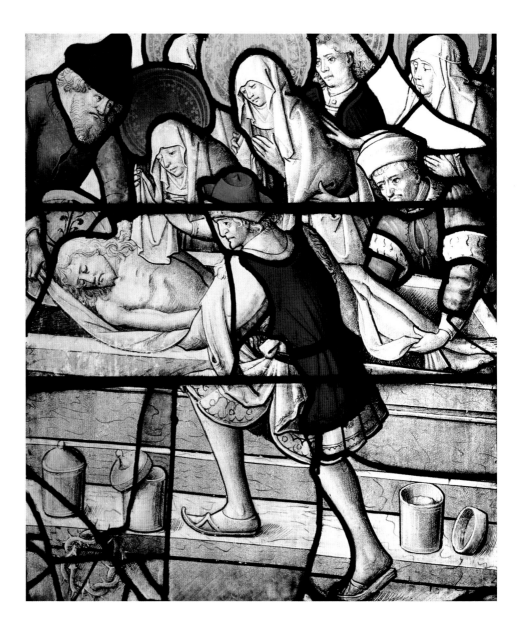

of Songs, holds "*Commedite amici et bibite z cat v*" (Eat, O friends, and drink: Cant. 5: 1). David, believed to have written the Psalms, holds a scroll that praises nearness to God: "*Sic letatiu om hia e i te ps 86.*" Although the Latin is confusing, the reference appears to be "The dwelling in thee is as it were of all rejoicing" (Psalm 86: 7).

In the organization of these vast programs, donor panels often filled the lowest register in each light, New Testament subjects the second register, and Old Testament ones the third. Each subject is a discrete entity, although also an element in a series. The stained-glass framing devices, such as the representation of sculptured pilasters, originally slid out from behind stone jambs like a stage curtain behind a proscenium arch. Thus the frames encapsulate the figures within the landscape background, so that the scenes can be envisioned as happening in the cloister garden.

One of the most active workshops is known as the St. Cecilia Workshop, after the now-destroyed cloister of the abbey of St. Cecilia, whose panels have been grouped in the Sacraments Chapel of

Cologne Cathedral. Duplicates and triplicates of St. Cecilia's cloister panels have migrated to British and American collections. The original panels were created by the workshop for contemporary installations in the Rhineland. Two panels in Trinity Cathedral (Episcopal), Cleveland, Ohio, show the *Nailing of Christ to the Cross* and an *Entombment*. The similarities between programs from this era have caused scholars to reassess their ideas on the production of art and the genesis, development, and propagation of distinctive styles. Such work has assumed the value of the identification of a master's work and the ability of the art historian, in the absence of written records, to apportion artistic responsibility on the basis of purely visual analysis. Glazing workshops, however, do not appear to be structured in the manner that is assumed in many studies of "masters" in painting. That is, organizational hierarchy is not evident in stained-glass workshops in most cases. The interaction among the various members of the shop appears to have often been fluid, with considerable variety in the execution.

The vivid and specific nature of such imagery was greatly indebted to devotional writings of the time, which were read for centuries. One of the most influential was the *Meditations on the Life of Christ*, about 1374, attributed to an Italian Franciscan, Johannes de Caulibus. The Latin text was translated into English and arranged for a lay reader by a Yorkshire Carthusian, Nicholas Love, as the *Mirror of the Blessed Life of Jesus Christ* (1410?). Another influential source was Bridget of Sweden, who lived in Rome from 1349 until her death in 1373. Her *Revelations* were known in England even before her death, and early translated into English. The order she founded, commonly known as the Bridgettines, was favored by Henry V, who in 1415 established Syon Abbey at his manor in Isleworth, a double monastery

of men and of women, which became an important center of fifteenth-century English spirituality. Bridget made several pilgrimages, among them one to the Holy Land in 1373. She described a vision of Christ's Passion, which she experienced in the Church of the Holy Sepulchre, Jerusalem.

He ascended gladly like a meek lamb led to the slaughter (and) extended his arms and opened his right hand and placed it on the cross. Those savage torturers monstrously crucified it, piercing it with a nail through that part where the bone was more solid. And then with a rope, they pulled violently on his left hand and fastened it to the cross in the same manner. Finally they extended his body on the cross beyond all measure; and placing one of his shins on top of the other they fastened to the cross his feet, thus joined, with two nails ... Then the crown of thorns, which they had removed from his head when he was being crucified they now put back, fitting it onto his most holy head. It pierced his awesome head with such force that then and there his eyes were filled with flowing blood and his ears were obstructed.

ABOVE *Curiosity and distaste appear on the faces of the onlookers who view Christ struggling under the weight of his Cross. They are presented as a crowd of unbelievers. The viewer therefore is encouraged to examine his or her own actions and to consider how they attest Christian belief. Formerly in Cologne, the window is now in the parish church of Great Bookham, Surrey, England.*

BELOW *Meditation on the Passion was often structured around thinking on the Five Wounds—Christ's hands, feet, and side—as exemplified by Great Malvern Priory, of about 1440.*

(Marguerite Tjader Harris and Albert Ryle Kezel, *Birgitta of Sweden: Life and Selected Revelations*. Paulist Press: Mahwah, NJ, 1990, pp. 188–89)

PARISH CHURCHES

Imagery designed for parish churches demonstrates the artistic and devotional sensibilities of a new class of patron. The church was the most important communal building of the village, the site of legal, social, and artistic as well as religious activities; these shared practices produced common architectural features. Distinct from the cathedrals, which were sites of great ecclesiastical power, parish churches frequently depended on the support of ordinary lay folk—the farmers, craftspersons, and merchants of the locality. By the mid-fifteenth century, most parish churches exhibited similar features: a western tower and an entrance porch, then a tall timber-roofed nave with aisle and clerestory windows. A chancel, often of lower elevation and differently roofed, was marked off by a screen (called a rood screen) crowned by a freestanding cross. Additional interior divisions appeared as chapels, sometimes to the left and right of the chancel, and sometimes set in the aisles. Stained glass adorned the many windows, usually portraying standing figures or scenes framed by light-colored borders of depicted architecture, allowing considerable light into the interior space.

The themes as well as the design of the windows reflected the desire to communicate to an audience of ordinary men and women. Organized like a sequence of pages, almost like a comic strip, the scenes are clear and easily read. A great deal of uncolored glass treated with silver stain increased the legibility of the image. Themes of moral instruction were common. A window of *Corporal Works* (Acts) *of Mercy*, ca. 1410, All Saints, North Street, York, shows the actions enjoined upon the Christian. At the base are donor representations. Each scene is envisioned with a practical model. In visiting the sick, a well-dressed bearded man, in cloak and hat, stands at the bedside of another man. He lays coins on the bedspread, received with a happy gesture by the ailing man's wife. Giving shelter to the homeless is shown as welcoming pilgrims, easily a scene that could illustrate Chaucer's *Canterbury Tales*. Indeed, the image of the host recalls Chaucer's description in the Prologue of the Merchant "with forked beard and … motley gown … upon his head a Flemish beaver hat."

Such images, which speak directly to parishioners, reflect the concern for educating the laity with such manuals as *The Lay Folks' Catechism*, issued in both Latin

BELOW *The late Middle Ages saw an increasing role for the laity. Merchant wealth began to rival that of landed estates, and parish churches were increasing decorated with high-quality artwork exemplified by the church of Saints Peter and Paul, East Harling.*

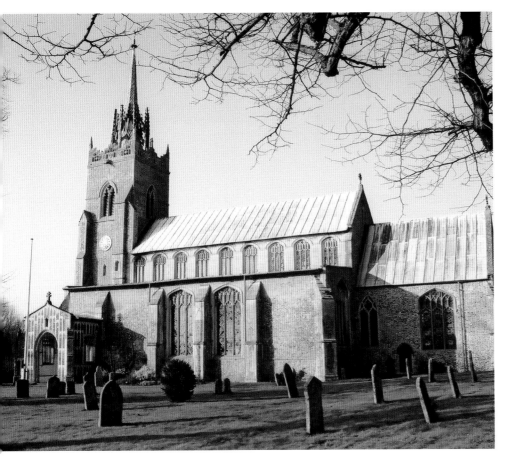

and English versions by William Thoresby, archbishop of York, in 1357. The text, in use until the Reformation, stated that the seven works of mercy will be "rehearsed" by God from each Christian soul on the day of doom. The *Catechism* gives the list, of which the first six are represented in the window.

Of whilk the first is to fede tham that er
    hungry.
That other, for to gif tham drynk that er
    thirsty.
The third, for to clethe tham that er
    clatheless
The ferthe is to herber tham that er
    houseless.
The fifte, for visite tham that ligges in
    sekenesse.
The sext, is to help tham that in prisoner.
The sevent, to bery dede man that has
    mister.

Of which the first is to feed those that are
    hungry.
The next, to give drink to those who are
    thirsty.
The third, to clothe those who are without
    clothes.
The fourth is to shelter those who are
    homeless.
The fifth is to visit those who lie in sickness.
The sixth is to help those in prison.
The seventh is to bury the dead who are
    churched.

Popular literature, such as *The Pricke of Conscience*, ca. 1340, a poem on the Last Days of the World, also inspired windows. In the early fifteenth century, copies of the poem are known to have been in the possession of important members of the laity, one being Alice Bolton, who gave windows to All Saints, North Street, which has a window on the theme. The poem lists fifteen days of destruction in vivid detail, including on Day Four: "Sea monsters rise up and roar and invade the earth."

The fierth day, sal swilk a wonder be
The mast wondreful fisshes of the se
Sal com to-gyder and mak swilk roryng
That it sal be hydus til mans heryng
Bot what that roryng sal signify,
Na man whit, bot God almyghty (lines
    4770–75)

The fifth day, there shall be such a wonder.
The most marvelous fishes of the sea
Shall come together and make such a
    roaring
That it will be hideous to hear.
But what that roaring shall signify
No man knows but God Almighty.

The window retains a fragmentary inscription: "Ye iv. daye ye fisches sal."

ABOVE *Themes that referred to the direct education of the laity, such as images encouraging good works, appeared in wall paintings and windows in parish churches. The* Corporal Works of Mercy *in All Saints, North Street, York, shows specific actions. One injunction is to visit the sick, here shown as a wealth man coming to the sick bed of another man and leaving money to aide his wife to care for the invalid.*

Stories of the saints were not forgotten. Saints with spectacular powers to heal and protect, such as Christopher, patron of travelers, were common. Christopher was frequently presented as a massive wall painting close to the entrance of a church. St. Martin, a charitable Roman military officer who divided his cloak with a beggar and who later became a bishop, was highly honored. A large window of multiple rectangle scenes, similar to the arrangement of the Corporal Works of Mercy, graces St. Martin-le-Grand, York; the vivid imagery includes St. Martin banishing a devil.

Stories of the lives of Christ and the Virgin still dominated representation. Anne Harling,

ABOVE *The Passion was, of course, the central element of lay piety. At Holy Trinity Church, Long Melford, the depiction of the Virgin of Pity from the 1490s showed the suffering aspect of Mary's role. At her feet is the clerical donor.*

wealthy heiress and patron of Saints Peter and Paul Church, East Harling, represented her three husbands in various ways in the church, including the east window, 1463–80, whose theme is the *The Joys and Sorrows of the Blessed Virgin Mary*. Beginning with the Annunciation and ending with the coronation of the Virgin as queen of heaven, the images are filled with homely details. In the Visitation scene, St. Elizabeth wears maternity clothes with a laced front to allow expansion as the pregnancy progresses. Scenes such as St. Anne teaching the Virgin to read, as seen in All Saints, North Street, 1412–28, were repeated.

The Virgin of Pity, or Pietà, is a subject not found in the Bible. The Gospel describes Joseph of Aramathea demanding Christ's body and arranging for burial, and adds laconically that "the women … saw the sepulcher, and how his body was laid" (Luke 23: 55). With the growth of lay devotion in the later Middle Ages, the faithful demanded a more personal means of evoking Christ's family, in particular his relationship to his mother. The image of the Virgin holding Christ's body became one of the most popular visual motifs in the fifteenth century in northern European art. Its juxtaposition to the image of the Virgin holding her infant son on her lap constructed an opening and closure to the Christian epic of human redemption through a God made flesh.

Details of such representations confirm these sentiments. Christ's face is gaunt, his brow furrowed as if contracted in pain, while the circlet of thorns causes droplets of blood to fleck his skin. Mary's hand tenderly cradles the body that has suffered its last agony. Margery Kempe, a woman of the merchant class from Lynn, Norfolk, dictated a personal spiritual autobiography, *The Book of Margery Kempe*, 1440. In Chapter 80 she describes a long meditation on the Passion of Christ in which she felt that she could see and hear

all that happened. She concentrated on the last moment of Mary with her son. She heard Mary beseech St. John and Joseph of Aramathea not to "take away from me my son's body" and ask them not to "part my son and me from each other" or, if he was buried, to bury her with him for she could not live without him.

Devotional images responded to these needs. That of the Five Wounds, in decorative pattern as well as a badge, further abstracted the representation of the suffering body. The *Arma Christi*, signs from episodes in the Passion of Christ, such as the lance that pierced his side or the pliers used to draw out the nails and remove his body from the cross, became widespread. The image of God the Father holding the body of Christ crucified (called the Throne of Mercy) with the dove of the Holy Spirit became one of the most common means of representing the Trinity in the fifteenth century.

An east window from a small parish church, Holy Trinity, Goodramgate, York, which includes the Throne of Mercy has survived relatively intact. The pastor of the church, John Walker, gave the window, in which he shows his personal as well as shared associations, in 1470. In the center Walker is seen at the foot of God the Father, who is holding the Son in his arms. The dove of the Holy Spirit hovers between the two heads. Next to Walker a Latin scroll reads: "I adore and worship you O, Holy Trinity." Around the window: "Have mercy on the soul of John Walker, Rector. He caused this house and window to be made in the year 1470 in Thy honor, O King." Flanking the image of the Trinity are John the Baptist and John the Evangelist, and at the far sides are St. George and St. Christopher, patrons of York guilds. Below is the Virgin Mary with the extended family of Christ. Christian legend, contained in sources like the late-thirteenth-century *Golden Legend*, told of St. Anne's two

FAR LEFT *At the foot of Christ, the diminutive form of the donor, John Walker, makes his petition for grace in Holy Trinity Goodramgate, York. Christ's body is often shown bearing the marks of his scourging and the holes where the nails pierced his feet vestiges of his blood.*

LEFT *The fifteenth-century worshipper wished to give to Christ the loving support of family that was dear to them. The Holy Kinship was conceived in order to provide Mary with two half sisters and numerous cousins for Jesus. Mary Cleophas, with a halo, appears with her husband Alpheus and four sons. This small scene was on the lower level of the John Walker's window, making it more accessible to the church's parishioners.*

subsequent marriages after the death of Joachim, the Virgin Mary's father. From these marriages came two half-sisters, Mary Cleophas and Mary Salome, who bore St. James the Less, St. Simon, St. Jude, St. James the Greater, and St. John the Evangelist, making these apostles Jesus's cousins. Thus the window displays lineage and personalized relationships: God the Father, his Son Jesus, and the human family that surrounded Jesus while on earth. John Walker's relationship to his church, his fealty to God, and the protection of the special saints of York are all depicted.

Donors, seen as diminutive figures at the foot of a saintly patron, were intimately linked to such personalized display. They were often shown, as in English illuminated manuscripts, kneeling before altars or desks with open prayer books or holding a model of their donation, such as Robert Skelton of York, offering his window (about 1350). As attested by Skelton's image, and that of his wife in the companion lancet of the window, the laity began to claim positions of prominence by such self-imaging or prominent inscriptions. John Barett, responsible for the rebuilding of the roof of St. Mary's, Bury St. Edmund's

LEFT *God the Father is shown as compassionate as the Virgin as he holds his dead son in his arms. This Throne of Mercy in York Cathedral was formerly in St. John, Michelgate. It was commissioned in 1498 by Richard York, mayor of York from 1469 to 1482. The quarry design in uncolored glass is original to the window.*

ABOVE *The donor portrait of Robert Skelton, St. Denys Walmgate, York, shows full use of silver stain in the yellow tint of the hair, alternating silver and gold lions in the border, and the detailing of the bees in the quarries of the background. Introduced in England 1307–12 at York Minster, silver stain became a staple of York glazing practices by 1350.*

BELOW *The church of the Holy Trinity in Long Melford, Suffolk, was reconstructed in the 1480s–90s. Inscriptions on the exterior asked for prayers for the donor John Clopton and his extended family.*

OPPOSITE TOP *Kentwell Hall, a Tudor building, still extant, was the Clopton residence in Long Melford.*

OPPOSITE BELOW LEFT AND RIGHT *In the fifteenth century, families of the merchant classes and lesser nobility began to appear in glazing programs. John Clopton included his relatives, ancestors, and many important acquaintances. The figures have been reinstalled in the aisles in modern windows of uncolored quarries.*

(Cambridgeshire), in the 1450s, painted his motto on the roof braces, and John Clopton, the renovator of Holy Trinity Church, Long Melford (Suffolk), invoked prayers for himself and his family on the decorative banding on the exterior of the church. The windows of Long Melford, dating from the 1490s, escaped the destruction of so much English glass by Protestant iconoclasts; they show family members and associates of Clopton.

The program shows not only piety and family association but also the growing importance of professions. Clopton depicted his grandfather Sir Thomas Clopton (d. 1383), the first Clopton to occupy Kentwell Hall, Long Melford, having married the heiress Catherine Mylde.

Sir Thomas is placed between his wife and his daughter-in-law, Elizabeth Pygot. The heraldic dresses of the women display the arms of Clopton on one side and on the other those of their own families. In heraldic terms Clopton's arms *impale* those of their families. By such representation, the women are seen in their roles of transferring family connections and inheritance. Their bodies literally are their family's lineage since they bear their family's representation, just as they bore the family's progeny. The men display their family's arms on heraldic dress only when they are in armor. When in secular dress, they are depicted representing their professions; for example, Sir William Howard, a chief justice, wears the sober robes of a jurist.

Such family alliances were of great importance in the shifting political atmosphere of the late Middle Ages, as attested by the correspondence of the Paston family of Norfolk between 1422 and 1509. John Paston was often away from home attending to legal matters, and in his absence, his wife, Margaret, supervised his estates. Their correspondence, however, suggests intimacy set within the piety shared by the Cloptons. She wrote to him during her first pregnancy to ask him to buy a girdle, for she had only one that fit, and added, "I pray that ye will wear the ring with image of St. Margaret that I sent you for a remembrance till ye come home" (*Paston Letters*, December 14, 1441).

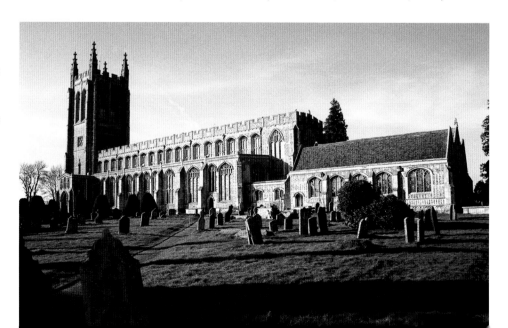

POST-REFORMATION SWISS PANELS: THE SIXTEENTH AND SEVENTEENTH CENTURIES

By the 1550s the Reformation had so changed the structure of artistic patronage in the institutional church that large-scale stained glass became rare. The armorial window, however, came into its own in a new era. Typically measuring about 16 inches high and 12 inches wide, these panels were suitable for almost any window, for they were meant to be set within a clear glass lattice, often formed of circular segments, or bull's-eyes. Since they demonstrated family and community pride, they were very popular.

These small independent panels were ubiquitous in public buildings such as town halls, law courts, inns, or even religious buildings from the fifteenth through the seventeenth centuries in Switzerland, southern Germany, and the upper Rhine. That the panels were considered obligatory elements of public architecture is borne out by textual evidence. In 1542, for example, the *Bürgermeister* of Stein-am-Rhein, surveying the newly finished town hall, expressed the "earnest wish that our gentlemen and distinguished individuals would each claim a window in which to install an honorific shield." One can suppose that the kinds of panels expected might resemble the representation of fourteen members of the law court of Goldach, near St. Gallen, of 1580. Executed by Niklaus Wirt of Wil in a common format, the panel shows the jurists at table, being served in a large hall with musical instruments hanging on the wall. All fourteen heraldic badges of the members, and their names, surround the scene. Unlike in many other areas in Europe, heraldic badges were not restricted to the nobility. Indeed, when called to civic duty Swiss citizens were obligated to use their family shields or to construct one for themselves.

Other frequent themes include the standard-bearer representing the arms of a city or canton, as in the arms of Uri in the cloister of Muri. Panels representing individuals, whether a couple (the "marriage" or "welcome" panel), a bishop or abbot, or donors of a religious institution, were produced in quantity in both Catholic and Protestant areas. Overtly confessional references often accompanied the images, such as Catholic patron saints or Protestant liberation themes. Additional images from classical literature and history combined with local references to produce an extraordinarily rich picture of Swiss Renaissance culture.

The marriage panels testify to the increasing role of the middle class in the commissioning of art. Husband and wife appear in the central scene sometimes with their children. Often the wife holds a beaker for the husband and he is dressed in parade armor or full citizen's dress and holds a halberd or banner. Above is often a scene of plowing with a team of horses or oxen, the transport of goods, the production of honey, fishing, or another image of agriculture or commerce. Below the representation of the couple are their coats of arms, the husband's on the dexter side (the viewer's left) and the wife's on

the sinister. Sometimes the shields stand between the couple, or at their feet. The lowest panel is an inscription, usually identifying the couple by name, with a description of the husband's status, such as mayor or captain, and the woman's as his wedded wife, *"sin Ellich hus Frouw."* The format varied little throughout the sixteenth and seventeenth centuries for this was a truly popular art, one dominated by individuals keen on preserving their family traditions, and therefore eager for the reassurance that their own marriage panel reflected the format and design of that of their grandparents'.

An early testimony to the ideals and politics of the Reformation appears in the panel of 1530 showing William Tell shooting an apple from his son's head (Schweizerisches Landesmuseum, Zurich). The donor, Christopher Froschauer, named in the inscription was a patriot printer in Zurich who was responsible for publication of the writings and Bible translation of the reformer Ulrich Zwingli. Not only does the central image show Tell's famous exploit but the scene above depicts Tell's assassination of the governor of Wolfenshiessen in his bath while the governor's wife sits spinning yarn. The frog on the shield is a "canting arms" play on the name Froschauer as *Frosch*, German for "frog."

Protestant Switzerland produced images that were sometimes overtly anti-Catholic, such as the panel dated 1574 given by three tradesmen. Images on the shields at the bottom of the panel identify a baker (pretzel hanging from a tree), a butcher (cleaver), and a vintner (two vinedresser's knives). The panel is based on the woodcuts of the *Passional Christi und Antichristi*, a Protestant book published anonymously in Wittenberg in 1521. Martin Luther's letters indicate that the text can be credited to Philip Melanchthon, a noted theologian, and Johann Schwetfeger, a jurist, and the illustrations to Lucas Cranach the Elder. The year 1521 also saw Luther's excommunication by the pope and his condemnation by the Diet of Worms. The organization of the text juxtaposes two images across the page: to the left an act of Christ, to the right an act of the pope. The *Passional* enjoyed wide popularity, undergoing a number of printings in various forms, including a Latin translation. In the *Washing of the Feet* panel borrowed for the stained glass, Cranach shows Christ humbly washing the disciples' feet while the pope demands that rulers honor him. Melanchthon's text associates the pope not only with "all tyrants and pagan princes" but also with the beast of Revelations 13, which "could both speak and cause that whoever should not worship the image of the beast should be killed." The stained-glass panel does not quote directly from the text but restructures the message into rhymed couplets, similar to those found in the illustrated Bibles of the time. In translation:

> Christ out of heartfelt humility washed the feet of his disciples.
> Out of pride, the pope makes emperors and kings kiss his feet.

The lower images are not from the *Passional*, but repeat standard iconography of the Last Supper and the elevation of the host during the Catholic mass. The verses, however, are decidedly critical.

> Christ through his Last Supper gives us strength of our faith
> The Mass is an invention of the pope and a disgrace to the Passion of Jesus Christ.

In general, however, the imagery was subtler. Often panels presented scenes from the Old Testament and the parables of Christ, especially didactic themes such as Joseph fleeing Potiphar's wife, the sufferings of Job, or the Good Samaritan. "Liberation" themes like Daniel in the

Paſſional Chꝛiſti vnd **Antichꝛiſti.**

Chꝛiſtus.
Szo ich ewie fueſſe habe gewaſchen ð ich ewir herꝛ vñ meyſter bin/vill mehꝛ ſolt yr einander vnter auch die fuſſe waſchen. Hie/ mit habe ich auch ein anzeygung vñ beyſpiel geben/ wie ich ym than habe/ alſzo ſolt yr hinfur auch thuen. Warlich warlich ſage ich euch/ ð knecht iſt nicht mehꝛ dan ſeyn herꝛe/ ſzo iſt auch nicht ð geſchickte botte mehꝛ dã ð yn geſandt hat/ Wiſt yr das! Selig ſeyt yr ſzo yr das thuen werden. Johan. 13.

Antichꝛiſtus.
Der Babſt maſt ſich an igluchen Tyrannen vnd heydniſchen furſten/ ſzo yre fueſz den leuten zu kuſzen dar gereicht/ nach zu/ volgen/ damit es waer werde das geſchꝛieben iſt. Wolcher dieſer beſtien bilde nicht anbettet/ ſall getöd werden. Apocalip. 13. Dis kuſſens darff ſich der Babſt yn ſeynē decretalen vnbotſ ſchꝛimbt rümen. c. cũ oli ð pͬ. cle. Si ſummus poͬ. ð ſen. excõ.

lion's den and Jonah and the whale were also popular. The Swiss and German panels, then, present a vivid picture of the beginnings of Protestant iconography. It not only countered Catholic imagery but reflected the themes of the Protestant reform: the belief in the sacred text as the prime authority and the belief that Protestant reformers were not so much breaking away from a tradition as returning to a purer tradition exemplified by the first centuries of the Christian era.

In Catholic Switzerland the glass was often connected to explicitly Roman Catholic traditions. The most frequent themes were the great feasts of the Catholic calendar and images of the saints. In addition, there was a strong tendency to emphasize Marian themes, very possibly because devotion to the Virgin Mary was an aspect of Catholic teaching vehemently rejected by Zwinglian reformers. One finds images of the Assumption of Mary into Heaven, or the Immaculate Conception, the Annunciation, the Circumcision of Christ, and the Adoration of the Magi (the Feast of Epiphany). Often included in the borders are saints connected to

ABOVE *The availability of prints, as woodcuts or engravings, broadened the sources available to the window designer. The illustration by Lucas Cranach for the* Passional Christi und Antichristi, *printed in Wittenberg in 1521, was widely disseminated.*

OPPOSITE *At the end of the wars of religion, Switzerland was apportioned into Protestant and Catholic states. Lutheran literature, in particular the* Passional Christi und Antichristi, *was the basis for the panel given by three men, very probably for a civic placement such as a town hall or parish building. The panel is now in the Mead Art Museum, Amherst College, Massachusetts.*

RIGHT *Catholic patrons continued their devotion to the saints. Lawrence Wissenback and Margaretta Schwitzer, husband and wife could be spiritually present through the depiction of their patron saints, Lawrence and Margaret. The panel was produced about 1575–1600, in Fribourg, Switzerland, and is now in the Mead Art Museum, Amherst College, Massachusetts.*

BELOW RIGHT *The abbey of Muri, Switzerland, has an extensive glazing program. The windows show a large variety of donors, including civic authorities such as the city of Uri, installed in 1557. The stance of the standard bearers on either side of the shield was a popular composition in Swiss heraldic practice.*

a local devotion or the name saints of the couple commissioning the panel.

A panel from the last quarter of the sixteenth century has been attributed to Fribourg and its Catholic milieu. The panel is a moving example of the religious and familial sentiment in the Catholic cantons. In 1529, Fribourg and Valaais joined with the five original Catholic cantons (Zug, Uri, Unterwalden, Lucerne, and Schwyz in central Switzerland) to form a Christian alliance with Ferdinand V of Austria. The donors, Lawrence Weissenbach and Margaretta Schweizer, present their patron saints, Lawrence in his deacon's robes and grille, and Margaret standing over the dragon. (St. Lawrence was martyred on a grille and St. Margaret was freed from an attack by Satan in the form of a dragon when she made the sign of the cross and the dragon's body split and released her.) Between the two saints is a prayer: "Oh, human being, think during all of your life on your last hour so you will not sin against eternity. Amen." Above is an image of Gabriel's annunciation to Mary that she would bear the Messiah with a prayer below: "O Lord Jesus Christ,

I desire that your holy face is the first thing that I see when my soul departs from my body, Amen."

Catholic patrons continued to support the monasteries, whose glazing programs were impressive. Muri in the mid-sixteenth century installed a brilliant series of cloister windows by the Zurich glass painter Carl von Egeri. In each triple-light cloister bay, the center opening frequently displayed the arms of a state, such the *Standesscheibe* of Uri showing a black bull's head on a gold ground. The right and left openings contained associated saints, such as St. Michael holding both the scales to weigh souls and a sword to defeat Satan. In another bay a prominent man, Beat von Fleckenstein, and his wife, Anna Mutschlin, are associated with three members of

the Fleckenstein family. Beat's patron, St. Beatus, a legendary hermit who evangelized Switzerland and dispelled a local dragon from a cave, is shown in action. A brilliantly executed panel of St. Blaise commands the central image in a bay funded entirely by a neighboring monastery. Stained glass takes on the role of talisman, uniting and safeguarding the community.

Cloister Wettingen also constructed its glazed cloister in the post-Reformation climate. Its extensive program extended from the 1520s to the early seventeenth century. Many of the panels are donations of cities, for example, such as that donated by Basle in 1579. A figural representation of the city includes its patron saints, the Virgin standing on a crescent moon holding her child, and Emperor Henry II, who holds

a model of Basle Minster. The highly accomplished painting style includes vigorous delineation of architectural motifs such as the dolphin heads at the base of the columns. At the bottom are small scenes of St. Matthew, guided by the angel and writing his Gospel, and to the right is St. Mark with his symbol of a lion. Both are modeled after the picture Bible by Tobias Stimmer published in 1576.

The new cloister of the Cistercian convent of Rathausen near Lucerne was completed in 1591, and during the next thirty-two years, the sixty-seven openings were gradually filled with glass in a clearly articulated theological program. The windows demonstrate the cooperation between Church, state, and wealthy citizens. Each panel shows a similar

BELOW LEFT *St. Michael, along with St. Oswald, was the patron saint of the city of Zug. Clad in brilliant armor, the archangel who has defeated Satan weighs a soul in the form of a naked child. Heavy with good works, the soul will be allowed entrance to heaven.*

BELOW RIGHT *Typically, private donors would include their patrons. Beat von Fleckenstein honors Beatus, an English monk who was thought to have been the first Christian emissary to evangelize Switzerland. The elaborate shields on either side of the panel reflect the family alliances of von Fleckenstein.*

ABOVE *The panel of St. Blaise is one of the most complex and richly executed of Muri's entire cloister. It was executed in 1558, presumably by the glass painter Hans Füchslin.*

OPPOSITE *Scenes taken from classical literature were reinterpreted in the Renaissance with moralizing Christian interpretations. The stories of the Judgment of Paris, and Death of Pyramus could be seen as exemplars of decision making and of acceptance of the unexpected. The panel is now in a private collection, California.*

organization of a highly detailed image set within an architectural frame. The donors' patron saints stand on the side of the frame and the donors' family heraldry appears at the bottom. The inscription at the top, a rhymed couplet in German, identifies the scene, and the inscription below gives the donor's name and the date.

Of the sixty-seven panels, twenty-one were donated in behalf of religious institutions by their officials; for example, the *Transfiguration* (now in the Metropolitan Museum) was given by the abbot of Muri. Secular institutions such as the cities of

Sursee, Lucerne, and Rottwyll were responsible for sixteen panels. Private citizens identified in the inscriptions as mayors, captains, ambassadors, governors, and other officials, often with their spouses, gave the remaining thirty. Sometimes it is possible to see a relationship between the narrative and the donor, as in the panel given by Barbara Hund von Wenkheim, abbess of Rottenmuster, which shows *Mary Magdalene Washing Christ's feet*, Schweizerisches Landesmuseum, Zurich. The inscription states that the sinner receives much grace because she has loved well.

Production of leaded stained glass continued well into the seventeenth century in Switzerland. A beautifully executed panel of 1628 shows the classical themes of the Wheel of Fortune, the Judgment of Paris, and the Death of Pyramus. Typical of its date, the panel shows a greater reliance on enamel paints, the scenes being defined through blue and purple enamel colors and yellow silver stain applied to uncolored glass. Traditional pot-metal colors, formed in the glass in its molten state, appear only in the border. A single donor is inscribed: Hans Hagnamer, Lucerne. The Wheel of Fortune, a late classical motif, was highly popular in the Middle Ages. It shows the ascent of an individual—here a man as a youth, then soldier, then ruler—and then his fall from grace as the wheel turns. Boethius's popular *Consolations of Philosophy* made a central use of this image. Equally literary are the reference to Paris, speaking with the god Mercury to decide whether Venus, Hera, or Minerva is the fairest, the legendary cause of the Trojan War, and below, a tale from Ovid's *Metamorphoses* used by Shakespeare in *A Midsummer Night's Dream*, the lovers Pyramus and Thisbe. Certainly the donor was an educated man. Given the changing social context of the time, he might have been a man of inherited privilege or equally a jurist or university professor.

Hauß Hagnaner, von Dietichen vß
dem Lucern, gebiedt 1 6 Z 8

ROUNDELS

The roundel is a phenomenon of northern Europe, with its greatest popularity in the Lowlands; it is intimately linked to the tradition of printmaking in the Lowlands and Germany. It often resembles a drawing with line, shading, and tints of yellow wash. The artists of the southern Lowlands, such as Jan Swart van Gronigen, Bernard van Orley, and Dirick Vellert, lived and worked in major commercial and political centers like Antwerp, Brussels, and Mechelen. The busiest European port in the first half of the sixteenth century, Antwerp was also an important center for art production. Panel paintings were mass-produced and sold commercially, and roundels may very well have been marketed in the same way. Artists worked in many formats. Vellert

painted and produced designs for monumental compositions at King's College Chapel, Cambridge, and for smaller panels such as *Esther before Assuerus*, discussed below, as well as roundels.

The roundel, a new object in glass, a single pane painted with vitreous paints and silver stain, emerged as a major element in glazing programs. It was in part a response to the increased value of the graphic media of drawings and prints, but also responded to a new market for glass in more intimate settings. Distinctions between the secular and the ecclesiastical, as used in modern times, are as inappropriate for the Renaissance as they are for medieval settings. A prominent ecclesiastic might install a roundel in his private quarters, just as a magistrate might commission an image for his parlor, or for

RIGHT *Roundels, single sheets of glass treated with paints and silver stain were often the choice for heraldic display. Very possibly from Nuremberg, this small shield with its shining helm and elaborate mantling would have been set in a grid of uncolored glass in round or trellis leaded panels. The panel is now in a private collection, California.*

the windows of a hall of justice, as may be supposed for Vellert's exquisitely painted judgment scene of the *Son of Zaleucus Accused of Adultery*. Rather than trying to force modern distinctions on the past, it is preferable to define the issue as one of scale. The roundel must function within an intimate setting, one where the viewer has a feeling of importance within the space.

The subjects of the roundels reflected many of the themes treated by the small leaded panels *(Kabinettscheiben)* and also by large panel paintings. Often documented as originating from halls of justice *(Gerichtssaal)*, many of the scenes show images of law and justice, such as the law court of Goldach mentioned above. Panel paintings for justice chambers include examples by Derick Bouts (*The Justice of Otto III* for Louvain, 1470–75), Gerhard David (*The Judgment of Cambyses* for Bruges, 1498), Albrecht Dürer (*The Calumny of Appelles* for Nuremberg, 1521), and Peter Paul Rubens (*The Last Judgment*, *The Judgment of Solomon*, and *The Judgment of Cambyses* for Brussels, 1622; destroyed in 1695). Dirick Vellert continued such judgment scenes in Lowlands glazing, exemplified by a *Judgment of Solomon* from the Great Cloister of the charterhouse of Louvain, 1525–30, now in the Cleveland Museum of Art. Swiss panels frequently show themes of justice taken from the Bible rather than classical history. Christ and the Woman Taken in Adultery, Susanna and the Elders, and the Judgment of Solomon were frequent themes.

The theme of justice is emphasized in the roundel of *Christ Being Led Away from Herod Antipas*, about 1515–20, from the north Lowlands, possibly Amsterdam. It carries a Dutch inscription in the form of a rhyming couplet typical of the picture Bibles popular at the time: "Love justice, hate injustice, and employ the light of moral wisdom. Then that which you begin you will succeed in, you who rule over the people and the

country." The representation is encoded as a reference to issues of justice and human action, just as the inscription specifically addresses "you who rule." Christ is not the central figure; he is led off to the side and is a relatively calm and passionless form. Herod is larger, dressed in ermine-trimmed robes. Their complex folds across his lap attract our attention. Framed by the canopied throne and flanked by advisors, he is the embodiment of the secular ruler.

ABOVE *Roundels could also carry detailed scenes, exemplified by a panel attributed to Dirick Vellert, now in the Martin D'Arcy Gallery of Art, Loyola University of Chicago. Seen at close range, the intricate detail of a panel such as the* Son of Zaleucus Accused of Adultery *spoke directly to the onlooker.*

ABOVE *Whether a classical example of justice of an interpretation of a biblical event, the panels carried specific messages. A panel showing* Christ Being Led Away from Herod Antipas *is now in the Metropolitan Museum of Art, New York. The inscription painted on a separate border makes it clear that the image is meant to exemplify issues of justice and not simply narrate Christ's Passion.*

Thus the inscription and the construction of the image argue that the intent was to emphasize justice as a specific virtue.

Justice, in medieval and Renaissance thought, was one of the Four Cardinal Virtues (with Prudence, Temperance, and Fortitude) that could be achieved through human reason. In contrast, the Theological Virtues—Faith, Hope, and Charity—were beyond human learning and accessible only through the mystery of God's Grace. In the panel of Christ and Herod, Justice is personified by action rather than by the traditional isolated female form. Specific aspects of narrative, then, could be structured as moral tales according to the emphasis and position of standard elements in the story. The roundel has

neither added nor subtracted any iconographic feature common to the story of Christ's confrontation with Herod. Rather, the manner of depicting the story has changed. It has received an identifying label, designed to convey a pointed moral to the viewer.

Although many roundels appear to come from well-defined series, others raise several questions. Patrons of a stained-glass studio selecting a panel design for personal or corporate placement often isolated an exemplary scene: David confronting Goliath, as in a panel dated 1646 from Toggenburg, Switzerland, and now in Harvard University's Fogg Art Museum (Naumburg Room) is such a scene. It could be integrated, as in the Harvard example, into a personal matrix of patron saints, biblical citations or other confessional texts, and lengthy biographical inscriptions including location and profession. Series of the Prodigal Son were also popular, frequently presented in four scenes as are the panels in the Fogg Art Museum and the Los Angeles County Museum (45.21.36), showing the *Departure, Gambling, Herding Pigs,* and *Return.*

The popular Lowlands tale Sorgheloos (Careless), a variant on the theme of the Prodigal Son, demonstrates the evils of gambling and loose living, using allegorical figures such as Careless himself, Fickle Fortune *(Lichte Fortune),* Luxury *(Weelde),* and Poverty *(Pouer).* Sorgheloos has a protagonist whose life is ruined by his unrepentant dispersal of fortune among loose companions. There is no return to a forgiving father, the final message being the harsh reality of poverty as the result of a morally dissolute life. This type of theme was developed in conjunction with morality tales of the Power of Women. In 1541 a series of woodcuts with a lengthy poetic description defined six stages of the story: Sorgheloos setting out; Sorgheloos and Luxury dancing; Sorgheloos and Fickle Fortune; Sorgheloos beaten by Indigence and bitten by Poverty; Sorgheloos, Poverty, and Indigence rebuffed; and finally Sorgheloos destitute. The image of the foolish young man gambling in the tavern is one of the more readable in the series. The survival of a large number of roundel versions of the episode may suggest that this scene, showing the turning point from a life of wealth to one of poverty, was the one in the cycle that best exemplified the entire import of the story. Thus a Sorgheloos series could be expanded or contracted, as long as this event was included.

A roundel of the *Last Supper,* Detroit Institute of Arts, after the print cycle of scenes of the Passion by Jacob Cornelisz.

van Oostsanen, was probably executed by a workshop in Amsterdam about 1514–25. Van Oostsanen's woodcut series of the Passion comprises twelve scenes: Last Supper, Agony in the Garden, Kiss of Judas, Taking of Christ, Mocking of Christ, Flagellation, Crowning with Thorns, Ecce Homo, Carrying of the Cross, Crucifixion, Lamentation, and Resurrection. A later edition amplified the woodcuts through lavish architectural frames with figural inserts. It is impossible to know precisely what model was employed by the glazing studio or for what context the Detroit *Last Supper* was created. It might have been part of a full cycle of twelve images, perhaps even juxtaposed with images creating a typological context with Old Testament scenes. It is equally, and perhaps even more likely that the *Last Supper* was commissioned as a single piece portraying the centrality of the eucharist in Christian worship as well as the image of Christ's compassion for his followers. Only one extensive series of roundels after the van Oostsanen print series has been identified—eight installed in the Church of the Holy Trinity, Bradford-on-Avon, Wiltshire. The subjects include the *Agony in the Garden, Kiss of Judas, Mocking of Christ, Flagellation, Ecce Homo, Crowning with Thorns, Christ Carrying the Cross,* and *Crucifixion.* Of the other extant roundels associated with this series, six are images of the *Last Supper.* Four roundels each show the *Resurrection* and *Crowning with Thorns,* three each depict the *Kiss of Judas* and *Ecce Homo.* The *Crucifixion* and *Flagellation* have been found only once.

It seems reasonable to see the dynamics between patron and workshop, with its complicated process involving models, designers, and painters, as a part of life in late-medieval and Renaissance times. A wealthy or corporate patron like a prominent merchant or a cleric might commission an entire series of roundels on the Life of Christ. A less affluent client

OPPOSITE *Small leaded panels were often treated with the same careful draftsmanship as roundels. A panel of* Esther Before Assuerus, *about 1525–30, now in the Cleveland Museum of Art, is associated with the artist Dirick Vellert. Vellert, like others of his time, produced designs for tapestries, large-scale windows (in particular King's College Chapel in England), small-scale panels, and roundels.*

might select a single subject, perhaps the Last Supper or the Resurrection.

In these small panels, whether roundel or leaded panel, new and highly seductive ways of addressing the viewer are often explored. Challenged by the closeness of the viewer, the designer sought to evoke the architectural experience of the monumental glazing program within a small format. Recent analysis of literature and art has encouraged the study of the larger story embedded in a single image, such as the story of poverty and gender in the painting of *Two Laundresses* (1884, Louvre) by Degas, or Parisian class divisions and sexuality in Manet's *Olympia* (1863, Musée d'Orsay). Likewise, for studies of Italian Renaissance wall paintings and altarpieces, scholars have explored the coded messages and the languages employed by makers and receivers. The stories provide exemplars of individual heroism, social exclusion, romantic attachment, or judgment and retribution. The arrangement of elements within the composition allows the story to be told.

The story of Esther has drawn attention through medieval and Renaissance times. A panel showing *Esther before Assuerus*, probably by Dirick Vellert comes from the Great Cloister of the charterhouse of Louvain, 1525–30. In this composition, the perfectly coordinated perspective lines terminate at a point just above the head of the soldier to the left of the chest in the center. Sequential events are presented as if they are simultaneous but framed in different architectural placements. Knowing that her predecessor was exiled for violating protocol, Esther has come to see the king without an invitation (Esther 1: 12, 19; 4: 11, 5: 1–2). Three serving women accompanying Esther form a semicircle in front of the king, who touches her with his scepter. She will reveal Aman's plot to kill the Jews, of whom she, unbeknown to the king, is one (Esther 5: 4). The man to the left, whose head is on the same level as that of the seated king, is

Aman. He proudly flourishes the ring that the king has given him, the seal of the kingdom with which he has authenticated documents ordering the Jews' extermination. Seen between his head and the king's is a small box, surely the "ten thousand talents of silver" that Aman has promised to the royal treasury in return for the king's support of the pogrom (Esther 3: 8–15).

Through the door behind Assuerus, Esther lies on her bed. Aman kneels before her supplicating her favor and Assuerus strides in the doorway. Vellert has effectively illustrated the moment during the feast organized by Esther when the king goes out to walk in the garden and Aman asks Esther to mediate for him (Esther 7: 7–8). Assuerus is shocked at Aman's plot and outraged by the perception that his councilor is assaulting his wife. The outcome—Aman's hanging—appears on the right. The key personage, Aman, is represented three times: he sees his downfall, begs for mercy, and is executed. The conflict is played out through the representation of architecture. In the center, a profusion of riches, plates, cups, pitchers, surmounted by a nude idol, dominates the scene. On the same level, we see the back of the throne. Aman's cupidity and desire for wealth are shown as the cause of his destruction and become a warning for viewers of the panel.

These changes in the leaded and painted window herald the modern era with its diverse constituencies and locations for stained glass. Not confined to the churches, the windows show a broad range of human concerns; desire for justice, self-representation, pride in family, and delight in intellectual pursuits. Windows are addressed to very specific and divergent audiences, from the most sophisticated jurist in a cosmopolitan city to the laborer in a rural parish. Through the variety of formats and placements, imagery in glass permeated all aspects of life.

6

Large-Scale Renaissance Stained Glass

OPPOSITE *The fifteenth century saw a resurgence of interest in window narratives. New themes, however, showed an awareness of the new public. The section of the church that served the laity, the north nave of the Carmelite church, at Boppard-am-Rhein, was renovated in 1440. A window of the* Ten Commandments *carries inscriptions in German obviously directed towards the laity. In the window depicting "Thou shalt not commit adultery," couples cuddle in various compromising positions. The window is now at Salve Regina University, Newport, Rhode Island.*

For both its artistic brilliance and its intense production in almost all European countries, the stained glass of the Renaissance constitutes a major epoch in large-scale decorative art. During this time, cities assumed a larger role in economic and civic life, secular patronage of government officials grew substantially, and art was universally seen as a requirement of status, either as a personal possession or as a public statement of largess. Vying to attract such discriminating patrons, artists developed new modes of expression, the most important being systems of perspective that evoke three-dimensional space. Artists in stained glass were part of this accelerated production. From the end of the fifteenth century to about 1550, and in the Lowlands well into the seventeenth century, they provided large, important buildings with stained glass. Monasteries engaged in extensive programs for their cloisters, cathedrals added chapels and even new glazing, and the laity financed new or expanded parish churches. All strove for windows that spoke an artistic language of heightened drama, three-dimensional realism, and intense color.

GERMANY AND ASSOCIATED AREAS

A new interest in glazing began early, especially in the Rhineland. In the Carmelite monastery of Boppard-am-Rhein, a series of windows, 1440–46, were part of the rebuilding of the north nave, the part of the church used by the laity. Boppard's seven large three-lancet windows once displayed images of saintly protectors, the life of Christ, and themes honoring the Virgin. The glass was dispersed in the early nineteenth century and is now divided between the Metropolitan Museum of Art in New York, the Schnütgen Museum in Cologne, the Detroit Institute of Arts, the Burrell Collection in Glasgow, the de Young Museum in San Francisco, Salve Regina University in Newport, Rhode Island, and other collections. Despite its monumental scale, the program parallels parish churches in the importance of lay donors and vivid stories, including instructional series such as the Ten Commandments.

The *Commandments* window originally grouped St. Elizabeth of Hungary with donor shields of Albrecht II and his wife; Elisabeth of Luxemburg, held by angels; the

Madonna clothed with the Sun; and Moses on Mount Sinai with representations of the Commandments. A window of the Commandments in the church of Saint-Thiébaud in Thann, Alsace, 1430–50, parallels the Boppard program in its architectural housing of the various scenes. In Boppard's window of the Ninth Commandment, "Thou shalt not covet thy neighbor's wife," a splendidly dressed woman in an ermine-lined scarlet surcoat is approached by two men while a demon endeavors to draw their faces together. God, a bust-length figure with cruciform halo, is above, presenting the Commandment and gazing down at the group of virtuous men and women on the right. This format is followed for all the scenes. In the Seventh Commandment, "Thou shalt not steal," the sinners appear

on the left, where a barefoot man seizes his neighbor's purse. For the Sixth Commandment's warning against adultery, the injunction is broad, written, as are they all, in old German, "Du solt nut unkuis sin" (Thou shalt not be unchaste). To represent what not to do, a man caresses a compliant woman's breast.

This expressive style employs short bodies and round heads with plump cheeks, curly hair, and large facial features. The compositions are densely packed, with fully saturated colors bringing the action across the surface. Architectural detail with little figures augments the vivacity of the compositions. Presumably centered at Koblenz or Mainz, the workshops responsible for these windows also worked in Thann, Altthann (Vieuxthann), Schlettstadt (Sélestat), and Zetting in

France, Partenheim in Germany, and Zofingen and Staufen in Switzerland.

Within a short time, dramatic images began to engulf the entire window. Artists designed scenes extending across multiple lancets as if there were no architectural divisions. A window of the *Birth of Christ and Presentation in the Temple*, 1483, in the Church of Our Lady, Munich, places the scene over five lancets, crowning the event with an extraordinary effusion of living architecture, naturalistic foliage appearing to grow in stone. The Strasbourg Workshop Cooperative, which produced the window, had been formed of a group of stained-glass workshops that pooled their resources to search for work, designing, and fabricating windows in the upper Rhine, southern Germany, and even into Austria.

ABOVE *Donor portraits were common in churches and cloisters. The specific lines of the face of Prior Peter Bloomeveen, however, suggest that the glass painter was attempting an actual portrait. The Cologne glass painter Hermann Pentelinck, who fabricated the window of the cathedral's* Passion *and* Coronation of the Virgin, *probably produced the glass of Cologne's Carthusian Monastery of St. Barbara for Prior Bloomeveen. This panel is now in the Worcester Art Museum.*

Glass painters developed highly sophisticated painting techniques to render the three-dimensionality of panel painting. Techniques varied, but often stipple washes were applied in layers to give smooth transitions from light to dark. Dark line was used sparingly, often simply as an accent to strengthen the outline of the nose or ear. Sanguine, a russet color, was introduced to give a reddish tone to lips or a cheek. Often near-life-size figures in volumetric rendering appeared as if a sculptural presence in the lancets of a window.

Other artists, however, continued to head workshops. In Lorraine, the reknown Strasbourg glass painter Valentin Bousch is first noted producing windows at Saint-Nicolas-du-Port in 1514. His work exemplifies the ability of glass painting to incorporate both color and depth, as expressed in oil painting, and the graphic line that had become so prized an attribute of Renaissance engraving. His expressive intensity parallels that of Hans Baldung Grien, whom he probably knew. Bousch's success led to his being named the master glazier of Metz Cathedral, where he began work in 1518–20. During his long career, he developed a large atelier, and his numerous commissions included the church of Sainte-Barbe, whose windows are now in Metz Cathedral. The artist's majestic grasp of space and arrangement of figures can be seen in windows from Flavigny-sur-Moselle, 1531–32, now in the Metropolitan Museum of Art, and private collections in the United States and Canada. A remarkable Catholic theological program of seven windows on the history of salvation, showing *Adam and Eve* and the *Flood*, presents Mannerist treatment of the nude in large-scale figures. The window of *Moses Presenting the Law* bears Bousch's monogram, VB, in the classical architectural frame as well as the donor's motto, "Fravs inimica luci" (Deception is the enemy of light), highly appropriate for its placement in a window.

ABOVE *St. Adrian wears medieval armor distinct to Northern Europe. From Stoke Poges Manor, England, the window may have been made there by Rhenish artists about 1510–25. The panel is now in the John Woodward Higgins Armory Museum, Worcester, Massachusetts.*

The transformation of stained glass in Nuremberg within the circle of Albrecht Dürer has already been discussed. These artists usually entrusted their designs to glazing workshops. The work of the Master of the Holy Kinship and the Master of St. Severin in Cologne Cathedral for windows in the north nave is similar.

THE LOW COUNTRIES

The Low countries were one of the primary sites for Renaissance glass. One of the earliest great masters was Arnoult de Nimègue whose twenty-six scenes chronicling the history of the diocese of Tournai were severely damaged by an explosion in 1745. They were extensively restored with nineteenth-century replacements, yet the quality of the windows is discernible. Here is a dramatic new feeling of physical presence and weight of form, the renown of which brought Arnoult an invitation from patrons in Normandy.

The Habsburg rulers of Belgium, who were related to the rulers of Spain, Portugal, Germany, and Austria, employed stained glass as a political tool. The collegiate church of St. Wandrue, a foundation of canonesses in Mons, shows the ideal apportionment of representation. In windows dating from 1511 to 1630, the royal family and most important individuals of the empire appear in the choir, and local dignitaries in the nave. Nicolas Rombauts, master glazier of Brussels in 1524, put his signature on the harness of the horse in the window of St. Martin.

St. James in Liège, of about 1525, is one of the most renowned of Lowlands ensembles, published in exquisite detail in the nineteenth century. The program shows the donors and their patron saints in a lower level, in the upper level, figures of saints surrounded by heraldic shields. The Hornes family were the major donors. Jacques de Hornes wears the collar of the Order of the Golden Fleece, a chivalric association instituted by the Dukes of Burgundy and promoted by the Holy Roman Emperors. Marguerite de Hornes, Jacques's sister, appears in prayer before an image of the Virgin. Her patron, St. Margaret, with her identifying dragon at her feet, stands slightly behind her. Border initials *E* and *M* refer to Marguerite and

her husband, Everard de la Marck; their marriage brought reconciliation between two warring families.

In Brussels, the cathedral's north transept shows the Holy Roman Emperor Charles V presented by his patron, Charlemagne, in armor, and Isabella of Portugal with her patron, Elizabeth of Hungary. Under a huge triumphal arch, the couple kneel at prayer before a statue

ABOVE *After compositions by Peter Paul Rubens, the great painter of Catholic Europe, the 1654–63 windows of the chapel of Our Lady of Liberation in the cathedral demonstrate that glass painting remained important even into the Baroque age.*

LEFT *About 1540, Bernard van Orley was commissioned to depict the family of the Emperor Charles V under elaborate triumphal arches in windows for cathedral of Brussels. The couples are shown kneeling adoring the actual altar of the chapel they adorn. In the window of Francis I, king of France and his queen Eleanor of Austria, a dramatic St. Francis receives the stigmata behind the king, his namesake.*

of God the Father holding a reliquary of miraculous hosts. Across, in the south transept, is a window showing Queen Mary of Hungary, donated by Margaret of Austria, wife of the ruler of the Low Countries. Immediately to the north, and in a similar format, the Blessed Sacrament chapel contains windows dating from 1540–47 honoring the emperor's family and their adherence to the Catholic faith. In the upper level, a fabulous story about the theft of consecrated hosts, and below, rulers with their patron saints proclaim both religious orthodoxy and political hostility to the newly formed Reformed European states. Bernard van Orley, court painter to the Low Countries' rulers, designed and executed the cartoons (the full-scale drawings from which the glass painter would work) for most of these windows. The extraordinary architecture dominates the composition, while energetic figures silhouetted against a light blue background convey the subject.

In the mid-seventeenth century the chapel of Our Lady of Liberation was built on the south as a pendant to the Blessed Sacrament chapel. The windows display the same arrangement of monumental architecture framing donors below and narrative scenes above. The four immense windows, interpreted by Antwerp artists Th. van Thulden and J. de Labarre after the designs of Peter Paul Rubens, show exuberant Baroque ornament and fleshy, theatrical figural style typical of the master. The windows were installed between 1654 and 1663, the patronage stemming from the governor of the Low Countries, Archduke Leopold-Wilhelm of Austria, and his relatives, including Philip IV of Spain. Leopold-Wilhelm appears below the image of the Visitation, where putti swirl amid the columns.

ABOVE Called to Rouen from the Lowlands, Arnoult de Nimegue infused French glass painting with a new sense of graphic energy. His Tree of Jesse, 1506, for the church of Saint-Goddard transformed medieval tradition into a theatrical display of Renaissance three dimensionality and texture.

OPPOSITE A clerical donor, Celse Morin, is presented by his patron saint in a Tree of Jesse. Installed in Autun Cathedral about 1515, the window's white damascene background draws attention to contour, seen in the biblical kings above Morin, David with his harp and Solomon viewed from the back.

FRANCE

France supported major artists such as the Fleming Arnoult de Nimègue in Normandy and the Le Prince family in Beauvais. The area around Paris also experienced renewed activity in glazing, in the capital at Saint-Germain l'Auxerrois and Saint-Gervais-Saint-Protais, and in nearby towns such as Ecouen. In its color sensitivity, composition, and draftsmanship, painting on glass became the dominant pictorial medium of the French Renaissance.

Rouen around 1500 underwent a particularly distinguished period of church construction, reconstruction, and embellishment. The window of the *Tree of Jesse*, about 1506, by Arnoult de Nimègue (Arnoult of Nijmegen) in the church of Saint-Goddard, demonstrates the brilliance of color and power of figural representation that characterized the era. A theme demonstrating the lineage of Christ starting with the patriarch Jesse, the tree/vine houses massive, richly dressed kings and prophets within its branches. The scarlet, mauve, teal blue, gold, and variegated greens intensify the plasticity of the image. A theme known since the twelfth century, the Jesse Tree in its full-blown Renaissance format became one of the most popular depictions around 1500. Exceptional examples are found in the cathedrals of Autun, Auxerre, Evreux, and Troyes and churches of Saint-Julien-du-Sault (Yonne), Châtillon-sur-Seine (Côte d'Or), Vaudes (Aube), and Elbeuf (Seine-Maritime) among others.

The Le Prince family completed windows in Beauvais, including the *Tree of Jesse*, for the church of St. Etienne, about 1522, where Engrand Le Prince signed his name on the sleeve of one of the half-length busts of prophets. The window of the *Virgin of Pity*

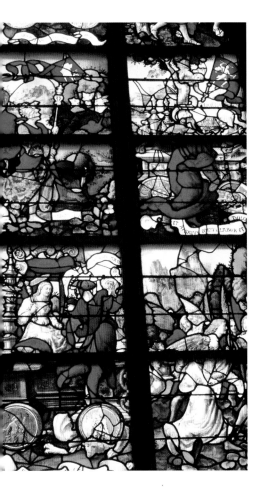

in Beauvais cathedral and the *Legend of Saints Crépin and Crépinien* in the church of Saint-Gervais-Saint-Protais, Gisors, about 1531, are among commissions in the region. At Rouen, the collaboration of Engrand and Jehan Le Prince, who signed the windows with their initials, has long been recognized in the *Life of John the Baptist,* the *Corporal Works of Mercy,* and the *Triumph of the Virgin*, made for the church of Saint-Vincent about 1525, reinstalled in the church of Sainte-Jeanne-d'Arc.

The *Triumph of the Virgin* shows just how cutting-edge glass had become. The detailed composition was designed within two years of the printing of Dürer's complex woodcut the *Triumph of the Emperor Maximilian*, which it emulates in the composition of a festival parade. Such processions, which included marchers, musicians, and tableaux set on wagons, became important city events in the sixteenth century. In three registers, innocence, fall, and redemption are presented through allegorical figures with inscriptions and symbolic attributes. The first register is the Triumph of Innocence, in which Adam and Eve ride through paradise in a chariot pulled by the virtues of Faith and Fortitude. The next depicts the Triumph of Evil, in which the chariot contains Satan in the form of a human-headed serpent entwined around the Tree of Knowledge. Adam and Eve, flanked by the personification of Pain and Sadness walk in front of the chariot. Behind the downcast couple are the bridge and cathedral of Rouen. Trailing the chariot are the Seven Deadly Sins, among them Pride mounted on a lion and Gluttony on a pig. Below, is the Triumph of the Virgin. Three angels pull her chariot, which is preceded by Moses and the personification of Truth mounted on a unicorn. To the rear are citizens, very probably the donors, passing by an exquisite image of the cathedral of Beauvais.

Jean Lafond, a pioneering scholar of Renaissance glass, suggested that the

quality of Normandy's windows was a result of the merging of the Lowlands interest in draftsmanship introduced by Arnoult de Nimègue with the compositions and palette of the French tradition represented by the family of Le Prince. Artistically significant glass is found in numerous parish churches and foundations. In the church of Saint-Foy, Conches-en-Ouche, 1540–50, the glass painter Romain Buron of Gisors signed windows with his monogram. In countries that had remained Catholic in the face of Protestant reform, windows often presented vigorous statements of doctrine and pious practices as promoted by the Catholic Counter-Reformation. Saint-Foy's themes include the story of the Gallic martyr St. Foy, the Eucharist, and the Litany of the Virgin, thus countering Protestant rejection of the cult of saints, sacraments, and veneration of Mary. In Auch, 1510, Arnaut de Moles executed windows of the axial chapel, showing solid Renaissance balustrades, pilasters, and columns framing standing figures.

The dramatic figural compositions of the glass of this region are exemplified by the *Martyrdom of St. Eustace* from Saint-Patrice in Rouen. Eustace was a popular saint throughout the Middle Ages and Renaissance. Protector against fire, in this life and in the next, as one of the fourteen auxiliary saints, he was also honored by hunters. The window is reputed to have been given by the first president of parliament, either François de Marsillac, or Pierre Rémon, in 1543 when they changed office. Originally the donor may have been identified by armorials at the base of the window, but during the French Revolution they were destroyed in the effort to erase the signs of nobility, and there are now stopgap replacements.

At some time, presumably in the early twentieth century, a French studio made an exact copy of the *Martyrdom* and sold the original to the American millionaire

newspaper publisher and collector William Randolph Hearst. Careful comparison of the original and the copy reveals the weaker draftsmanship of the copy. The original, now in the Detroit Institute of Arts, shows Eustace and his family sealed in a bronze bull and burned. Nineteenth-century critics likened the window's style to the very best of the Italian Renaissance, citing the virile energy of Michelangelo and Julius Romano. Remaining in the church are the replica and two additional episodes from the saint's life: the test of his faith as he witnessed wild animals carrying off his two sons, in the tracery, and the vision that led to

Eustace's conversion, a faithful rendition of Dürer's engraving of St. Eustace in adoration before a stag with a crucifix between its antlers.

Champagne rivaled Normandy for the brilliance of its Renaissance windows. The city of Troyes contained numerous parish churches, among them Saint-Jean-aux-Marché, Saint-Nizier, and Sainte-Madeleine. In the apse of Sainte-Madeleine, a series of windows, 1490–1518—the *Life of St. Louis*, *Creation*, the *Life of St. Rémi*, the *Tree of Jesse*, the *Passion*, the *Life of Mary Magdalene*— develop their stories in horizontal bands. Gold, red, and blue dominate the palette,

ABOVE *Traditional saints' stories took on new monumental form. The multi-medallion narratives of Chartres or Sens have given way to multi-figured painting. Installed in 1543 in Rouen, the* Martyrdom of St. Eustace *formed part of a window of three levels. Highly attractive to early collectors, the martyrdom section was replicated by a restoration workshop. The original entered the art market and was acquired by the millionaire publisher William Randolph Hearst. It is now in the Detroit Institute of Arts.*

resulting in compositions of great warmth. These compositions, especially those of the *Creation*, the *Tree of Jesse*, and the *Passion*, became models for a large number of other sites. The high demand for windows fostered creative responses by the studios, among them not exactly a cartoon, but a model of the same scale. With such a model, the glazing studios could vary the placement of leadline and expand or contract compositions depending on the size of the window opening.

In the cathedral of Châlons-sur-Marne, the Renaissance windows dating 1500–10 keep individual scenes in the rectangular format of the lancet. A great series ignoring lancet divisions appears at Notre-Dame-en-Vaux, 1520–50, by the artist Matthew Bléville of Picardy. In the window of *St. James Combating the Moors*, after an engraving by Martin Schongauer (ca. 1430-91), Bléville signed his name on the harness of the saint's horse. His *Glorification of the Virgin* uses print sources of Dürer, just as the windows of Sainte-Foy in Conches show reliance on prints by Dürer, Dirick Vellert, and Marcantonio Raimondi. At the imperial foundation of Saint-Nicolas in Brou, about 1530, however, patronized by Margaret of Austria, the windows are patterned after the Lowlands traditions. They show representations of donor figures

and figural composition similar to those in Mons, Liège, and Brussels.

In Paris, the windows are numerous. Saint-Gervais-Saint-Protais demonstrates the transformation of style during the course of the century. The window of *Saints Isabelle and Louis* reveals a sense of lingering Gothicism in its emphasis on outline and flatter treatment of drapery folds. Then follows the *Life of the Virgin* around 1520. The *Judgment of Solomon*, dated 1531, is completely imbued with Renaissance concepts in both figure and architecture. Clothes swirl dramatically around the figures and draw attention to the richness of costume. Exoticism is vividly present, especially in the male figures such as the soldier holding the child and reaching for his sword. Elaborate hairstyles and hats mark the costume of the women. Solomon's turban is made of "venetian glass" colored with strands of color, a novelty at that time. Solomon's dress is of flashed red glass abraded with extraordinary finesse to produce a design of thin white banding. Similarly, at Saint-Germain-l'Auxerrois in Paris, transitional windows such as the *Legend of St. Sixtus*, about 1500, gave way to full-blown Renaissance compositions such as *Christ Appearing to the Apostles* and *Doubting Thomas*, about 1530. Within the depictions of the apostles as they cluster under monumental architecture, there is a sense of individual portraiture.

The windows donated by François de Dinteville in 1525–45 or Charles de Villiers, 1524, in the collegiate church of Saint-Martin at Montmorency, and the huge program of windows in the church of Saint-Pierre, Montfort l'Amaury, show additional variants of the architectural frame, but all clearly place the Renaissance architecture as major elements in the design. One may also note the impressive architectural canopy

ABOVE LEFT *From the* Judgement of Solomon, *Solomon's red tunic is composed of glass with two layers. The artists abraded the red layer to reveal the uncolored glass, creating an impression of white embroidery. Such tour-de-force technical achievements appear throughout the window.*

ABOVE RIGHT *Exaggerated musculature, elongated proportion, and torsion of the body are hallmarks of the Mannerist school of Fontainbleau. The concepts also appear in one of the shepherds from the* Adoration of the Shepherds, *1545–50, formerly in Chaumont-en-Vexin, now in the Museum of the Legion of Honor, San Francisco.*

and base in the 1532 Tullier window by Jean Lécuyer in the cathedral of Bourges. France's acceptance of the soaring monumentality of Renaissance architecture appears in the window of the Tiburtine Sibyl, 1542, in the cathedral of Sens.

The concentration of artists working for François I (reigned 1547–59) at Fontainebleau deeply influenced stained glass between 1540 and 1550. In Italy, beginning around 1520, artists had shifted from the calm monumentality and ideal proportions of the High Renaissance to compositions displaying tensions, asymmetry, and dissonance. The human body was exaggerated, often elongated with otherworldly presence or heroically proportioned. François's highly

sophisticated court imported the Italian Francesco Primaticcio to decorate in stucco and fresco Fontainebleau palace. The Mannerist style was immediately disseminated, and the characteristic attenuated body, exaggerated musculature, and sinuous contours appear in the church of Sainte-Acceul, Ecouen, in the windows of the *Annunciation* and *Visitation*, 1544, and at the Sainte-Chapelle of Vincennes, on the outskirts of Paris. In Gisors, the window of the *Life of the Virgin*, 1545, in the church of Saint-Gervais-Saint-Protais, exemplifies the elegance of the style in pearly tones of grisaille. Windows of the *Meeting at the Golden Gate*, *Refusal of Joachim in the Temple*, and the *Adoration of the Shepherds*, 1545–50, now in the Museum of the Legion of Honor,

San Francisco, show typical Mannerist contours and fantastic architecture inspired by the School of Fontainebleau. The windows come from Chaumont-en-Vexin, about 12km east of Gisors, where scholars have suggested that copies were installed by the Bazin workshop, 1850–55. In the Parisian church of Saint-Gervais-Saint-Protais, about 1550, the window of the *Healing of the Paralytic* shows one of the most elegant of Mannerist groupings of figures against evocative ruins, domed temples, and imposing arcades.

The seventeenth century still saw some new commissions. Troyes' Saint-Martin-és-Vignes windows date mainly from the first quarter of the century. In Paris, Saint-Etienne-du-Mont's *Last Supper*, 1630, shows new techniques of enamel colors. The choir of Saint-Eustace, Paris, 1631, despite its late date, demonstrates one of the most evocative installations of glass and architecture. Apostles, priests, and doctors of the Church are depicted under monumental classical arches. The fictive architecture echoes the intersection of stone architecture as one moves about the actual church. Thus, by extension, the saintly choir appears to inhabit the viewer's own space.

LEFT *Saint-Eustace, Paris, embodies the transformation from Gothic to Renaissance styles. The vista of the nave from the south transept reveals Gothic ribbed vaulting intersecting classical arches in the triforium and fluted attached columns with classical entablatures at the crossing.*

ABOVE *At Saint-Eustace, the glass painter Antoine Soulignac signed his work with the date 1631. The sequential representation of arches evokes the experience of the church itself.*

ABOVE *Guillaume de Marcillat executed a series of windows for Arezzo Cathedral. In* Christ Driving the Moneychangers from the Temple *he demonstrates his command of Renaissance architecture and dynamic figural pose.*

OPPOSITE *The window of the Passion in Batalha monastery's chapter house shows Christ being nailed to the Cross, Christ's Death, and the Deposition. The brilliant colors enhance the flat, tapestry-like play of the composition. The sense of space emphasizes surface juxtaposition unlike the contemporaneous work of Lowlands' artists in England and Belgium.*

ITALY

Stained glass carried the primary decorative programs in selected Italian churches such as the cathedral of Florence. A window of the *Annunciation to the Virgin*, by Giovanni di Domenico, about 1500, in Santa Maria Maddalena dei Pazzi, Florence, shows the colors of olive, blue, gold, purple, and pinks familiar from panel painting. The French immigrant artist Guillaume de Marcillat was called to Rome as a result of papal interest in French glass painters, initiating the last major revival of monumental stained-glass painting in Italy. After work in Rome, including windows at Santa Maria del Populo dating from about 1510, he moved to Cortona in 1515. Supported by Cardinal Silvio Passerini, he produced frescoes and a great variety of stained glass for the city. The *Nativity* and the *Adoration of the Magi* once filled the space over the altar in Cortona's cathedral. They are now in the Detroit Institute of Arts and the Victoria and Albert Museum, London. Marcillat's work disseminated the art of the High Renaissance of Rome with its calm monumentality, symmetrical balance, and palpable weight, to central Italy. He exerted considerable influence on the decoration of the cathedral of Arezzo, producing five double-lancet windows on the Life of Christ, as well as frescoes. In Florence, he worked with the painter Jacopo da Pontormo in the coordination of his window of the *Deposition* within the fresco decoration of the Capponi Chapel of the church of Santa Felicità, 1525–28.

SPAIN AND PORTUGAL

Toledo reached the height of its power in the fifteenth century and the windows of its cathedral date from 1418. The names of the master glaziers have been recorded; first was the Frenchman Juan Dolfin,

followed by Loys Coutin, presumably also of French origin. The reference to a "maestre enrrique vedriero aleman" in 1478 identifies a glazier as coming from "German regions" which at that time could also include the Lowlands. Enrique's work, however, shows a definite stylistic affinity with the windows of the Strasbourg Workshop Cooperative active in southern Germany. His many windows in the nave of saints and prophets under architectural canopies show similar crisp contours and volumetric modeling via smooth washes. Eight lancet windows show half-length personifications of the liberal arts familiar to medieval thinking. Geometry holds calipers and a ruler, Astronomy a model of the heavenly spheres; Fame wears a winged headdress and sleeves to aid her swift dissemination of renown. The women are richly dressed and identified with inscriptions. Grotesques appear below, and above is a flattened arch molding. In the center of the west rose, the arms of the cathedral include a red cardinal's hat framing the escutcheon.

In Seville's cathedral, two brothers, Arnao de Vergara, beginning in 1525, and Arnao de Flandes, working after 1534, sons of the glass painter Arnao de Flandes the Elder, demonstrate Spain's consistent ability to incorporate foreigners into mainstream indigenous art. A window of St. Sebastian, shown holding bow and arrow, deviated from the more customary image of the unclothed saint pierced with the arrows of his martyrdom. The two tiers of architecture show perspectival illusion. Although accomplished earlier, they suggest the format used by Bernard van Orley in the chapel of the Blessed Sacrament in the cathedral of Brussels. These densely ornamented Renaissance forms also dominated architectural façades in Spain.

Granada's cathedral contains a highly focused program in its Capilla major by the artist Teodoro de Holanda. Fourteen windows, grouped in pairs, depict intensely human aspects of Christ's life are depicted; in the axial window the *Transfiguration* appears next to the *Last Supper*. Teodoro's dramatic but sober compositions, clearly revealing the subject, reflect Mannerist style as practiced in the Low Countries at midcentury. Eloquently simple, with ample space surrounding the figures, the windows show the pervasive influence of Mannerism across Europe.

The monumental works undertaken in Batalha around 1514 meant a dramatic change from the production of the established glazing workshop at the monastery. A new artist, Francisco Henriques, took the place of old master João. Well integrated in the artistic élite of his time, which then enjoyed a privileged status in Portuguese society, he was reputed not only as a panel painter but also as a glass painter (through his works in Évora and Sintra).

This younger artist was certainly seen by the king as the ideal interpreter of his purposes for Batalha, one who would move beyond the traditional workshop which had been there for more than seventy years.

The Descent into Hell from the choir is one of the works undertaken by Francisco Henriques. Its realism recalls earlier Flemish painting, whose influence extended throughout Europe, but the graphic style in which the figures were carried out is specific for Portugal. One need only look at similarities in contemporary Portuguese panel painting to see the regional flavor. The three-lancet window of the chapter house, dated 1514, depicting scenes of the *Passion* was probably designed by Henriques. The glass painter executing the work, however, evidences a less sophisticated painting style than the *Descent into Hell*. This is most probably the same painter who executed the window of St. Anthony in the choir.

Dirck Pietersz. Crabeth was a major designer of stained glass in the Lowlands of the mid-sixteenth century. His best-known works are a series of monumental windows for the church of St. John at Gouda, executed 1555–70. The medieval church had been struck by lightning and burned in 1552. Dirck and his brother Wouter were engaged to glaze the newly constructed church. The windows were of extraordinary height, the transept with Renaissance openings of 60 feet. The east window, on the subject of the *Baptism of Christ by St. John*, was given by George van Egmont, bishop of Utrecht, in 1555. Crabeth's responsibility as designer is documented by full-scale cartoons, still extant. The *Last Supper* window is also by Dirck Crabeth. The Gouda figures are thin and elongated, set into compositions with dominant horizontal and vertical organizational systems. In the cartoon as well as the executed window, John stands erect to one side. Christ kneels, and his legs and arms form horizontal counterpoints to the verticals of his torso and head.

The Crabeth brothers also produced a series of clerestory windows for the choir of the former monastic church of the Regulars in Gouda. The extant cartoons

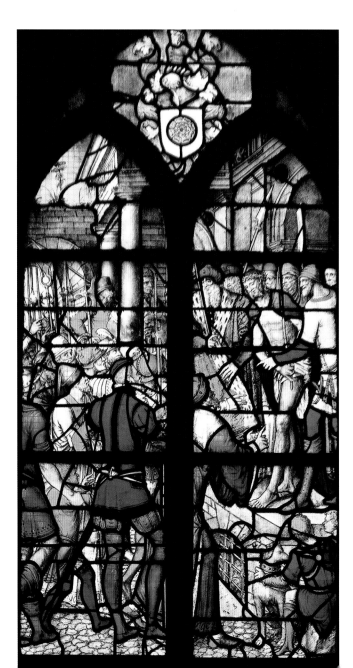

offer a fascinating contrast with the executed panels. Each window is divided into two lancets, with the narrative above. The actuality of the image is heightened by the stylish dress of the participants: colorful doublets, stockings, slashed pantaloons, and varied shapes of caps, bonnets, and helmets. The kneeling donor with his arms appears below, silhouetted against a Renaissance wall decorated with caryatids and classical arches. An inscription names the donor as well as commenting on the subject depicted.

Like other designers of the time, Dirck Crabeth also produced notable small-scale work on uncolored glass. A house at Pieterskerkgracht, Leiden, installed windows in 1543 containing twelve panels, each showing a central image panel leaded into an elaborate classical architectural surround. Swags, birds, monkeys, classical nudes, and friezes derived from Italian prototypes create an extraordinarily rich ensemble. Created for a prominent member of the government, Adriaen Dircxz. van Crimpen, the program is as sophisticated as the artistry. Seven subjects are from the First Book of Samuel and five from the Acts of the Apostles. They do not repeat medieval typology but rather express Protestant theology, which emphasized God's communion with the individual and the responsibility of each person to respond justly.

The story of Samuel, for example, focuses on Samuel's dedication to the service of the Lord since childhood. He slept in the temple where the Ark of the Covenant was kept, "and the Lord called Samuel. And he answered: Here am I" (1 Samuel 3: 4). The Christian hero Paul is shown in his conversion from persecuting Christians to God's service when God spoke directly to him as "a light from heaven shined round about him. And falling on the ground he heard a voice" (Acts. 9: 3–4).

LARGE-SCALE HERALDIC INSTALLATIONS

Stained glass in the sixteenth and seventeenth centuries was predominantly related to the individual donor, and donor representation was constant. Heraldry was a vital part of this representation, particularly in small-scale work, as we have seen. Heraldic display emerged in the thirteenth century with placements of shields of great families, such as the

ABOVE *The glazing of the immense St. John's church at Gouda represents the largest commission in the Lowlands. Dirck Pietersz Crabeth's* Baptism of Christ *shows typical vast scenes of many figures and landscape vista. The church's glazing was interrupted during the rebellion of 1572 and the conversion of the Lowlands from a Catholic to Calvinist government. The church's glazing was resumed in 1593, however, in a Protestant tradition with coats of arms and allegorical scenes.*

prominent gold and blue (*or* and *azur*) checker pattern of the house of Dreux-Bretagne throughout the south transept rose at Chartres. The heraldic-clad female donors kneel under the left two lancets and the males under the right; the armorial alone appears under the image of the Virgin and Child.

By the fifteenth century it had become customary to embellish domestic settings with heraldic glass, such as the great hall of Ockwells Manor, Berkshire, about 1460. The combination of densely colored shields and clear grisaille with inscriptions achieved both definition and illumination. Heraldry became virtually the dominant art of many Protestant countries, exploiting the Baroque love of ornament to create frames of dramatic impact.

Invariably retrospective, display allowed the creation of a desired lineage and the retrospective construction of family history. A patron might reincorporate an entire lineage of ancestors, reclaiming them, and even rehabilitating them, so to speak. Sir Edward Seymour, lord protector during the reign of Edward VI, and sympathetic to commoners and liberal

religion, was executed on an admittedly weak charge conjured up by his enemies in 1552. Almost fifty years later, however, he was an honored presence, his arms incorporated in a series of worthies depicted heraldically in windows of the Elizabethan Warkworth Manor, Northamptonshire. The manor house was dismantled in 1806 and the heraldic panels are now in the collection of the Detroit Institute of Arts.

This broad impetus to define and advertise self through the patronage of art and architecture may be as old and universal as the constructed monument. The dedicatory inscription and the portrait image have been common means of establishing such status. Despite its seeming specificity, however, the donor portrait, as used in the Middle Ages and the Renaissance, must be seen as an abstract distillation of symbols of class, gender, and social context, rather than as a portrait in the modern sense, for example, as projected in John Clopton's family and associates in Long Melford. Modern portraits, such as those of Martin Brimmer and Francis Channing Barlow in

Harvard University's Memorial Hall show recognizable, differentiating facial traits. Heraldry, through a vocabulary of signs, operates in the same premodern manner, connecting the memory of a past, ancestral presence with the depiction of a present within the image, and prospectively calling to a future of subsequent viewers.

The Lowlands included large displays of heraldry in the borders of scenes such as the window depicting Elizabeth of York installed in 1503 in the cathedral of Antwerp. The Dutch, in particular, developed glazing programs for houses of worship that were exclusively organized around heraldic shields. Often the areas were decorated with meticulously rendered floral imagery similar to that found in the new illustrated books of herbs and flowers that were executed with tour-de-force botanical exactitude.

Architectural sculpture with armorial badges such as the Tudor rose and portcullis at King's College Chapel, Cambridge, confirms the importance of such display in glass. Heraldry was ubiquitous. In the Tudor era, the arms of the ancient and the recently elevated nobility of Henry VIII often took the form of heraldic shields set in a cartouche of Renaissance architectural forms decorated with fruit. How such an installation might have looked can be seen in the glazing of Fawsley Hall, Northamptonshire, 1537–42. A typical heraldic panel records the early life of John Winthrop (1588–1649), the first colonial governor of Massachusetts Bay Colony, now in the United States of America. Winthrop's arms are impaled by those of his second wife, Thomasine Clopton. In all probability, the panel was made for a window in his estate at Groton Manor, Suffolk, before he converted his holdings into a cash income and set sail for Massachusetts in 1630. John Clopton, Thomasine's ancestor, is known from his

rebuilding of the church of Long Melford around 1480–1500 with extensive personal inscriptions and family heraldry, especially in the Clopton Chapel to the north of the chancel. Thomasine died, however, after giving birth to a child on December 8, 1616, little more than a year after her marriage. She and the child were buried in the chancel of Groton church, next to Winthrop's first wife. A moving account, deeply informed by religious sentiments, of Thomasine's last days was recorded by her husband: "The day before was 12 months she was married to me & now this day she should be married to Christ Jesus, who would embrace her with another manner of love than I could."

ABOVE *The arms of John Winthrop, the first colonial governor of Massachusetts, were created for an English setting before his departure for the colonies. They now reside in the colonies, at the Detroit Institute of Arts.*

RIGHT *The church of St. Mary, Fairford, reconstructed in the 1490s demonstrates the power of the mercantile elite to endow churches, as had the nobility in the past.*

OPPOSITE *Fairford's narrative windows, 1500–15, are divided into three segments, thematically, although not chronologically linked. One window shows the transfigured body of Christ: he appears to his mother after his death, to his apostles in the Transfiguration, and to his female followers.*

BELOW *The delicate gesture of the risen Christ and the hopeful astonishment of Mary Magdalene evoke the intimacy of the encounter.*

ENGLAND

In the mid- to late-fifteenth century active centers of glass painting such as Norwich and York had produced windows in a vigorous, late-medieval style. By the late fifteenth century immigrant artists in stained glass had begun to settle in England, causing the London Glaziers Guild to protest in 1474 against more than twenty-eight "alien glaziers" working in London; most were from the Lowlands. Although much of the glass documented by these artists has been lost, its is certain that they were responsible for major commissions, including windows in Westminster Abbey, the Pilgrimage Chapel at Walsingham, St. George's Chapel, Windsor, and the east window and choir aisles of Winchester Cathedral. Another is the church of St. Mary, Fairford, rebuilt in the late fifteenth century, finished by 1497.

The Fairford windows, 1500–15, are clearly in the style of Lowlands glaziers; the presence of the king's glazier, the Netherlander Barnard Flower, has been argued. In the Corpus Christi Chapel window, the vaulted space supported by attenuated columns in the scene of Christ appearing to the Virgin after his death contrasts to the flowing landscape of the scene of the Three Marys at the tomb. The figures move in believable space, and realistic detail abounds. Some have suggested that the Magdalene's distinctive facial features—high forehead, rounded chin, and faint eyebrows—and modish dress indicate a contemporary portrait of Princess Mary, daughter of Henry VII.

St. Mary's, like most of the parish churches built in the fifteenth century, depended on mercantile wealth. John Tame, who had made his fortune in the wool trade, and his son Edmund Tame are recorded as building and finishing the church. The imagery in the windows multiplies instances of personalized human

interest by giving attention to situations that resonate with everyday life. Christ reassuring his mother of his well-being after the Crucifixion, a scene outside Scripture, the births of both the Virgin and Christ, and the weary Virgin and Child resting on the flight to Egypt while the donkey grazes, are but a few examples. The scene of Christ being taking down from the cross has touched many a visitor. William Strode (1600–45) responded to the imagery in verse:

> See where he suffers for thee: see
> His body taken from the Tree:
> Had ever Death such life before?
> The limber corps, besullyd ore
> With meager paleness, doth display
> A middle state twixt Flesh and Clay:
> His arms and leggs, his head and crowne
> Like a true Lambskin dangling down.

The western part of the church contains images of saints and prophets as single figures under canopies. The apostles, who hold sections of the prayer the Apostles' Creed, reflect the row of prophets who hold banderoles with their prophecies.

"the Story of the Olde lawe and new lawe" patterned after the windows of the chapel of Henry VII in Westminster Abbey, now lost. Numerous artists were involved, many, such as Barnard Flower and Gaylone Hone, named in contracts, others, such as Dirick Vellert of Antwerp, identified through stylistic analysis. The windows established the acceptance of the Continental style since the work of documented native-born artists, such as Bond, Reve, and Symondes is virtually indistinguishable from that of the foreign glaziers. Windows sVII, sVIII, and sX have been attributed to Dirick Vellert. Once again, we must consider the different value systems operative for the early sixteenth century. Vellert, who was praised for his ability to paint on glass as well as to design, was involved with some of the largest glazing projects of his time, as well as with small panels for cloisters and the individual, highly personal roundels.

Lowlands artists furnished glass for William, Lord Sandys, Henry VIII's lord chamberlain, now in the chapel of The Vyne, his house near Basingstoke in Hampshire. Lord Sandys is documented as being in Calais in 1522 where he met with a group of ten glass painters from Antwerp. Apparently, he ordered windows made in the Lowlands, probably Antwerp, and shipped for installation for the Chapel of the Holy Ghost in Basingstoke, later transferred to The Vyne. Scholars have associated the work of the Lowlands artist Bernard van Orley, responsible for the windows of the transept and Blessed Sacrament Chapel in Brussels Cathedral, to the design. Three windows now in The Vyne show the *Carrying of the Cross*, the *Crucifixion* and the *Resurrection*, with Catherine of Aragon, Henry VIII, and Margaret, Queen of Scots below. The arrangement of the portrait section, as seen in *Henry VIII and His Patron Saint the Holy Roman Emperor Henry II*, is extremely close to the organization of windows in the church of St. James in Liège.

ABOVE *The largest and most prestigious glazing commission in the first half of the sixteenth century for England was King's College Chapel, Cambridge. Henry VIII supported the lengthy installation of windows in a typological program. The* Adoration of the Magi, *1535–47, presented here, was juxtaposed with an image of the Queen of Sheba presenting gifts to Solomon. The head of the Virgin has been replaced with one of St. Anne from another window.*

The upper windows show defenders of the faith, heralded by angels on one side and their persecutors encouraged by demons on the other. A monumental *Last Judgment* commands the western wall.

The huge series of windows for King's College Chapel, 1515–47, was designed by various artists, all working in some form of the Continental Renaissance style. Bishop Richard Fox was responsible for the program, described in the 1526 contract as

The separate lights carry: the standing patron saint, kneeling donor, and object of veneration, for Jacques de Hornes a sculpture of the Trinity, and for Henry VIII Christ as ruler of the world holding the same type of orb as Henry II. In the summits of the windows are lavish representations of arms.

With the break with Rome and the establishment of the Anglican Church under Henry VIII, monumental stained glass was discouraged, often destroyed. There was a brief revival, the so-called Laudian reform, under James I (reigned 1625–37). William Laud, archbishop of Canterbury, and bishops and clergy who shared his views on the importance of the sacraments and liturgy redecorated many churches. Laud was later impeached and, in 1644, put on

trial, accused of "countenancing the setting up of images in churches and the places of religious worship. That in his own chapel in Lambeth [in London] he had repaired the Popish windows" (Marks, p. 237). Two brothers, Bernard and Abraham van Linge, natives of Emden, Holland, were active at this time. They supplied a number of windows, particularly in Oxford colleges: Queens, 1635, Christ Church, ca. 1635, Balliol, 1637, and University, 1641. *St. George and St. Cyriacus*, 1632, in Magdalen College, Oxford, although not associated with the van Linges, shows the clear Baroque style of draftsmanship as well as the sobriety of the grisaille color schema.

A panel by Abraham van Linge showing the *Deposition*, from Hampton Court, Herefordshire, dispays both pot-metal

BELOW *As in the Lowlands, stained glass installations reflected concepts of royal power and religious orthodoxy. William, Lord Sandys, Henry VIII's Lord Chamberlain, commissioned windows of the Life of Christ and royal portraits about 1523. The crowded scenes show three-dimensional figures in dramatic action.*

and white glass with enamel paints. It is
signed and inscribed: "The truth hereof is
historicall devine and not superstistious
Anno Domini 1629." Clearly the artist and
his patron wanted to distance themselves
from any suggestion of popery or false
religion. The image of Christ taken down
from the cross is based on a fifteenth-
century painting by the Lowlands artist
Rogier van der Weyden. The selection is
further evidence of the importance of
tradition and the power of past images
propagated in later art, a tendency that
was to figure largely in nineteenth-century
revival ideals.

The Civil War that pitted Puritans
against the monarchy broke out in 1642
and renewed fears of religious imagery.
Cromwell's troops often engaged in
random acts of destruction. The taking
of Peterborough resulted in the almost
complete destruction of the windows of
the cloister and the church of the cathedral.
Later, possibly exaggerated, accounts
speak of Cromwell himself getting a ladder
and breaking down a little image of the
crucifixion he saw left over high up in the
church loft. York was fortunate. When it
was taken by Puritan troops under Sir
Thomas Fairfax in July 1644, the minster

and parish churches were protected from destruction. But systematic campaigns were prevalent elsewhere. In 1643 laws mandated the destruction of superstitious imagery, including crucifixes and pictures of the Virgin, the Holy Trinity, and the saints. William Dowsing left a journal of his vigorous breaking of windows and other forbidden items such as the inscription on sepulchral monuments of "Pray for us."

Stained glass next saw a period that equaled the output of the Renaissance: the stained-glass revival of the nineteenth century.

LEFT *The sobriety of uncolored glass treated with grisaille paint was appealing to Protestant taste as seen in Magdalene College's glazing, Oxford, 1632.*

BELOW *A window of 1525 in the Church of St. James, Liege, shows the model operative for Lord Sandys. Jacques de Hornes is shown with his patron, the apostle St. James. The print is taken from J. Weale's* Divers Works of Early Masters in Christian Decoration *of 1846.*

7 | The Revival of Stained Glass in the United Kingdom and the United States

ABOVE AND OPPOSITE *Thomas Willement of London was one of the pioneers of the Gothic Revival both in his own work and his publications concerning historic glass. His* Presentation in the Temple *of 1845 was made for Holy Trinity, Carlisle and is now in the Victoria and Albert Museum, London. The design shows an attempt to link the abstraction in the architectural frame with the more conventional modeling of the figure.*

With the Restoration of Charles II in 1660, glass painting was tolerated, but scarcely popular. There had been too long a hiatus since the monumental installations of the early sixteenth century for glass to be seen as truly important art. Examples of work from the early eighteenth century include windows by William Price (1703–65) in the south chancel of New College Chapel, Oxford (ca. 1735–40). William Peckitt (1731–95) of York produced windows in a Rococo style. The brilliant colors of Old Testament figures in the south transept of York Minster show the unusual attraction of his work. A controversial window, even at the time of its installation in 1783, is the *Nativity and Virtues* in the west window of New College Oxford. Designed by Sir Joshua Reynolds (1723–92), then president of the Royal Academy, the window was painted by the Irish-born Thomas Jervais (d. 1799). Medieval glass was removed to make way for the new window, which was executed as if it were an oil painting on canvas.

The great revival of stained glass in historic styles in the nineteenth century began with Romanticism and the inspiration of landscape. In the seventeenth and eighteenth centuries historicizing elements in buildings had been invariably picturesque, decorative touches consisting of pointed arches, cusped finials, and flamboyant tracery, such as the "Gothick" decoration done about 1750 in Horace Walpole's home at Strawberry Hill, Twickenham. Sham ruins as deliberate constructions were even part of eighteenth-century landscape architecture. The delight in the Gothic was primarily a visual one, and its lush complexities blended into the rich curves and intricacies of the Rococo floral designs and "chinoiserie" of the time.

The Gothic had in addition been associated with a raw and untutored expression. Even its name was a misconception, evoking the barbaric Germanic tribe of the Goths. Yet Gothic forms remained strangely a part of everyday experience in post-medieval Britain. After the dissolution of the monasteries in 1536 under Henry VIII, many monastic buildings were converted into residences for the newly created nobility. Cheek by jowl with the converted remains were the evocative ruins of great abandoned buildings,

and private chapels of Gothic construction, or viewed the vestiges of great Gothic buildings as noble ruins set in nature's frame. The long tradition is chronicled in literature from Shakespeare to William Wordsworth. To the latter the ruins suggested a pre-industrial age when reverence for God and nature was central to human experience, especially that of the common man, as in *At Furness Abbey* of 1845:

> Well have yon Railway Labourers to THIS
>   ground
> Withdrawn for noontide rest. They sit,
>   they walk
> Among the Ruins, but no idle talk
> Is heard; to grave demeanour all are bound;
> And from one voice a Hymn with tuneful
>   sound
> Hallows once more the long-deserted Choir
> And thrills the old sepulchral earth, around.
> Others look up, and with fixed eyes admire
> That wide-spanned arch, wondering how it
>   was raised,
> To keep, so high in air, its strength and
>   grace:
> All seem to feel the spirit of the place ...

Religious sentiment thus encouraged the revival of the Gothic style, which was seen

ABOVE *In Sir Joshua Reynolds' depiction of the* Virtues, *in New College Chapel, Oxford, Temperance pours water into wine to dilute its potency.*

ABOVE RIGHT *A portrait of Joshua Reynolds after Gilbert Stuart, now in the Ashmolean Museum, Oxford, shows the founder and first president of the Royal Academy.*

elements of the monasteries too large or ill placed for domestic buildings. Best known may be the Byron estate at Newstead Abbey, Nottinghamshire, inherited by the poet Byron at the age of ten. The great ruins of the west façade of the abbey still stand close by the manor house built into the conventual buildings. The English gentry either experienced Gothic architecture by their daily usage of halls as an expression of an age of faith; religion also impacted on the growth of collecting. English collectors showed a precocious affection for medieval art, reflecting, perhaps, continued use of medieval buildings by the English gentry. The interest in older art was also motivated by confessional needs. One of the major collections was formed around 1800 by Sir William Jerningham (1736–1809) at Costessey Hall, Norfolk, where he built a Gothic Revival chapel near his Tudor manor house and began to collect medieval glass to set in its windows. Sir William was staunchly Catholic and he built the chapel for the use of his own family and to serve as the parish church for a substantial portion of the population of the village of Costessey. Many panels appear to have been purchased through John Christopher

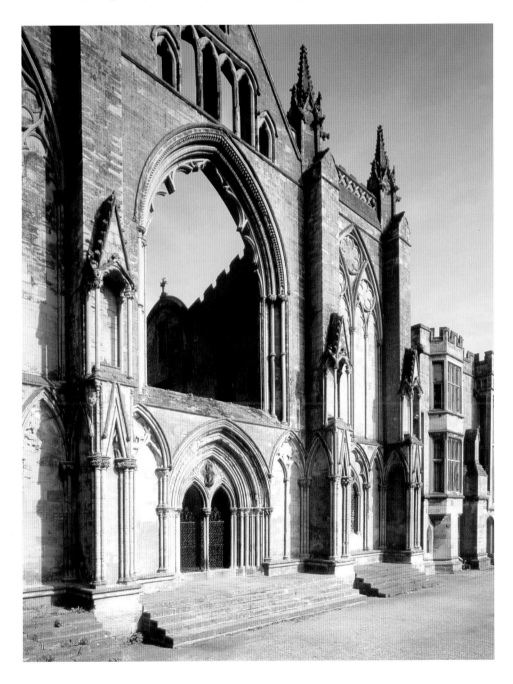

LEFT *Gothic remains were a constant presence in England. Many of the great monastic buildings dissolved during the reign of Henry VIII could be viewed either as romantic ruins or part of converted estates of the nobility such as the Priory Church, Newstead Abbey (Nottinghamshire), home of Lord Byron.*

Hampp (1750–1825), a Norwich wool merchant whose journeys took him to Antwerp and Bruges in the Lowlands, Paris, Amiens, and Rouen in France, and Cologne, Aachen, and Nuremberg in Germany. Hampp acquired large quantities of medieval glass from the monasteries disbanded during the secularization following the Napoleonic conquests, glass sold to many English churches; for example, sixteenth-century panels from the Cistercian convent of Herkenrode were sold to the cathedral of Lichfield. The Jerningham glass, numbering eighty-four subject panels, appears to have been fully installed by 1809, the year of Sir William's death. Two sales, one in 1885, which included a number of panels from other buildings on the estate, and another in 1918, when the chapel was dismantled, allowed the passage of many of these extraordinary works into great public collections such as London's Victoria and Albert Museum and New York's Metropolitan Museum of Art. In the early nineteenth century Sir Thomas Neave, of Dagenham Park, Essex, made a similar collection, now also dispersed.

The Jerningham and Neave collections are revealing as a record of what was considered medieval glass, and as an indication of the models available to contemporary painters who were struggling to revive the so-called lost art. Most of the pieces dated from the later medieval period and were of German origin, very unlike the French High Gothic model so often praised in the twentieth century. A panel showing *St. Benedict with the Shields of Salm-Reisserscheidt and Hoya* from Jerningham's collection is now in the collection of Portsmouth Abbey, Rhode Island. The panel is presumed to have come from the Church of the Maccabees, Cologne, 1505. The space is rendered with three-dimensional realism, and the figures are modeled to suggest the weight of garments and substance of the body. These devices were familiar to artists schooled in nineteenth-century academic principles of rendering. Many patrons and glass painters in the nineteenth century accepted such work as "medieval" and modeled their own work according to these principles.

The form of the "Gothic" revived throughout the nineteenth century was therefore extremely varied. Walpole included window glass in Strawberry Hill. He had begun by acquiring ancient glass, evidenced in letters to individuals such as his friend Sir Horace Mann asking for "any fragments of old painted glass, arms or anything." He also acquired over 450 pieces of sixteenth- and seventeenth-century roundels, which he installed throughout the house. He saw the pieces not as medieval but as totally appropriate for inclusion within his Gothic castle. These works on glass were fitted into what might seem to a modern eye a foreign style. However, stylistic uniformity was not

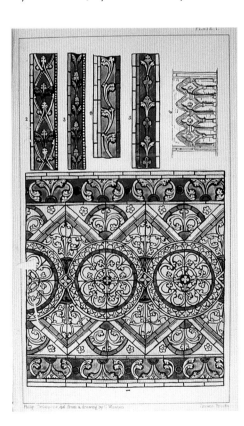

essential to many patrons or practitioners of the time as well. Indeed, what were often interpreted as Gothic, at least in the early years of the revival, were late-medieval or even sixteenth-century works.

Most essential to an understanding of the early manifestations of stained-glass revival, however, is the notion of the supremacy of painting as the primary art form. By the eighteenth century, oil painting had become synonymous with "art," and so for "art" to appear in windows it needed in some way to reference painting. Thus it is possible to understand how it could be that medieval glass was destroyed to install a "painted window" as was the case with Reynolds' *Nativity and Virtues* in New College, Oxford. This bias is reflected even in the supremely useful antiquarian work of Charles Winston (1814–64). Winston's writings were among the most influential for both the development of new windows and the appreciation of the variety of the old. He was a lawyer, an amateur of the history of glass painting, and also a designer of windows, an example being the west window of the church of St. Mary, Bushbury, Staffordshire, dated 1853, fabricated by Ward & Hughes (Thomas Ward, 1808–70 and Henry Hughes, 1822–83). His publications were illustrated with meticulously observed watercolors of important medieval examples. After Winston's death an exhibition of more than 700 of his watercolors was held by the Arundel Society in London. In his most influential work, a modest quarto published in 1847 and known by its short title of *Hints on Glass Painting*, he achieved a remarkably evenhanded evaluation of the characteristics of English period styles. In his articles, published posthumously as his *Memoirs* in 1856, he included both figural and decorative work so abundant in English churches, such as the thirteenth-century grisailles of Salisbury Cathedral. He also recorded German late-medieval and

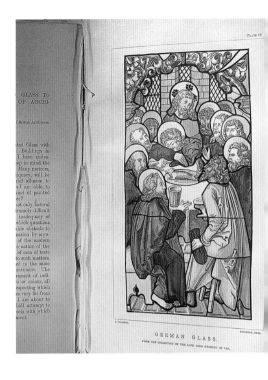

ABOVE *The three-dimensional realism of fifteenth and sixteenth century stained glass was particularly attractive to Charles Winston. His books illustrated works such as this* Last Supper, *apparently imported from the Rhineland and in a private collection.*

LEFT *Throughout the British Isles, members of the nobility, clergy, and other citizens began systematic study of the medieval past, including the time of the Roman occupation. Societies of antiquarians were formed, providing an audience for illustrated books such as Charles Winston's* Mémoires Illustrative of the Art of Glass-Painting. *These works began to define the varieties of specific period styles.*

OPPOSITE *Collections of medieval and Renaissance glass began early in the nineteenth century. Panels such as* St. Benedict with the Shields of Salm-Reisserscheidt and Hoya *were acquired from the Continent, often to embellish Gothic Revival chapels for Catholic patrons such as William Jerningham. The panel is now in Portsmouth Abbey, Portsmouth Rhode Island.*

ABOVE *Three-dimensionality was also prized by early practitioners of stained glass such as William Jay Bolton who designed and fabricated all the windows in the church of the Holy Trinity Brooklyn. The panel of the* Awakening of Lazarus *shows the linear graphics used to create shading characteristic of artists who worked around 1500 in Nuremberg under the influence of Albrecht Dürer.*

Renaissance glass in English collections, such as a panel from the Rhineland showing the *Last Supper* from the collection of George Herbert Winston. He was convinced of the superiority of early-sixteenth-century glass painting, in a full-blown Renaissance style with three-dimensional modeling, which he called the Cinque-Cento style, yet his publications meticulously analyzed all periods.

The United States, in the early nineteenth century with its population and wealth concentrated on the eastern seaboard, retained an intense relationship with British law, culture, and religious expression. The colonies might have gained political independence, but culturally they were still indebted to Britain. An Anglo-American artist, William Jay Bolton (1816–84), working in the United States, produced the largest and most devoted emulation of Winston's most admired style. Over fifty windows were set into Minard Lafever's (1789–1854) Episcopal church of the Holy Trinity, Brooklyn, built between 1843 and 1847. The church's design was influenced by the Ecclesiologist movement, which will be discussed later in this chapter. Planned in the Perpendicular Gothic style of the fifteenth century, it was modified as construction progressed to incorporate more of the early Decorated mode. The stained-glass program, the first major commission on American soil, was not in the same historical style as the building but patterned after the early-sixteenth-century glazing in King's College Chapel, Cambridge .

The context of Bolton's commission and his training reveals much of what was typical of the time. Robert Bolton, William Jay's father, a representative of a Savanna cotton company, married Ann Jay, daughter of a prominent Evangelical Anglican minister. The family settled in Bath, England, and the young Bolton grew up under the influence of his grandfather

and father, who had also taken holy orders. During his school holidays William came to know King's College while visiting an aunt, Arabella Jay, in Cambridge. When William Jay was twenty, Robert Bolton moved his family to Pelham, New York, just outside of New York City. The author Washington Irving was a close neighbor. The Boltons constructed a mansion, built in Gothic Revival style, that they named The Priory, and a family church, now Christ Church, Pelham. For the Boltons, patronage, artistry, and religion were combined. William Jay had begun painting while still in England and, in America, enrolled in Samuel F. B. Morse's courses at the National Academy of Design. He returned to Europe and toured both England and the Continent, returning in 1842. Presumably on this trip he gained not only additional artistic education but guidance in the techniques of producing painted and leaded windows. He set up a glazing kiln in a shed behind The Priory and in 1843 began to produce the first of the windows that now fill Lafever's church. Bolton's own writing reflects his passionate belief in nineteenth-century progress: that his century could surpass the art of the past. "If Gothic we must have, let it be an enlightened, progressive, nineteenth-century Gothic ... when we possess better materials, a less superstitious religion, and a more cheerful taste, with all the experience and examples of the past to guide and correct."

William Jay was inspired by both the iconography and the style of the windows in King's, many of which were designed by the Lowlands artist Dirick Vellert. Bolton thus incorporated what we now term Northern Renaissance style into a late-Gothic building. Today Vellert is viewed as a major Lowlands printmaker and designer of panels and glass, influenced by Dürer and the Italian Renaissance. To the mid-nineteenth century he represented the last and greatest phase of a medieval tradition, orchestrating scenes with large numbers of three-dimensional figures against vast architectural backdrops. Bolton's *Christ's Entry into Jerusalem* reflects the same acceptance of the three-dimensionality and pictorial tradition. Bolton adapted the compositions from the immense windows at King's and restructured the iconography to fit the smaller openings and more intimate spaces of Lafever's building. Significantly, Winston had criticized King's College Chapel for what he felt was its use of overcomplicated compositions too crowded with figures extending into the extreme distance. Bolton's adaptations are simpler and more easily read from a distance. He also adapted a painting style and brushwork that took into account the difference of scale between this work and the easel work or drawing to which he was accustomed. The windows exhibit broad sweeps of smear shading and bold hatchwork to model the forms. This is particularly visible in the organ loft window, now installed in the garden court of the Metropolitan Museum. The Brooklyn program was an extraordinary achievement; more than fifty windows designed, painted, and installed within eight years. It remains today, even in the context of contemporary European programs, a major monument of post-medieval glazing.

Bolton also provided a series of windows in a Renaissance mode—not that of the large architectural composition, but that of the small roundel. The installation was for the Church of the Holy Apostles in Manhattan, 1846–48, designed by Minard Lafever in an Italianate Renaissance Revival style. Bolton's windows consist of small circular medallions containing a painted roundel. A lush adaptation of classical foliage motifs surrounds each medallion and functions as a transition to the square format of the three panels in each lancet.

ABOVE *Bolton's image of the Entrance into Jerusalem, 1844–48, demonstrates his volumetric handling of space. His windows took their inspiration from the program at King's College Chapel, but divided the Old Testament imagery to the clerestory and the New Testament to the gallery levels of the church.*

LEFT *King's College Chapel inspired Bolton's compositions and proportions of the figures. The* Entrance into Jerusalem, *dating to the 1530s, however, shows the dramatic Renaissance ability to orchestrate multiple figures and to achieve palpable mass of drapery forms.*

Inscriptions above each panel identify the iconography depicted in the roundels. This roundel design was based on Bolton's knowledge of the Renaissance roundel imported from the Continent during the first half of the nineteenth century and installed in many English churches. The roundel functions aesthetically as drawing on glass that can retain a viewer's interest in the delight of draftsmanship as well as iconographic subtleties and yet be set within a decorative frame of window glazing, in Bolton's decision, embellished with floral motifs.

The roundel has enjoyed a long tradition, even to the present. In a world accustomed to realistic imagery and the photograph, the three-dimensional, careful recording of the world as seen appears to keep a

tenacious place. In the stairwell window of about 1900 produced for the Fairhaven High School, Fairhaven, Massachusetts, the authorities wished to represent all the seals of the American states. The seal of North Carolina shows Liberty and Plenty as majestic female figures set amid the "waving fields of grain" known in the popular song *America*. Using enamel as well as vitreous colors, the artist gives faithful renderings of the framing mountains, sky, and classically garbed women.

During the nineteenth century both architect and artist became more informed about precedent. Many believed that they could define the Gothic style according to its principles of construction. They saw in its purported natural logic a style pre-eminently suited to both urban centers of Christian worship and intimate domestic settings. Energetic debate among the many pretenders to the "true principles" of Gothic style was as much a part of the era as were the varied forms of the constructions themselves. The stained-glass studio, like the architect's office, collected an unprecedented amount of information about the past. At first printed and later photographic sources expanded the pool of information on which "modern" glass could be based. In this climate, heterogeneity was absolutely normative. It was from the architectural precedence that the structure of the window independent of the model of oil painting took its strength.

There were early attempts at figural imagery in the Gothic style. James Henry Nixon (1802–57), of Ward & Nixon, designed a triple-light east window showing Christ, St. Peter, and St. Paul, for the church of St. Martin, Owston Ferry, Lincolnshire, in 1836. The figures stand in three-dimensional solidity like statues set in niches. Their bases are semiclassical in form while the canopies are late Gothic with silver-stained yellow crockets and finials. Thomas Willement (1786–1871) was

BELOW *Often roundels were favored for secular installations, just as they had been popular during the Renaissance for law courts and private homes. The Beaux-Arts architecture of High School of Fairhaven, Massachusetts displays a series of emblems of the States of the Union in its stairwell.*

one of the early designers who emulated medieval windows. His panel of the *Presentation in the Temple*, made for Holy Trinity, Carlisle, 1845, now in the Victoria and Albert Museum, is a good example of fourteenth-century inspiration, similar to the architecture framing the knights in Tewkesbury Abbey. Almost all three-dimensionality is avoided and the elaborate canopy is as vital as the figural grouping.

His pupil William Warrington (1786–1869) served even more impressively. Warrington restored windows as early as 1833 and designed windows for Augustus Pugin in 1838 for St. Mary's College Chapel, Oscott, Sutton Coldfield, Warwickshire. In 1848 he published at his own expense a lavish folio volume, *History of Stained Glass from the Earliest Period of the Art to the Present Time* (London, 1848). Although the text is said in the subtitle to be "illustrated by coloured examples of entire windows in the various styles," all the examples are taken from Warrington's own designs. For instance, in the section on the twelfth century, the expected references to Abbot Suger of Saint-Denis and the glass of York Minster are followed by plates illustrating Warrington's work "in the twelfth-century style." The author explained this decision: "It is necessary to improve public taste or the art itself can never be generally improved. But it is by the production of good modern works that this must principally be effected. Hence the Author has chosen to give a series of his own designs which have actually been executed by himself (knowing, as he does, that they are all composed on the most rigid principles of ancient art)." Warrington divided his text into seven sections, progressing in a chronological development from pre-twelfth-century through Renaissance work. The largest numbers of illustrations appear in the sections devoted to the fourteenth and fifteenth centuries, or Perpendicular style.

The greatest influences on developing the Gothic as a style of choice were Augustus W. N. Pugin (1812–52) and the Ecclesiological Society. Pugin, best known for his contributions to the design of the Houses of Parliament, was a prolific architectural designer and polemicist. In 1836 he published his *Contrasts, or a Parallel Between the Noble Edifices of the Middle Ages and Corresponding Buildings Showing the Present Decay of Taste*, in which he argued that both religion and social values could be invigorated through a rebirth of the Gothic

ABOVE *Arguably the most influential architect of the Gothic Revival, Augustus W.N. Pugin wrote* The True Principles of Pointed or Christian Architecture *in 1841 at the age of twenty nine. His fervor for the revival of the style encouraged his illustrating Gothic inspired architecture and furnishings even for domestic settings.*

Pugin also designed stained glass. In 1845 he prevailed upon John Hardman, who had founded an ecclesiastical metal works firm at Birmingham in 1839, to begin fabrication of his windows. This image of the Crucifixion *is part of a series of medallions on the Passion in Jesus College, Cambridge 1849–50.*

style. He maintained a close supervision of the decorative aspects of his buildings, even designing and cartooning windows himself, in this aspect paralleling the practices of the French Viollet-le-Duc. The chancel windows of Jesus College, Cambridge, fabricated by John Hardman & Co. (John Hardman, 1811–67) of Birmingham, provide excellent testimony to Pugin's

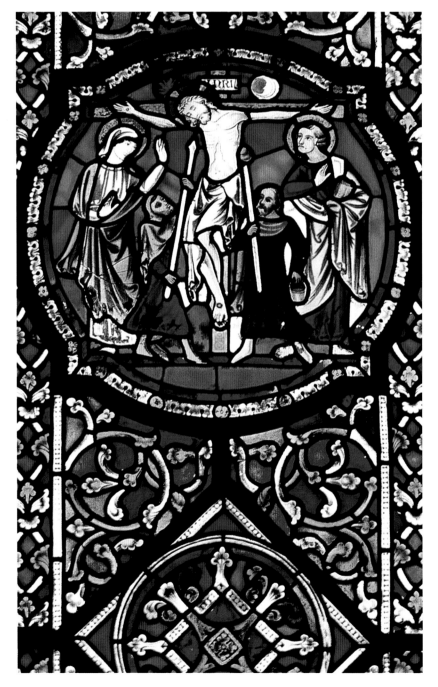

understanding of French High Gothic medallion pattern and figural compositions. For Pugin, a Roman Catholic convert, the Gothic style represented the rediscovery of the unity of man, nature, and God as understood by the Middle Ages. His publications and commissions were major forces in the development of Gothic Revival in England and its cultural extensions, particularly the United States.

Richard Upjohn (1802–78) was inspired by Pugin's writings in his design for Trinity Church, Episcopal, New York. Trinity was finished in 1846 in the English Perpendicular Gothic style, the historicizing mode then advocated by Pugin as ideally suited to church building. Galleries, so common in Georgian buildings, had been eliminated. A raised chancel area reflected the liturgical requirements of the prevailing English taste. Upjohn himself provided the Gothic Revival design for the chancel window executed by Abner Stevenson in 1844–45. The Upjohn–Stevenson window presents Christ flanked by figures of the four evangelists and Saints Peter and Paul under Gothic canopies. The single figure under a canopy, complemented by nonfigural designs in either grisaille or pot-metal glass, became the standard mode of much figural glass painting at midcentury.

The Ecclesiological Society was dedicated to the reform of church worship and architecture. Founded in 1839 as the Cambridge Camden Society, in 1845 it moved to London, taking the new name. Under the direction of Benjamin Webb, John Mason Neale, and Alexander Beresford Hope, the society endeavored to promote architectural design that would enhance liturgically oriented space, with clearly defined areas that reflected increased religious ritual. Its journal, *The Ecclesiologist*, published between 1841 and 1868, included both scholarly articles and criticism. The Ecclesiologists developed precise definitions of ideal medieval models and demanded a high level of accuracy in their replication.

They favored at first English Perpendicular but later restricted the choice to the Decorated style of about 1300, especially as reflected in the English parish church.

The construction of St. James the Less, Philadelphia, also Episcopal, from 1846 to 1849 shows the influence of Ecclesiological ideology in America as well as increasing patronage across geographic boundaries. Samuel Farmar Jarvis, the second Episcopal bishop of Connecticut, who had lived in England, received in 1844 plans of St. Michael's, Long Stanton, Cambridgeshire, dating to 1230, from Cambridge Camden Society. Although generally recommending the more elaborate Decorated style of the later thirteenth century, the Ecclesiologists decided to urge an Early English model for "the colonies." The simplicity of the style made it more suitable for limited funds and restricted construction expertise.

Jarvis conveyed the plans to Robert Ralston, a wealthy merchant living in a rapidly developing suburb of Philadelphia, who also immersed himself in Ecclesiological literature and corresponded with the Reverend Benjamin Webb. St. James the Less is a faithful replica of the Early English model. The pulpit, lectern, rail between nave and chancel, and all of the window sashes were to be imported from England. The window above the high altar was fabricated in 1849 by Alfred Gérente of Paris. Alfred and his brother Henri were connected to England through their mother, and built impressive careers producing stained glass in the archaeological revival mode.

St. James's tall, narrow lancets are similar to Pugin's design for the windows at Jesus College. The subject matter, a Tree of Jesse, is as traditional as the style. The lineage of Christ is based on the prophecy of Isaiah that "there shall come forth a rod out of the root of Jesse" (Isaiah 11: 1). Kings of the Old Testament are seated within tendrils of a vine that springs from

the recumbent figure of the patriarch Jesse, as in the west windows of Chartres. The style is a meticulous reproduction of an early-thirteenth-century mode. Blue and red, the typical stained glass palette of France, dominate the window. The single figures are silhouetted against an unmodulated background and perform stylized gestures. The garments are constructed of solid pot-metal colors on which are applied simple strokes of grisaille paint in linear patterns. Three-dimensionality is scrupulously avoided.

The studios soon became avid spokespersons for thirteenth- and fourteenth-century styles. Heaton & Butler, in the 1864 catalogue of their work, claimed that, during the Decorated style of 1280–1380, "Glass Painting attained its purest and most perfect development." Obviously the studio was happiest when working with abstracted forms, pot-metal colors against grisaille, and schematized architectural frames. (This is the style represented in the *Presentation in the Temple* by Willement, discussed above.) The studio faults the sixteenth-century work at King's College Chapel and Lichfield Cathedral, the style most admired by Winston, arguing that the windows "cannot be regarded as architectural decorations, but as independent works of art." The Chance Brothers of Birmingham in *Church Windows: A Series of Designs Original or Selected from Ancient Examples by Sebastian Evans, M. A.*, of 1862, like Heaton & Butler advertised their ability to work in the full range of period styles, including Perpendicular, Decorated, late Gothic, and Tudor. The English studios' output was vast, and its distribution extended to Canada, Australia, and New Zealand, as well as to the United States.

Before continuing to review some of the major firms, it is useful to look at the pragmatic issues of glazing within a building, especially the apportioning of figural and ornamental windows. Model

ABOVE *English designers were well aware of work on the continent. Efforts at correct replication of thirteen-century Gothic appears in work by Alfred Gérente made for the church of St. James the Less, Philadelphia, in 1849.*

books proved important on both sides of the Atlantic. The first book advocating the Gothic style in the United States was the 1836 *Essay on Gothic Architecture* by John Henry Hopkins, Episcopal bishop of Vermont. Hopkins was a firm supporter of stained glass to modulate light in order to produce an atmosphere conducive to prayer. Aware, however, of the limited technical and financial resources available, he suggested that "a very beautiful effect may be produced at small expense, by transparencies painted on linen or muslin in the Gothic style and fixed inside the windows." Hopkins's own church of St. Paul in Burlington had such substitutes until true stained glass of a quarry design was installed during renovation in 1851.

Even when architects used leaded glass, it was most commonly quarry glazing, small sections of glass in a lattice pattern, a style very popular in fourteenth- and fifteenth-century English country churches and Tudor secular buildings. Not simply expedience but a general tendency to distrust imagery appears to have encouraged these choices in the first half of the century. Hopkins devoted a chapter in his *Essay* to the issue of pictures in churches. He argued that "it would seem that ... events [from Scripture] might lawfully be presented to the eye by pictures and statues, since these would assuredly aid to fix them in the memory." He concluded, though, that the danger of superstition and idolatry had been so great in the history of Christianity that on the whole he would recommend only "appropriate architectural enrichments, and ... judicious and edifying selections from the word of God."

Later renovations of many buildings have destroyed these early windows. St. Michael's Episcopal Church, Litchfield, Connecticut, however, houses a window possibly dating from as early as 1825. The window shows lozenge-shaped quarries framed by borders of russet and blue squares in the side lights, and oak-leaf and stem in pot-metal and silver stain in the central light. The central light also contains two medallions with standard religious symbols, the pelican piercing her breast to feed her young, at the top, and the Paschal

Lamb at the bottom. These traditional windows were popular throughout the century with American and English studios alike. An early example in England is an 1840 quarry design by C. E. Gwilt, *St. George and the Dragon*, now in the Victoria and Albert Museum. The same kind of glazing of grisaille quarries with emblems was installed in St. Paul's, Burlington, as part of Hopkins's 1851 renovation, so we can conclude that the style met with his approval. The system has remained a viable and popular choice throughout the history of stained glass.

The New York studio of Sharp & Steele, also known as Henry E. Sharp and, later,

Henry E. Sharp and Son, was a prolific enterprise, producing windows from at least 1850 to the end of the nineteenth century. Typifying service to the architect, Sharp appears to have become the glazier of choice for Richard Upjohn, the most influential architectural firm at midcentury. His windows showing figures under arcades, or medallion inserts in grisaille quarries, are very much in the tradition of English glass of a generation earlier, such as the 1836 window by Ward & Nixon in St. Martin's Church, Owston Ferry, Lincolnshire. Edward Tuckerman Potter, who was responsible for the lavish Hartford home of the author Mark Twain, engaged Sharp in 1868 for the Church of the Good Shepherd, a richly endowed Episcopal church in Hartford, Connecticut. The church was supported entirely by Elizabeth Colt, widow of Samuel Colt and manager of the firearms company he founded, which made the "gun that won the American West." Elizabeth lived for forty-two years

ABOVE *Studios provided wide choices for nineteenth-century clients. In the 1870s Cox & Son of London presented a typical catalogue showing many patterned windows with suggested figural or symbolic inserts.*

ABOVE LEFT *Nineteenth-century churches, like their medieval counterparts often apportioned figural glass to the entrance, chancel, and the transepts and grisaille to the aisles. Windows with etched inscriptions and stenciled quarries comprised the original aisle program by Henry Sharp in 1869 for the church of the Good Shepherd, Hartford Connecticut.*

after her husband's death, at which time she had inherited a business and fortune equivalent to over $200 million today. She was an active philanthropist and patron of the arts, amassing a collection of decidedly Victorian taste of European academic paintings of sentimental subjects, American landscapes, Japanese pottery, and the like. Religion, especially for a woman who lost four of her five children in infancy, was a dominant aspect of life, and her devotion to church building and service was typical of her generation.

Nonfigural designs, even in such well-funded commissions, were a standard aspect of Sharp's production, as they were for the windows carried in English studio catalogues. Heaton & Butler, London, advertised in its 1860 catalogue fourteen varieties of "geometrical lead work, glazed in strong lead, and in any tint of Cathedral glass with coloured borders, and occasional pieces of colour." A second plate showed ten choices of "grisaille glass." The text reads as follows:

> Grisaille and ornamental quarry glass is now favourably received as a decoration for the aisle and clerestory windows of churches, especially when subdued light is required. The general effect is warm and silvery, and, when a little colour is added, it is a most pleasing decoration. Grisaille glass often forms the groundwork for a window in which subjects, figures, or heraldry are introduced ... This treatment will afford all the colour that is requisite, at an inconsiderable expense.

In the 1870 and 1872 catalogues for Cox & Son, London, most of the choices are nonfigural, with a variety of quarry designs in lattice systems of vertical or diagonal formats. Often the windows were provided with figural or pattern inserts. One design of diagonal format, interspersing lines of text and stenciled foliate pattern quarries, is based on fifteenth-century Tudor windows similar to those found in the great hall at Ockwells Manor.

The same systems appear in Sharp's work. An aisle window from the Church of the Good Shepherd shows verses carried on blue diagonal bands alternating with stenciled quarries of uncolored glass. Sharp's technique in other windows is similar to that of his English counterparts, employing patterns that were used during the fifteenth century, for example at Ockwells. Often the quarries are stenciled

TOP LEFT *In the chancel windows of the Church of the Good Shepherd, Christ stands in the center of the twelve apostles modeled after designs by Heinrich Overbeck, founder of the German Nazarene movement. Sharp converted the black and white prints after Overbeck's work into intense beacons of color that compete successfully with the patterned polychrome interior.*

BELOW LEFT *The architectural vigor of glass painting can often been seen in unidentified American studios and in small parish churches. In St. Mary's Church, Wharton New Jersey, in 1873 deep color focuses attention. The multi-sectioned rose window was well suited to symbolic themes such as the* Sacred Heart of Jesus *and* Emblems of the Passion.

OPPOSITE TOP *The Church of the Good Shepherd, 1868, was funded entirely by Elizabeth Colt, in a manner not unlike the patronage of the church of Saints Peter and Paul in East Harling, England, endowed by the fifteenth-century heiress Anne Harling. Originally named the Church of the Holy Innocents, the church imposed no pew rents and served as a memorial to her husband, Samuel Colt and three of their four children.*

OPPOSITE BOTTOM *The wealth of the Colt Fire-Arms Manufacturing Company enabled Elizabeth Colt to hire an architect, Edward Tuckerman Potter, renowned for his creative use of varied materials and sculptural ornament. Both within and without, the church displays rich surface detail within simple architectural profiles.*

in a flat application of grisaille paint. Sharp relieved the design, frequently a stylized flower or leaf, by a tiny grid pattern in the background. The pattern was emphasized and the intensity of light subdued by the density of the paint. The organization of the entire church, not simply the individual details, links the English and American experience. The "favourably received"

system of grisaille and ornamental quarry glass in aisle and clerestory, mentioned by Heaton & Butler in 1860, typically concentrates figural work in the chancel, transepts, and entrance wall. This appears in Sharp's work for St. Paul's Episcopal church, 1868, Wallingford, Connecticut, and the First Universalist Church, 1871, Providence, Rhode Island, as well as the

Church of St. Mary, Wharton, New Jersey, designed by architect Jeremiah O'Rourke (1833–1915), presents windows set in the same relationship of grisaille and figural program. The rose of the entrance wall shows the image of the Sacred Heart of Jesus, a Catholic devotional image of great popularity. A brilliant hand-colored lithograph of the Sacred Heart by Currier and Ives, about 1848, demonstrates the kind of illustration used in a domestic setting, linking the experience of church with that of the home. The medallions are surrounded by geometrically abstracted flower and leaf motifs popular in the Aesthetic Movement (1870–85). The aisle windows continue these patterns in grisaille, in many ways evoking the medallion patterns in Winston's watercolor of the medieval windows from Salisbury Cathedral. St. Mary's windows were produced with stencils. In the simplest kind of work, the glass painter "obscured," in the term of the time, the uncolored glass with a wash of paint. When the first layer was dry, the stencil was placed on the glass and full-strength paint applied.

ABOVE *Writing in 1836, Henry Hopkins, Episcopal Bishop of Vermont encouraged stained glass in grisaille quarries such as those of 1873 in St. Mary's Church, Wharton, to manipulate light in order to produce an spiritual effect. For many congregations opposed to imagery, such as Baptists, non-figural grisaille remained the glazing of choice throughout the nineteenth century.*

Church of the Good Shepherd. The vigor of the American window's brilliant color, retaining but intensifying the English gold, blue, and white harmonies, is set against a figural repertoire taken from pattern books. Sharp's images of the apostles in the Good Shepherd cycle are based on the Apostles series by Friedrich Overbeck, founder of the German Nazarene movement. Such images were widely distributed in single sheets and bound collections of popular religious pictures.

Similar brilliant color and strong pattern appear at many other sites. The Catholic

In other instances, the patterns are hand-done and more scintillating, such as the windows set in 1874 by Page, MacDonald, & McPherson of Boston (Donald MacDonald, 1841–1916 and William J. McPherson active ca. 1845–88) in the transepts of Harvard University's Memorial Hall. The *Virtues* window consists of a huge rose of foliate designs in pot-metal and grisaille glass and lancets containing ornamental medallion designs with Latin inscriptions of the virtues essential to the scholar, such as *Disciplina*, *Patientia*, *Fortitudo*, and so forth. The window's refraction of light through irregularities of material and of paint enlivens the visual experience. The glass has been discovered to be of an extremely durable variety, a thick, richly colored type,

with variegated surface texture. The analysis confirms the opinion of early American writers on the decorative arts, such as Roger Riordan (1848–1904), who stated that the firm was one of the first to make quality glass in America. There appears to have been absolutely no corrosion during

OPPOSITE RIGHT *Correspondence across media appeared in the nineteenth century as it did in the Middle Ages. The vivid color of stained glass also characterized popular prints, exemplified by a Currier and Ives image* Sacred Heart of Jesus.

ABOVE *Grisaille pattern in the nineteenth century was most commonly achieved through the use of stencils such as these tin examples probably from the 1890s.*

LEFT *Ornamental windows could also be quite complex and executed by hand, such as those produced for Harvard University's Memorial Hall. The* Virtues Window *was installed in 1874 to honor those who had given their lives in the American Civil War. The trapped air bubbles and irregularities in the surface enhance transmission of light.*

the century of exposure to New England weather and the more recent toxic elements of the atmosphere of urban environments.

The links between England and the United States continued in the latter half of the century in the same ways as they had earlier. Artists emigrated to America, one being Charles Booth (1844–93), a Liverpool-born artist who moved to New York in 1875. Booth contributed to the growing popularity of Aesthetic-style glass, most notably in his windows of about 1877 for the Jefferson Market Courthouse, now the Jefferson Market Region Library, a branch of New York City's public library system. The motifs of the geometrically transfigured natural forms appear in Booth's *Modern Surface Ornament* of 1877 and an article in the *Art Worker*, February 1878, making the patterns even more widely understood by patron and designer alike. Booth also produced impressive figural windows, as seen in the draftsmanship of a bearded head, about 1880, from Christ Church, Philadelphia (see frontispiece).

At the same time, British firms continued to export glass to the United States by Charles Eamer Kempe (1834–1907), Henry Holiday, Daniel Cottier (1838–91), and a host of others. Kempe founded an extremely successful firm, active until 1934, which developed a distinctive style inspired by fifteenth-century glass and panel painting. Brilliant use of uncolored glass tinted with yellow silver stain and the emulation of jeweled textiles characterize windows of this firm, which continued under his chief designer, John William Lisle (1870–1927). The firm's adherence to Victorian High Church embellishment is exemplified by the lavish sculpture, painting, and carved woodwork of the interior of the church of St. Mary Magdalene, Sandringham (Norfolk), 1911. Henry Holiday's career encompassed illustration and painting as well as stained-glass design, and he was arguably one of the greatest draftsmen of his era. His work is

ABOVE *Charles Eamer Kempe had been deeply involved with the conservative Tractarian movement while studying at Oxford and the windows, sculpture, and other liturgical furniture and interiors produced by his firm were popular with high church congregations in the United Kingdom and abroad. Kempe had studied the Renaissance glass of Troyes, Rouen, Nuremberg, Liège, and Cologne but his own characteristic style remained constant throughout the long history of the firm. Evoking late medieval English color harmonies and meticulous draftsmanship, the Kempe style is evident in an image of St. Michael, 1890s, Emmanuel Church, Boston.*

OPPOSITE *Charles Booth was a London artist working in the United States. Known for brilliant aesthetic style designs, he also produced highly traditional imagery, exemplified by an apostle, about 1880, for Christ Church, Philadelphia, Pennsylvania.*

distinguished by a superb command of anatomy and a perfect understanding of the demands of the medium of glass. Whether the nude figure or the swirling draperies of the angel of the Resurrection, his work balances the demands of legibility, image, and graphic structure of window design.

Scotland saw a resurgence in the field with artists of high artistic individuality. Daniel Cottier was born and apprenticed in Glasgow. He gained firsthand experience of the windows produced by the Royal Bavarian Manufactory (Königliche Glasmalerei Anstalt) in Glasgow's

RIGHT *Henry Holiday's work, while retaining illustrative abilities, still addressed the demands of stained glass to achieve legibility over considerable distances. An angel for Grace Episcopal Church, Providence, Rhode Island of 1891 commands attention, suggesting triumph even by gesture.*

OPPOSITE TOP *Unlike many studios of the later nineteenth-century, Daniel Cottier understood the difference between oil painting and glass. As seen in a detail of the Sower, Trinity Church, Boston, 1877, he was able to present the dynamics of the brushstroke and contour as expressive, not imitative principles.*

OPPOSITE BELOW *John Hardman & Co., like all of the surviving studios of the Victorian era showed great flexibility in design. By the twentieth century the firm was marketing successfully to the United States. A large program was installed about 1910 in the now destroyed St. Peter's Church, Lowell, Massachusetts, a city that supported a thriving textile industry. The sophistication of the painting is revealed by the detail of an angel, now in the collection of the Archdiocese of Boston.*

cathedral, discussed in Chapter 8. His own direction was linked to that of Morris & Company and he attended classes by John Ruskin (1819–1900) and Ford Madox Brown (1821–93). He set up an important branch in New York City, which supported progressive artists such as Albert Pinkham Ryder (1847–1917) as well as providing decorative work. His windows for Trinity Episcopal Church, Boston, where he was also consulted for the interior decoration, show the subtle olive, ocher, blue, and gold palette used in much of his work. The 1877 *Sower and Reaper* (Matthew 13: 3–8) constructs a Protestant allegory of beginning and end, age and youth, as well as Father and Son of the Christian Trinity. Stephen Adam (1848–1910) was similar

RIGHT *After World War I, many individuals chose stained glass to commemorate loved ones lost in the conflict. A memorial window in St. Clement Church, Terrington (Norfolk), reads: "To the glory of God and in memory of John Henry Brown volunteer of Kitchener's Army who died in hospital January 12, 1917 aged 19 this window is erected by his sorrowing parents Charles and Edith Brown of Hay Green House in this parish." The window is signed by the studio Jones and Willis.*

to Cottier in many ways, but remained in Scotland, establishing his own studio in Glasgow in 1870. He produced a series of twenty windows of the trades and professions, 1877-78, for the Burgh of Maryhill, now in the People's Place collections, Glasgow, as well as numerous ecclesiastical windows, for example New Kilpatrick parish church, Bearsden. His Henderson Memorial, 1909, in Bearsden masterfully arranged the figural composition across four extremely narrow lights, preserving the poignancy of Christ as Man of Sorrow and the intimacy of the Virgin and Child. The upper areas of the windows contain angels of the same proportion as the figures below, thus meshing divine and human action.

Many firms continued a more painterly approach, taking Victorian illustrative work well into the twentieth century. Hardman's Birmingham studio changed from the faithful thirteenth-century model that it executed for Pugin to more pictorial compositions. The shift can be seen in the delicate angel from a window for St. Peter's Church, Lowell, Massachusetts, about 1910. Through the last half of the nineteenth century many firms, for instance

Burlison & Grylls (John Burlison, 1845-1913 and Thomas John Grylls, 1845-1913, and later Thomas Henry Grylls, 1873-1953), continued a Victorian approach, mixing careful draftsmanship and reminiscences of later-medieval sensibilities. Clayton & Bell (John Richard Clayton, 1827-1913, and Alfred Bell, 1832-95) featured a wide range of styles. Nathaniel Hubert John Westlake (1833-1921), who designed with Lavers, Barraud & Westlake, produced glass and also a four-volume work, *A History of Design in Stained and Painted Glass*, 1881-94, the first truly comprehensive overview of the medium.

Memorials were a major aspect of window production where these conservative approaches were often successful. A window by Heaton, Butler & Bayne (Robert Tirnhill Bayne, 1837-1915) places a late-Gothic frame around an image of a young woman to commemorate Maria Burnham, who died at the age of six. The window was installed shortly after 1896 in Boston's Emmanuel Church. The technique of paint application is conservative using carefully graduated washes very similar to academic painting of the time. Expertly fired and enduring, the modeling is completely

ABOVE *Morris & Co.'s six subjects for the bay window of the Combination Room, Peterhouse, Cambridge were based on Chaucer's* Legend of Good Women. *Burne-Jones provided the drawings. The subject was a popular one and Burne-Jones designed other series on the theme; three panels are now in the collection of the Victorian and Albert Museum. Burne-Jones's designs for tapestry on the subject, never completed, were commission for John Ruskin, the historian and critic who championed Pre-Raphaelite painting.*

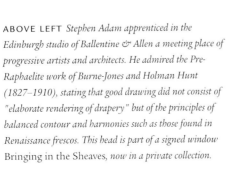

ABOVE LEFT *Stephen Adam apprenticed in the Edinburgh studio of Ballentine & Allen a meeting place of progressive artists and architects. He admired the Pre-Raphaelite work of Burne-Jones and Holman Hunt (1827–1910), stating that good drawing did not consist of "elaborate rendering of drapery" but of the principles of balanced contour and harmonies such as those found in Renaissance frescos. This head is part of a signed window* Bringing in the Sheaves, *now in a private collection.*

ABOVE RIGHT *A window by Heaton, Butler & Bayne, about 1900, for Emmanuel Church, Boston exemplifies the lasting attraction of Victorian realism. The studio inserted a three-dimensional figure in voluminous robes under a complicated Gothic canopy. Similar to late-medieval representations, the figure is relieved by a richly worked cloth with hints of blue sky and foliage at the head level.*

LEFT *In 1861, Morris, Marshall, Faulkner & Co. had been formed with the association of artists including Ford Maddox Brown, Dante Gabriel Rosetti, and Peter Paul Marshall who designed for stained glass. With the reorganization of the firm, in 1875, under Morris exclusively—Morris & Co.—Burne-Jones became virtually the sole designer in stained glass until his death in 1898. The linear elegance associated with Burne-Jones's works appears in the panel of* The Magi Led by a Star, *1879, All Hallows Church, Allerton, Liverpool.*

BELOW *William Morris has emerged as one of the most influential figures of the nineteenth century, author of arguably the first fantasy novel of the modern era, preservationist, printer, designer, and catalyst for enabling the work of many great artists such as Edward Burne-Jones in the medium of glass.*

smooth. No marks of the brush disturb the soft illusionism of the faces of the subject and framing angels or the careful emulation of a stone. After World War I, a spate of memorial windows appeared to commemorate those who had lost their lives in the "war to end wars." Parish churches such as St. Clement's in Terrington (Norfolk) installed windows like the Brown Memorial Window, which shows a soldier expiring on the battlefield, his prone body juxtaposed with that of Christ's extended vertically on the cross.

The firm of Morris, Marshall & Falkner (changed in 1874 to Morris & Company) remains one of the major innovators of the later nineteenth century, fusing its work with that of the Pre-Raphaelite painting movement. It affected all the decorative arts, including illustrated books, carpets, tapestries, wallpaper, embroidery, and decorative furniture, as well as stained glass. Morris's work set the level for both domestic and ecclesiastical work. The firm was particularly adept in blending figure panel and grisaille in the best tradition of the Middle Ages. The Combination Room at Peterhouse, Oxford, 1869, depicting "Good Women" of classical lore, demonstrates the sweep of the series of windows, similar to the firm's 1866–68 installation in the Green Dining Room of the Victoria and Albert Museum, London. *The Magi Led by a Star* for All Hallows Church, Allerton, Liverpool, 1879, shows the Three Kings striding forward in

RIGHT *Edward Burne-Jones's design for* David Conferring on Solomon the Plans for the Temple, *Trinity Church, Boston shows extraordinary linear fluidity. The composition unifies all aspects of the surface yet allows individual elements to be read. For example, specific details convey humor as well as narrative. The severed head of Goliath carried on the banner by David's soldiers is actually a portrait of William Morris.*

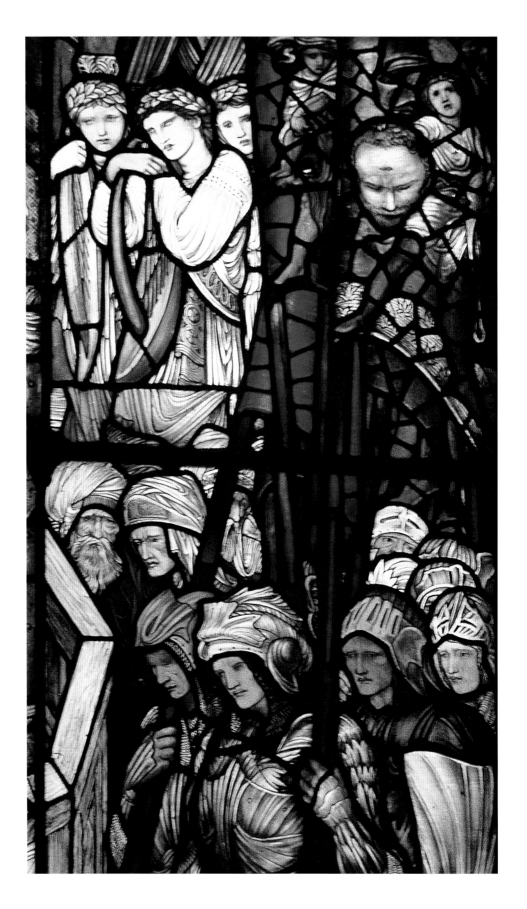

turquoise, russet, and emerald cloaks. The sweep of the robes accentuates the forward motion of the attendant figures. Above and below the image, dense green, olive, and emerald foliage is accented by russet fruits.

Martin Brimmer (1829–96), the founding director of the Museum of Fine Arts, Boston, was responsible for the first stained-glass commission by Edward Burne-Jones (1833–98) and William Morris (1834–96) in the United States, at Trinity Church, Boston. The firm produced the north transept window of the *Early Life of Christ* in 1880. The church's window of *David Conferring on Solomon the Plans for the Temple*, installed in 1882 in what is now the baptistery, was mentioned in Burne-Jones's account book: "This work may be said to represent the culmination of my power."

Burne-Jones designed the window but its color harmonies were developed by Morris, and the actual fabrication, including the painting of the glass, was done by studio personnel. Despite the division of labor that was to prove problematic to less cohesive meetings of the mind, the window is one of the studio's most brilliant productions. The design was also used for a tapestry now in the possession of Christ Church, Cranbrook, Bloomfield Hills, Michigan. It shows the young Solomon kneeling before an aged David who holds a drawing of the Temple. Around the figures, gifts from the faithful are being tallied by scribes and witnessed by maidens and military. The theme would have particular relevance for congregations who had themselves banded together to finance the construction of their church.

Morris became increasingly frustrated with the problems of restoration, and in 1877 founded the Society for the Protection of Ancient Buildings. He was distressed by the haphazard nature of repairs to older monuments and took the uncompromising decision to refuse to design windows for ancient buildings. He issued a circular explaining his motives: "We are thus driven into this course by the necessity we feel of keeping ourselves clear in future from any appearance of participation in the so-called restoration of ancient buildings, which, in ALL cases where more is done than repairs necessary for keeping out of wind and weather, means really nothing but vulgarization, falsification, and destruction."

Morris's opinions were a direct about-face from practices early in the century. In 1821 the studio of John Betton (1765–1849) and David Evans (1793–1861) restored the late-fourteenth-century east window of Winchester College Chapel by taking out the old, cracked glass and replacing it with copies. When the original panels are compared with the Betton and Evans product, it is clear how faithfully the studio tried to reproduce the contours and application of paint.

By the twentieth century, the ethos of retention of the original, despite its fragmentary or damaged state, had become paramount, resulting in the reinstallation of the original medieval panels in the chapel. Indeed, English and Continental practices had both stressed concern for a unity of style and a belief that the modern practitioner had achieved a level of competence on a par with or even superior to that of the past. During the 1848–62 restoration of Canterbury Cathedral, George Austin frequently removed old, cracked portions, substituted new glass, and kept the original panels for himself. Two thirteenth-century panels from the *Jesse Tree* window remained in his shop while he created copies for installation in the cathedral. However, the process of copying period windows and repairing ancient glass laid the groundwork for the ability of the artist to feel capable of producing different styles throughout the nineteenth century. This intersection of the creation of new work with the study and restoration of the old is a theme that continues in the study of the revival of stained glass on the Continent.

ABOVE *Early publications of Gothic monuments encouraged restoration programs for windows. R. Ackermann published this aquatint by William James Bennett of Winchester College Chapel in 1816, as part of his* History of the Colleges. *Restoration of the windows began in 1821.*

Historic Revivals in Germany, France, Belgium, and Italy

GERMANY

Throughout Europe interest in the medieval past increased dramatically in the early nineteenth century. Nation states began to consolidate along modern boundaries, and increasing industrialization and the growth of cities brought into question traditional ways. In the face of change, leaders in government and culture began to look to the medieval past as a time when national character was formed and when a common Christian culture united Europe. Many felt that these qualities were in need of revival in the present. Self-imaging by Europe's elite in medieval settings can be seen in a painting (about 1820) of Prince Friedrich of Prussia in the Armory Room of his Wilhelmstrasse Palace, now Berlin, Schloss Charlottenburg. A collection of roundels, fragments of windows, and heraldic panels are integrated into a large window dominating the room. Above the mantelpiece is a copy of Stephan Lochner's *Dombild*, 1440–45, a cherished image of the patron saints from Cologne Cathedral. Like Horace Walpole in England, progressive intellectuals constructed precocious Gothic

edifices. Prince Leopold Friedrich Franz of Anhalt Dessau (1740–1813), imbued with ideas both of the Neo-Gothic and of English landscape gardening, built the Gotisches Haus (1773-1813) in Wörlitz. Its windows are filled with a collection of historic German, French, and Lowlands stained glass, and the building that once served as private refuge of the nobility is now a public treasure.

The revival of stained glass in German-speaking territories, within this atmosphere of princely awareness, was linked to governmental policy. Bavaria played a leading role as Ludwig I (1786–1886) supported a revival of crafts, including mural painting and glass painting. He commissioned major artists and funded research into glazing techniques. Yet, as in England, the interest in the revival of stained glass had first been awakened by collectors interested in old glass. Sulpiz Boisserée (1783–1854) and his brother Melchior (1786–1851) were major influences in the German Romantic movement, combining a love of beautiful objects with a deep Catholic faith and a conviction that great art would transform

ABOVE *In the general enthusiasm for art and faith, Stefan Lochner's 1440s* Dombild *of the Adoration of the Magi was revered for its continued function as an altarpiece in Cologne Cathedral.*

RIGHT *The profound changes accompanying the invasion of Germany by Napoleon ended abruptly what has been a general decline in the viability of monasteries. Church was separated from state and many religious establishments, without sources of income, were abandoned. Some sites were destroyed in an effort to recycle materials; their works of art and furnishings then entered the art market. Collectors/dealers who assembled works often published them. An example is the* Life of St. Lawrence, *Ahrweiler, about 1240, from the publication of Christian Geerling,* Sammlung von Ansichten alter enkaustischer Glasgemälde nebst erlauterndem Text, *Cologne, 1827.*

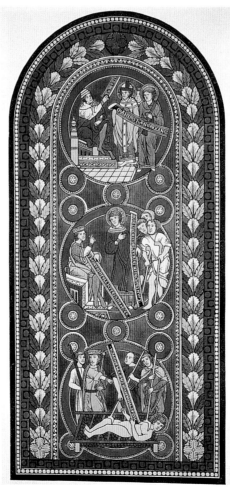

its beholder into a better human being. In Paris in 1803, they were mesmerized by the collections amassed by Napoleon from conquered territories and began to form their own collection of medieval works, which they published with lithograph illustrations in 1821. Edmund Lévy, a Belgian historian and critic, commented, as did Adolph Didron about Henri Gérente's studio in Paris, that artists were invited to come to the Boisserée gallery to study the works. Study, in nineteenth-century terms, invariably involved copying. For example, the Boisserées' *St. Columba Altar*, 1455, by Rogier van der Weyden (then attributed to Jan van Eyck), showing the *Annunciation*, the *Adoration of the Magi*, and the *Presentation in the Temple*, was reproduced in stained glass by the Königliche Glasmalereianstalt (Royal Bavarian Manufactory). In 1827 the Boisserée collection of over two hundred paintings by German and Lowlands artists was sold to King Ludwig to form the core of his Munich museum, opened in 1826 and later known as the Alte Pinakothek.

Some collectors and dealers specialized in glass. Christian Geerling (1797–1848), a Cologne wine merchant, developed a collection of works of extraordinary quality available in the Rhineland from secularized churches and monasteries. In 1827 he published his collection, subscribed to by many prominent persons including King Friedrich Wilhelm of Prussia and Ludwig of Bavaria. Colored lithographs of windows such as panels of the *Life of St. Lawrence* from Ahrweiler, south of Bonn, convey reasonably well the period styles. Geerling, whom a later generation has often seen as a plunderer of monuments, was a contradictory figure. As the self-appointed "conservator of Rhenish antiquities," he presented the ancient glass as a source of both religious restoration and the renewal of glass painting, which, he argued, could achieve artistic success only when windows were fabricated in a "true, religious, mystical manner." The high quality of the objects in Geerling's possession is attested by their presence in major museum collections today—the Germanische Nationalmuseum, Nuremberg, the Landesmuseum, Darmstadt, the Metropolitan Museum of Art, the Victoria and Albert Museum, and the Burrell Collection, Glasgow.

The development of the Bavarian/Rhenish style of glass painting, perhaps more than that of any other European country, was a part of contemporary trends in painting, in turn expressive of new ideas of religious purpose and nationalism. The Romantic movement of the early nineteenth century was deeply motivated by a renewed sense of the greatness of the Germanic past and a feeling of collective purpose in the face of

French hegemony, so clearly evidenced by the Napoleonic conquests. Goethe's 1772 essay *Von deutscher Baukunst* (On German Architecture) was an early manifestation of a desire to see a national ethnic character in "Germanic" art of the medieval world. In Nuremberg in 1828, the ceremony for the laying of the foundation stone marking the 300th anniversary of Dürer's death, attended by representatives from all German-speaking territories, took on the character of a national revival. Ludwig of Bavaria's vigorous support of the liturgical arts, especially glass painting, must be seen in relationship to this general reevaluation of the medieval past as a high point of German artistic, religious, and political power. As first announced in Goethe's essay, the medieval art most frequently

*Sulpice Boiserée (**TOP**) and his brother Melchior (**ABOVE**) influenced the development of the modern museum as well as the Gothic revival. Their collecting of the works of previously neglected masters of the fifteenth century, such as Stefan Lochner directed attention to the art of panel painting in Northern Europe.*

LEFT *Displaced panels of stained glass migrated, often losing all trace of their original provenance. At one time the panels of the* Life of St. Lawrence *were prominently incorporated into the Gothic room of Marble House, a vast Newport Mansion built 1888–92 by Alva Erskine Smith Vanderbilt, then surfacing in a lot of "American glass," identified as medieval, recognized through Geerling's publication, sold at auction, and purchased by a private collector, Switzerland.*

cited was that of the fourteenth through the early sixteenth centuries. Dürer and his contemporaries were characterized as the last great flowering of the Middle Ages.

This view animated the development of the Nazarene school of painting, without question the most significant influence for German nineteenth-century glass. Friedrich Overbeck (1789–1869) set the movement's initial philosophy by founding the Brotherhood of St. Luke and moving with his followers into a secularized monastery on the outskirts of Rome in 1810. The Nazarenes produced images melding Catholic religious sentiment with a Raphaelesque air of idealism and sweetness; they favored glowing colors, Renaissance figural types, and smoothly polished surfaces. See, for example, Johann Scheffer von Leonhardshoff's *Death of St. Cecilia*, painted in Rome between 1820 and 1821 (Osterreichische Galerie, Vienna). The images thus fused the deeply felt religious sentiment of the north with the idealized Renaissance forms of the south. Above all they were imbued with the concept that moral teaching was the essential purpose

of art. Heinrich Hess (1789–1863), who later became prominent in the design of frescoes and glass painting, was part of the first generation of artists grouped around Overbeck. Peter Cornelius (1763–1867) and Wilhelm Schadow (1789–1862) were to reorganize the study of oil painting at the Academy in Düsseldorf in 1826, and Hess became the artistic manager of the Royal Bavarian Manufactory founded by Ludwig I in 1827.

That the Nazarene painting style could be translated on glass was facilitated by the technical experiments of Michael Sigmund Frank (1770–1847). He began as a porcelain painter but around 1810 began to produce paintings on glass after antique sculpture and Renaissance prints, such as Dürer's *Last Supper* and Hendrick Goltzius's *Circumcision*. In 1818 the young Prince Ludwig of Bavaria secured Frank's appointment as painter for the royal porcelain establishments in Munich, where he developed sophisticated enamel colors. An example of the high quality of the techniques ultimately developed by the Munich painters is shown by a panel of the *Visitation* by Johann Schraudolph (1808–79) for the church of St. James in Burghausen an der Salzach. Painted in 1857, the panel uses green, yellow, and blue pot-metal glass and a variety of translucent enamel colors. The Virgin's dress is flashed red, St. Elizabeth's gray dress and brown shawl, the flooring, garden with roses, and background are all achieved through enamel paint.

One of the first commissions directed by Hess with Frank's new techniques was the glazing of Ratisbon Cathedral in the purported "style of the building." Seven windows were made between 1826 and 1829. Two were exhibited in Munich before installation, a window of the life of St. Stephen and another containing a scene of St. Beno converting the Slavs. The cartoons and fabrication of the figural images were by Christian Ruben, among others, and the

architectural ornament by Max E. Ainmiller (1807–70). These paintings show a close relationship to late-fifteenth-century stained glass by the Strasbourg Workshop Cooperative and Peter Hemmel von Andlau for richly draped figures under an elaborate architectural framework. In 1828 the west wall of the cathedral of Regensburg received stained glass, now lost but recorded in an oil sketch of the cathedral by Ainmiller.

Probably the most influential commission was that for the nineteen windows for Our Lady of Help in the new suburb of Au outside Munich. The church was designed by Ohlmüller in a fifteenth-century style and the glass produced under Hess' direction, in what was believed to be a complementary mode, between 1834 and 1843. All the costs for the windows were borne by King Ludwig. Two folio publications, one of black-and-white and later another of chromolithograph plates, made the windows of Au accessible to a broad European audience. Although brilliant in color, the windows allowed a

ABOVE LEFT *The artist, Johann Schraudolph, knew that the glass painter could achieve realistic detail with careful enamel painting.*

ABOVE RIGHT *As in previous centuries in Germany, the art of stained glass and the art of painting shared similar values. The* Visitation, *1857, shows the Virgin greeted by her cousin Elizabeth, pregnant with the child who will become John the Baptist. The image could easily be conceived as being executed in oil on canvas.*

high degree of light to enter the building. The elaborate architectural frames were based on the intertwining of organic and architectural forms, like those produced in such numbers in the fifteenth century by the Strasbourg Workshop Cooperative. The brilliant color and detailed draftsmanship were also found in the medieval prototypes, but the actual figures and the three-dimensional settings were far more indebted to Italianate models.

The German windows were the touchstone against which both French and English manufacture measured their progress. It is not surprising that one of the major voices of the Oxford Movement in England, A. J. B. Beresford Hope, commissioned Munich windows for Christ Church, Kilndown, Kent, in 1843. The windows were designed by Franz Xavier Eggert (1802–76) and executed by the Royal Bavarian Glass Painting Manufactory of Munich. Like the windows in Au, they were reproduced in a folio publication in 1852. In 1845 Georges Bontemps, director of glass manufacture at Choisy-le-Roi in France from 1823 to 1848, spoke of the German windows at Au in laudatory terms: "No other windows in our time have been so well executed by more skillful hands."

The Au commission was followed in 1844 by the windows on the south side of the nave of Cologne Cathedral. The completion of the cathedral impacted on revival styles in both architecture and stained glass. Although the choir had been finished in 1322 and the north nave by the 1560s, the façade was a truncated stump, and south nave, transept, towers, and radiating chapels had been left unfinished. A national and religious effort to complete the cathedral was supported by the Boisserée brothers, the scholar and journalist Joseph Görres (1776–1848), and the lawyer and politician August Reichensperger. Rebuilding began in 1823 and the dedication took place in 1880.

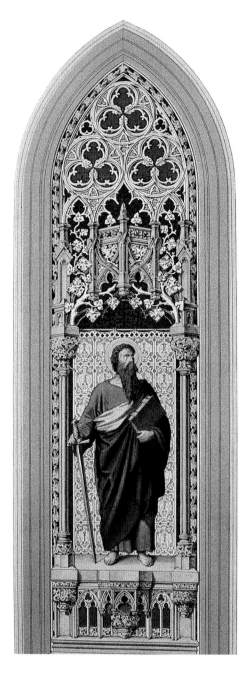

ABOVE *A. J. B. Beresford Hope was one of the driving forces of the movement to reform church worship and architecture in England through the Ecclesiological Society. Admirer of the German religious revival, Beresford Hope advocated the glazing by Munich glass painters of Christ Church, Kilndown, Kent, in 1843. The image comes from his publication on the windows in 1852.*

The windows in the south nave, testimonials to Bavarian royal largess, exemplify the brilliance of the "Munich" style. In the *Pentecost* window a complex figural composition stretches over all four lancets. The clustered figures are framed by a lavish three-dimensional canopy housing an image of Christ giving the keys of heaven to St. Peter. In the base, four doctors of the Church are framed like statues in shallow niches. The silhouetting of the figures against damascene ground and the subtle balance of color increase the visibility of the meticulous painting. One of the most cherished windows honors Joseph Görres, the inscription naming

RIGHT *In the transept window honoring Joseph Görres, Boniface is paired with Charlemagne as protector of the Christian faith in Germany. St. Boniface, an English monk, is widely regarded as the Apostle to the Germans, founding schools and monasteries and being named archbishop of Mainz in 744. He is often shown with a fallen oak tree, a reference to his encounter with Druids and confrontation of pagan beliefs.*

OPPOSITE *The nave window of the Nativity for the cathedral of the Holy Cross in Boston is part of the largest single installation of stained glass in New England for its time. Its format closely parallels German realistic figural depiction and colorful architectural framing.*

him "noble defender of the Catholic faith in Germany." The two-lancet window shows him in typical medieval format, kneeling before the Virgin and Child while St. Joseph, his patron saint, stands behind him. Below this image are the great medieval defenders of the faith in Germany, St. Boniface and Charlemagne. Set in the south transept of the cathedral in 1856, the window displays a brilliant handling of the paint, meticulous attention to detail, and harmonic contrasts of often acid colors.

Given the interest in Munich glass, as evidenced by Beresford Hope's installation in Christ Church, Kilndown, Kent, other commissions followed in Great Britain. A series of eight windows on the Life of Christ were commissioned for Peterhouse, Oxford, 1852–58. Designed by Claudius Schraudolph (1813–91) and Andrea Mayer (1813–93), they evoke large paintings on canvas. Stories such as the *Sermon on the Mount* take place as if the mullions of the triple-light window were a grille beyond which the three-dimensional world was visible. St. Mungo's Cathedral, Glasgow, received a series of windows installed between 1856 and 1865 by the Royal Bavarian Manufactory. The project was undertaken with the advice of Charles Winston and after inquiries among Continental studios, including Capronnier of Brussels and Lobin of Tours. Controversy raged over the slighting of English firms, but also over matters of suitable style: how archaeologically faithful windows should be to medieval forms, and how much should they adapt to nineteenth-century pictorial aesthetics.

The relationship of Munich and Austrian studios to glazing in the United States was profound. Catholic patronage gravitated to these firms, which were not only adept in high quality work but also familiar with Catholic traditions and piety. The windows of the cathedral of the Holy Cross, Boston, Massachusetts, installed in the 1870s,

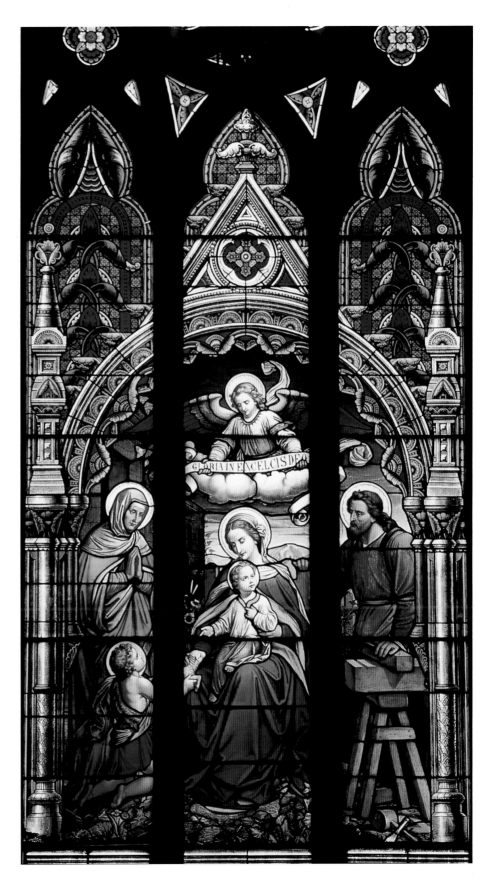

are remarkably similar in composition, palette, and figural style to the Bavarian windows of Cologne. The painting of the figures shows the same meticulous detail and subtle use of enamel colors. The purveyor of the windows, Morgan Brothers of New York City, established in 1847, may well have subcontracted to a European studio. There is a marked difference in the figural and decorative work. A documented commission with such a division of fabrication is noted for the German-Catholic church of St. Joseph in Detroit. The program shows integration of decorative forms in glass, sculpture, and architecture. The building was designed by Francis G. Himpler (d. 1916), a native of Trier who had studied architecture at the Royal Academy of Berlin in 1854–58. The large brick Gothic Revival structure evokes the German hall church design. Following accepted custom, the windows of the chancel were the first installed. The geometric patterns are shown in color on an architect's drawing labeled "Chancel Windows, St. Joseph's Church, Detroit Michigan, New York, Febr. 11, 1873, Fr. G. Himpler Architect." Apparently, the decorative work was fabricated by a local studio. The figures, however, were commissioned from the Franz Mayer studio of Munich. A signature, *"Mayer'sche Kunstanstalt Munchen,"* appears on the inscription band below the figure of Christ giving the keys to Peter in the central window. The tapestry pattern at top and bottom, enclosing figures framed in architectural canopies, was known to architect and audience alike through medieval precedents as seen in the cathedrals of Cologne and Regensburg or the abbey of Heiligenkreuz, Austria.

Most of the larger studios set up American business offices. The Tiroler Glasmalerei was known as the Tyrolese Art Glass Company at 50-61 Park Place, New York. Mayer signed the studio's windows in

America as "Mayer and Co., Munich, New York," and Zettler also had an American branch. Foreign studios also associated with American firms; for example, the Daprato Statuary Company of Chicago and New York advertised itself in 1910 as the sole representative for Zettler in the United States and Canada.

A reflection of these years can be found in publications by the studios themselves, such as the 1894 volume by Josef Fischer commemorating forty years of business by the Tiroler Glasmalerei Anstalt. The text reveals the studio's ideas of which were its

LEFT *As in medieval churches, the windows directly behind, or above the altar were the most honored. In St. Joseph's Church, the central image of* Christ Giving the Keys to St. Peter, *by the Mayer Studio, demonstrates the claim of Peter's primacy, a key doctrinal issue for Catholics.*

OPPOSITE *Rich treatment of natural forms often enhanced windows designed in the German tradition. Such is seen in a detail of the north transept window of the* Return of the Holy Cross to Jerusalem *in Boston's Cathedral of the Holy Cross, about 1880.*

BELOW *William Worden, a Detroit preservationist, discovered drawings by the architect Francis G. Himpler for the ornament design for the chancel windows of St. Joseph's Church, Detroit. Architects of this era were involved with the ornament as well as the structure of buildings.*

RIGHT *Franz Pernlochner was one of the most distinguished of the designers for the Tyrolese Art Glass Company. His work is exemplified in the window* Abraham greets the Three Angels, *1886, for Providence Cathedral, Rhode Island.*

flagship commissions, and a section was devoted to windows installed in the United States. One of the firm's largest commissions was for the cathedral of Hartford, Connecticut, by Patrick C. Keely (1816–96), now lost to fire; *Christ Calming the Sea*, installed in 1888, was illustrated in Fischer's book. At the time, the diocese extended from Hartford through Rhode Island, and many churches in Providence received windows by the Tiroler Glasmalerei Anstalt. The studio's chief designer, Franz Pernlochner (1847–95), imbued with Nazarene painting traditions, designed windows for the cathedral of Saints Peter and Paul, Providence. Elegant treatment of draperies and shades of turquoise, emerald, and scarlet contribute to the dramatic impact of the installation. The studio's books indicate its working methods. Dimensions of the window openings, organization of subject matter, and specific directions were supplemented with photographs of the building.

Mayer's windows and those by Franz Xavier Zettler (1841–1916), son-in-law of Joseph Gabriel Mayer (1808–83), founder of the Mayer firm, whose businesses ultimately intertwined, are ubiquitous in American Catholic churches. Mayer's commissions include over seventy-six cathedrals, twenty-six of them in the United States. The studio often incorporated imagery from Great Master paintings as well as compositions of the nineteenth century, a standard practice in public decorative work of the era. For example, a window in the cathedral of St. John the Baptist, Charleston, South Carolina, installed in 1907 or 1925–26, shows the *Transfiguration of Christ* modeled after the 1517 painting by Raphael in the Vatican. Since highly predictable rendering of the figures reassured American buyers, windows from many different locations exhibit strong similarities. A detail from the *Miracle of Cana* in Charleston's cathedral shows a young woman entertainer seated and gazing at the transformation of water into wine. The positioning of the figures, with their layering into a progressive stage of three-dimensional space, and the exquisite detailing of fabric recall the earlier work for Peterhouse, Oxford. Similar treatments of fabric appear in saints from St. Francis de Sales, Charlestown, a suburb of Boston and site of anti-Catholic riots in the mid-nineteenth century. Charlestown subsequently built a series of Catholic churches all embellished with Munich glass. The windows of St. Francis de Sales were installed in the second phase of construction in about 1913. The church of the Sacred Heart, now the Sacred Heart Cultural Center, Augusta, Georgia, however, installed its Mayer windows in 1900 for the opening of the building. Even a small detail such as a cherub high in the tracery of the organ loft window shows the reassuringly consistent arrangement of bright colors, especially streaky reds, and of realistic rendering.

Glazing studios included "Munich"-style windows in many ways. The Ford Brothers Glass Company with offices in Kansas City, Minneapolis, and Chicago advertised in

BELOW *A kneeling female musician appears in a* Miracle at Cana *made for the cathedral of Charleston, South Carolina by the Mayer studio. This theme was extremely popular because it related to the concerns of contemporary parishioners—the importance of marriage and the relationship of a mother and son who responds to her request.*

ABOVE *Cherubs are depicted on either side of St. Celica, patron saint of music, in the choir loft window of Sacred Heart church, Augusta, Georgia. The disused church has been rescued by its community and refurbished to serve as a Cultural Center.*

OPPOSITE *In the 1840s Jean-Dominique Ingres was the most respected painter in France. In the tradition of royal commissions, he was called upon to design windows for the Royal Chapel at Dreux and the Chapel of Saint-Ferdinand in Paris. Here St. Louis holds the Crown of Thorns. The architectural canopies framing the figures at Dreux were designed by the Gothic-Revival architect Eugène Viollet-le-Duc.*

the *Official Catholic Directory*, as "makers of all style of Catholic church windows." Their catalogue included English and German styles, both identified as "windows in the style of the middle Fourteenth Century as executed … by artists of European training and experience." In the twentieth century European studios provided windows sold through American firms. Windows by the Van Treeck Studio of Munich, founded by Gustave van Treeck in 1887, were commissioned by the Conrad Schmitt Studio, Milwaukee, founded in 1889, for a large number of churches in the Midwest in the 1920s. "Munich" as a label was even incorporated by an American firm. The Munich Studio, Chicago, founded by Max Guler, originally from Bavaria, operated from 1901 to 1932 with numerous commissions throughout the United States, among them the church of Saints Cyril and Methodius, 1913, Chicago.

The need for advocacy on the part of craftspersons supporting the stained-glass revival appears to have been slightly less in Bavaria, given the monarchy's strong support. It was the later generations of German glass painters who wrote, as had their counterparts in England and France, the first serious studies of medieval glazing in Germany. Heinrich Oidtmann (1861–1912) was a member of the family-run Oidtmann studios. His monumental work published in 1916 and 1922 on glass of the Rhineland from its origins through the sixteenth century still stands as an indispensable reference. Josef Fischer was associated with the Zettler Studios of Munich and produced a solid, comprehensive book in 1914, *Handbuch der Glasmalerei*, as well as a commemorative volume tracing forty years of glass-painting experience for Zettler in 1910. Heinrich Derix, of Derix studio, Kevelaer, published as well as restored the windows at Xanten at the turn of the century.

FRANCE

French taste began to parallel that of the English by the third decade of the nineteenth century. Given its extraordinary wealth of twelfth- and thirteenth-century stained glass, however, France's revival was deeply linked to restoration experiences. The decision to restore rather than replace in France followed the transformation of the political structure through the conservative monarchy of Louis-Philippe in the 1830s. The Orléanist monarchy was anxious to bolster its legitimacy by establishing its links to the Capetians of the twelfth and thirteenth centuries, who had first welded the diverse provinces of France into a unified state. Louis-Philippe supported the explorations of stained-glass technique by the Sèvres company and installed windows by the studio in his refurbishing of the royal chapel at Dreux in 1843–45. The strangely eloquent mingling of classical and Gothic systems in its sculpture and glazing programs was intended to evoke the heritage of the monarchy. Designed by the dominant classicist painter, Jean-Auguste-Dominique Ingres (1780–1867), a series of 1843 shows the patron saints of the royal family. St. Philip appears with the facial traits of Louis-Philippe, St. Amélie resembles the queen, and St. Ferdinand resembles the Duke of Orléans. The Sèvres manufacture of these costly and complex enamel paintings on glass was brought to a close with the revolution of 1848 and the resignation in 1847 of Alexandre Brongniart (1770–1847), the engineer mainly responsible for perfecting the enamel techniques and the company's director since 1800.

A series of restoration campaigns, both to repair old glass and to augment fragmentary windows with new panels, began in all of the major religious monuments. In 1830 the Service des Monuments Historiques was founded, and in 1834 the Société Française d'Archéologie.

In 1833–35 a campaign to restore Saint-Denis's glass, including the replacement of the panels taken out by Alexandre Lenoir (1762–1839), was under way. These windows and those of numerous other churches in the Parisian region had been gathered in a romantic ensemble from 1799 to 1816 in a Museum of French Historic Monuments, directed by Lenoir, formed by the revolutionary government, and continued under Napoleon. Etienne Thévenot (1797–1862) repaired the windows of the cathedral of Bourges and, with the help of Emile Thibaud (1810–96), those of the cathedral of Clermont-Ferrand. Both glass painters publicized their work through books about what they had come to see as "true" methods of Gothic Revival work. They indicate in these general comments and in specific plans for the restoration of Clermont-Ferrand that they felt capable of producing windows in different period styles.

The most important event of the decade, however, was the creation in 1838 of the first modern window in a meticulously researched and publicly accepted medieval style: the *Passion* window of the church of Saint-Germain-l'Auxerrois in Paris, whose design was based on the unrestored windows of the Sainte-Chapelle. It represented the collaborative efforts of the supervising architect, Jean-Baptiste Lassus (1807–57); Adolphe Napoléon Didron (1806–67), editor of the *Annales archéologiques* and founder of the Didron atelier, who provided the iconography; Louis Charles Steinheil (1814–85), designer and cartooner; and Reboulleau, a chemist and author of a manual on glass painting, who fabricated the work. In an 1844 article for the *Annales*, Lassus stressed that this commission proved that the contemporary glass painter was capable of reaching the quality of the art of the past, "for one reproduced for the new window, or more accurately for the renewal of the example of ancient glass, the same armature, context, and dimensions" (Lassus, p.17). In France the Saint-Germain-l'Auxerrois commission marked the coming of age of the archaeological revival: it proved that the modern painter had absorbed the principles of his medieval predecessors and could therefore produce a Gothic window that participated in the stylistic continuum from the thirteenth century.

Didron, Lassus, and the architect and author Eugène-Emmanuel Viollet-le-Duc (1814–79) were joined around 1841 by an unusually adept but unfortunately short-lived glass painter, Henri Gérente (1814–49). At first Gérente designed windows fabricated by other studios, such as the 1843 *Life of the Virgin* by the Choisy-le-Roi studio for Notre-Dame-de-la-Couture in Le Mans. In 1844, assured of the support of his architect patrons, Gérente set up his own shop, and commissions rapidly followed. In 1845–46 he restored the windows of the cathedral of Saint-Jean in Lyon; from 1846 to 1848 he made five windows for the chevet of Saint-Germain-des-Prés; in 1847 he won the much-publicized competition for the commission to restore the Sainte-Chapelle; and in 1848 he provided three windows for Ely Cathedral, England.

Gérente's knowledge of iconography and medieval draftsmanship made him appear to his architect patrons as the hope for a rebirth of the medieval aesthetic. In his 1844 essay, Didron described the *Life of the Virgin* window as the finest window he had ever seen, especially in contrast to Munich-style work and Renaissance enamel painting of the Sèvres atelier that had produced windows earlier in the century. He still had reservations, however, regretting that Gérente had emulated too closely the courtly style of 1280–1300 rather than the more vigorous style of the early thirteenth century. By 1848, Gérente was designing windows in an earlier style, close to the forms of the Sainte-Chapelle, as evident

the panels he made for Ely Cathedral. He even employed paint in a mat effect to suggest the patination acquired with age by genuine medieval glass.

The principle of harmony appears to have been perceived as an essential element of design, a harmony that did not permit the restorer to disrupt an ancient window with discordant elements and also suggested that new windows be conceived in an archaizing style to accord with the medieval architectural forms of the building. Didron criticized, in particular, the mixture of architectural styles common to the Munich style of essentially Renaissance-inspired scenes in Gothic canopies: "But please let us not take decorative ornament of the thirteenth century to frame scenes of the nineteenth ... harmony is the first and most important law of beauty."

The principle of harmony also appears to have been a major factor encouraging the retention of fragments of windows in the studio after the restoration was concluded. That such a practice was common, even praiseworthy, is verified by the comments of Bourassé and Manceau, two canons from the cathedral of Tours, who visited Gérente's studio while researching a book on the stained glass

ABOVE *A detail of the Passion window at Saint-Germain-l'Auxerrois, 1838, demonstrates how closely the nineteenth-century artist strove to work within the systems of the Middle Ages. At this time the Sainte-Chapelle of Paris, the most cohesive and unified medieval site in the city, had become the primary exemplar of medieval glazing art.*

OPPOSITE *The church of Sainte-Clotilde, Paris, strove to create a medieval ensemble that unified architecture and stained glass. Yet St. Christine, installed in 1854, retains nineteenth-century ideals of three-dimensionality.*

ABOVE *Charles Maréchal de Metz headed an extremely versatile studio. He retained a three-dimensional realistic style for the windows of Saint-Vincent de Paul, Paris. Most showed single saints. For the* Baptism of Christ, *we see John the Baptist in the act of pouring water on Christ, testifying to his mission.*

of the cathedral's thirteenth-century choir, published in 1849. They stated that they had seen the "magnificent collection of M. Henri Gérente, among which several examples date to the early years of the eleventh century, these having been found among fragments of glass from later periods." One of the most impressive examples was a late-twelfth-century head recorded by Viollet-le-Duc and reproduced in 1869 in the ninth volume of his *Dictionnaire raisonné de l'architecture française.* The authors elaborate that the dating can be verified by comparison with the draftsmanship of contemporaneous manuscripts. Bourassé and Manceau were specific that the works in Gérente's studio had been found in the midst of fragments of glass from later periods. Unconnected to an aesthetic or iconographic program, they were of little service to the church, since their retention, however "authentic," was at odds with the oft-cited principle of ideological and visual harmony.

Such evidence is of enormous importance for our understanding of the training of the nineteenth-century glass painter. To the ecclesiastics, architects, and critics of the day, Gérente's retention of sections of medieval windows in his shop was understandable (although it seems clear that after the financial troubles toward the end of the century, many of these study pieces found their way to dealers and collectors). The detached elements of heads, hands, or isolated medallions could be studied by "amateurs" like Bourassé and Manceau, and also could play an educational role in the formation of the young artist. Bourassé and Manceau exhorted artists to study the art of the past, as had Gérente of Paris, Lusson of Le Mans, and Lobin of Tours. The painter must "find his inspiration in the pure sources of the Middle Ages, remain faithful to the style of the past, and adhere to good archaeological traditions, all while retaining one's own

originality and remaining a man of one's century" (p. 15). In announcing the founding of the Gérente studio in 1844, Didron called to the youth of France: "M. Gérente will need, and searches everywhere for, young people who can understand his lessons and advice" (Didron, p. 149). The studio was to be the training ground where theory and practice could once again meet in the formation of the "new" medieval artist.

Henri Gérente's premature death in 1849 at the age of thirty-six momentarily stopped work in the studio. The restoration of the Sainte-Chapelle was given to Antoine Lusson of Le Mans (d.1853), the runner-up in the competition of 1847. Alfred Gérente (1821–1868), a sculptor, encouraged by the wealth of designs left by his brother and by the strong support of the restoration community, went on to take over the studio. He immediately formed a solid working relationship with Viollet-le-Duc, clearly the single most influential figure in French nineteenth-century restoration and revival efforts.

France's revival of stained glass supported a number of different styles. It produced not only the *vitrail archéologique* (historical window) but also the *vitrail tableau* (picture window), quite similar to the multiplicity of styles supported in England. In the windows of Sainte-Clotilde, we see a mingling of conceptions. Sainte-Clotilde was the first new church built in Paris entirely in the Neo-Gothic style, its construction extending from 1846 to 1857. That decision marks a significant rise in the popularity of the Neo-Gothic—in the first part of the century most new buildings embodied classical styles. Sainte-Clotilde's architect was François-Christian Gau (1790–1853), a native of Cologne who had witnessed the rebuilding of that city's medieval cathedral. The windows were the products of several major firms. Those of the nave were executed by Antoine Lusson, the Le Mans artist who had begun restoration of the

Sainte-Chapelle in 1849. Paul Jourdy (1805–56) and August Galimard (active 1848–75), who had worked with Ingres, furnished the cartoons. The program presents male and female saints designed to reinforce the legal and moral continuity of Christian France through its monarchs and early saints. In the window of St. Christine, a virgin martyr of the third century, Jourdy's academic training is revealed through the three-dimensional modeling of the body. The windows of the apsidal chapels, designed by Nicolas-Auguste Hesse, and fabricated by Laurent (d. 1892) and Gsell (1814–1904), show an even stronger pictorial mode. In the window of St. Louis embarking for the crusade, the surround lattice is perfectly flat and the background a diaper pattern, but the figures interact and pivot as if on a small stage.

A more rigidly medievalizing style was employed in Jean-Baptiste-de-Belleville. Built in 1859, the church was necessitated by the burgeoning working-class population that had gathered on the periphery of Paris. The architect was Jean-Baptiste Lassus and the windows were designed by Edouard Didron (1836–1902), nephew of Adolphe. The windows emulate the late-thirteenth-century format of Saint-Urban of Troyes, or Saint-Ouen of Rouen, discussed in Chapter Four. Grisaille panels combining larger circles and smaller squares of interlace frame rectangular figural panels. Borders show a deeply saturated combination of red, blue, white, and gold. Defining iconography is used, such as an elephant equipped with his tower of fighting men to illustrate the battles of Joshua. Clarity is achieved, even in panels in the upper levels.

At the same time, Charles Maréchal de Metz (1802–84), a master glass painter from Lorraine, could produce windows in a highly pictorial mode. A former pupil of Delacroix, Maréchal de Metz headed one of the most technically proficient stained-glass studios of the time, adept at engraving and the use of enamel paints with great subtlety. His aisle windows of Saint-Vincent de Paul, 1844, present three-dimensional figures against a deeply colored tapestry background surrounded by a pale grisaille frame of large naturalistic leaves. The church is in a Neo-Classical style, and the windows harmonize with the architecture in scale and in style. The studio of Maréchal de Metz was begun in 1837, and in its thirty years of operation, before it was

taken over by Charles Champigneulle in 1867, it is estimated to have produced 12,000 windows in 1,600 buildings. The vitrail tableau as used by Maréchal de Metz remained highly popular throughout the nineteenth century and well into the twentieth. Indeed in many respects, when providing modern glass in churches glazed predominantly in the Renaissance style, the pictorial window was historically correct. An example is Vincent Larcher's (1816–94) and Jean Prosper Florence's (active 1883–1917) windows in the church of Saint-Rémi in Troyes. The city's great glory is its windows of the sixteenth century. The *Sacrifice of Isaac*, 1894, by Florence shows brilliant color in the deep red of Abraham's robe and the green of his tunic, paralleling Renaissance compositions. The greater three-dimensional effects of nineteenth-century painting traditions are evident. Yet they are mitigated by the designer's understanding of the material nature of glass as a two-dimensional medium through the simplification of the imagery to set the figure against the background.

Like the studios in England, French makers of stained glass exported their work around the world. Catholic clients were particularly eager for windows from French studios. Louis-Philippe gave windows produced by the Sèvres studio to the archdiocese of New York around 1846; six are now installed in the chapel of Fordham University, Bronx, New York. Two French studios, Henry Ely (active 1863–84) of Nantes and Nicolas Lorin (1815–82) of Chartres, provided windows for St. Patrick's Cathedral, New York. In 1873, the University of Notre Dame, Indiana, commissioned 116 windows from Eugène Hucher (1814–89) of Le Mans for its Neo-Gothic chapel. The French heritage of New Orleans drew it strongly to French art. In 1878–80, Hucher was employed by the French Jesuits in New Orleans to provide a series of windows showing the history of the Society of Jesus for the church of the Immaculate Conception. The cathedral of Santa Fe, New Mexico, was built under the authority of Archbishop John B. Lamy, a native of Clermont-Ferrand. It was designed after a French Gothic model and the windows purchased from the long-lived firm of Félix Gaudin (1851–1930), also of Clermont-Ferrand. Installed in 1885, the windows make an intensely European statement in the midst of southwestern traditions of folk painting and sculpture. The aisles received a series of apostles and saints that hover between academic realism in the figure and two-dimensional pattern. The sharp contrast of the complementary

colors red and green, demonstrate the visual excitement of the palette.

Baltimore houses one of the oldest Catholic populations in the United States. Its brick-built St. Mary's Chapel, 1806, has been termed the oldest Gothic church in the country. Serviced by the Dominican order, it installed windows by Nicolas Lorin in 1881. The painting of flesh is accomplished with exquisite three-dimensional realism, but the garments and the architectural frame are in a more schematic rendering. The vast output of these nineteenth-century studios, as evident, makes analysis of individual designers or stylistic trends extremely difficult.

In the face of such a burgeoning market, the artist or architect was often also his own critic. Didron's *Annales archéologiques* served as a forum for the very artisans whose livelihood depended on the acceptance of the archaizing style for modern windows in medieval buildings such as Saint-Germain-des-Prés or Notre-Dame of Paris, and for commissions of new buildings and windows in the Gothic Revival style, such as the windows of Saint-Jean-Baptiste-de-Belleville. We are reminded that Lassus was responsible for the restoration of Saint-Germain-l'Auxerrois when he wrote the detailed article praising the *Passion* window accomplished under his supervision. Possibly one of the most memorable instances of self-justification is Viollet-le-Duc's description of the axial window reconstructed in large part by Alfred Gérente for Saint-Nazaire of Carcassonne. The window is an unusual composition, probably based on a manuscript illustration of St. Bonaventura's *Lignum vitae*. Viollet-le-Duc understood the images of figures holding banderoles to refer to a typological Crucifixion and a confrontation of Adam's sin and Christ's redemption. Thus he "completed" the lower segments in a manner that seriously distorted the window. He wrote in his *Dictionnaire* of the splendor

BELOW *The windows of the Basilica of the Sacred Heart, University of Notre-Dame, Indiana, were installed between 1870 and 1892 by the studio of Carmel du Mans, France.*

draftsmanship, firm modeling, worthy of the most beautiful windows of the thirteenth century" (Viollet-le-Duc, p. 440).

The vehemence of the Gothic Revival, especially in France, stems to a great extent from the grounding of the revival artists in early nineteenth-century rationalism. The artists and critics were convinced that great art necessitated an adherence to abstract principles inherent (however controversial the definition) in the nature of materials, the function of a building, and the cultural and geographic context. To revival artists, the Gothic system was the style that most correctly fulfilled the demands of the nineteenth-century urban context and provided the most morally uplifting setting for the new urban classes. Practitioners and their patrons viewed eclectic revivals not as copies but as authentic continuations of the rediscovered tradition. Thus its adaptation in its purest form, including the restitution of a purported original unity to a Gothic building during its restoration, was an ethical imperative. The mingling of the functions of restorer, creator of new structures, and polemicist was a logical extension of these principles.

BELGIUM

Belgium played a major role in both the nineteenth-century restoration of ancient glass and the creation of revival styles, especially in the work of Jean-Baptiste Capronnier (1814–91) and Baron Bethune. The taste of the Lowlands was able to reconcile both English and French tendencies with a respect for German glass—probably an advantage of the country's geographic location. The production was varied, showing glass as archaeologically faithful as that produced by Didron, and also as representational as that of the best of the Germany romanticists.

of the early-fourteenth-century glass at Saint-Nazaire without so much as mentioning the issue of the massive restorations or his own participation: "Among the windows of Saint-Nazaire, one must mention the Crucifixion with Adam's temptation as one of the most remarkable for its composition, selection of colors, solid

Capronnier was the great mid-nineteenth-century glass painter and restorer of this region. He provided the plates for Edmond Lévy's 1860 publication on the history of glass painting, one of the most comprehensive and explicit analyses of the relationship between religion and images on glass. In introducing his study, Lévy declared that Gothic architecture, "l'architecture ogivale," was in perfect harmony with the Christian faith. Windows were at first subordinated to architecture, but as the centuries passed, and the age of faith waned, the windows detached themselves from their architectural function. By the sixteenth century they had become completely deflected from their religious ends to serve a goal of personal artistic expression and worldly display. He praised the nineteenth century as the time when glass painting resumed its true spirit and character, subservient to the architectural frame and to the expression of ardent faith. This perspective was revived by adherents of America's Gothic Revival movement in the twentieth century, especially in the articulate polemics of Ralph Adams Cram (discussed in Chapter Ten).

Lévy said the goal of his book was the awakening of the young painter to the service of the adornment of buildings through this public art. Such statements might suggest a Didron-like adherence to windows copying thirteenth-century designs, but Lévy's support for Capronnier mitigates such an interpretation. The architectural framing and religious priorities, not the specific figural style, were the primary determinants of a window's success. Capronnier's draftsmanship had been conditioned by his restoration of sixteenth-century glass, such as the windows of Saint-Jacques of Liège, published in chromolithographic splendor, which should be compared with the later analysis of authenticity by the scholars of the Belgian Corpus Vitrearum. The restorer received high praise for creating restorations where one could not distinguish the new from the old. The windows of Tournai Cathedral, ca. 1500, attributed to Arnoult de Nimègue, display an extraordinary percentage of restoration. Capronnier expanded the medieval core, sometimes even substituting new segments for fragmentary work, especially in decorative areas. For example, in the panels showing a delegation of church dignitaries from Tournai before St. Bernard, only the head of St. Bernard, the heads and torsos of the two monks in the background, the horses, about half of the garments of the man standing to the extreme left, and a few other elements are authentic; all the rest has been provided by Capronnier in a similar style. Lévy's list of Capronnier's works is broken down into period styles, indicating his belief that the artist had achieved the ability to work in a number of different modes.

Capronnier's studio was capable of producing windows that competed well with the best of the English pictorial styles. Some reached the United States, for example in the First Presbyterian Church, Philadelphia, which houses a series of high-quality windows. One of them, designed

OPPOSITE *Philadelphia was a thriving city with a long history of interest in quality architecture and the decorative arts. American Protestants had no issues with Catholic Belgium, demanding subject matter such as Christ's parables, exemplified by Jean-Baptiste Capronnier's* Wise and Foolish Virgins, *for First Presbyterian Church, Philadelphia. Dated 1873, the commission probably resulted from a visit to Belgium by the donor, a common pattern of studio selection in the late nineteenth century.*

BELOW *The studio of Jean-Baptiste Capronnier produced work in many period styles. Some were archeologically faithful to the art of the later thirteenth century, such as a window that includes St. Louis of France, in the center and St. Elizabeth of Hungry, to the right. The delicate canopy design is characteristic of the medieval era.*

RIGHT *The importance of oil painting, especially for the portrait, was pervasive during this era. The very earliest manifestations of the revival of stained glass were associated with porcelain painting with its glowing colors and surface sheen. Enamel remained an option throughout the nineteenth century, often for the most prestigious commissions. Jean-Baptiste Capronnier executed double portraits of the King Leopold I of Belgium and his Queen Louise-Marie in enamels between 1836 and 1840.*

BELOW *The fine detail of the application of color and silver stain is a tour-de-force of the brush and the kiln. The oak leaves surrounding Leopold I have long been a symbol of strength. They are also an attribute of the Roman emperors, sometime depicted crowned with oak leaves.*

by Capronnier and signed and dated 1873, depicts the Prodigal Son, the Good Samaritan, and the Wise and Foolish Virgins. Technically superb, as pristine as when it was installed, the window shows a masterful balance between realism in the figures and two-dimensional energies of the deep colors of the glass and medieval pattern. A window in an early-fourteenth-century Gothic style in the north nave of the cathedral of Brussels shows three standing saints under canopies. The lacy architecture dominates the composition. Capronnier used the same tonalities of red and blue both within the framed niche and as background, effectively making the pattern a transparent screen, well suited to a large architectural installation. He used a very different technique for a set of panels portraying the Belgian king, Leopold I, and his queen, Louise-Marie, daughter of Louis-Philippe of France. They married on August 9, 1832, in Compiègne, Belgium, and the panels date from between 1836 and 1840. Here superbly applied enamel paint as well as the flashed and etched red animates the image. Such enamel work, especially for portraits, is also found in Italy.

Other important Belgian glass painters, such as Gustave Ladon (1863–1842) and Jean-Baptiste Bethune (1821–94), were deeply imbued with admiration for the Gothic. Bethune was aware of Gothic-Revival work in England and was a friend of the architect Augustus Pugin. In 1853 he collaborated with Capronnier on the great east window for the chapel built around 1330 and dedicated to the Holy Blood in Bruges, and he later established a studio first in Bruges, then in Ghent. Both Bethune and Ladon were devout Catholics and associated with Catholic revival efforts. Ladon was part of the Guild of St. Thomas and St. Luke, linking clergy and laymen, continuing, as Lévy had advocated, to conceive the Neo-Gothic—in all its forms—as an ideal of artistic and spiritual expression for glass.

ITALY AND SPAIN

Italy, like Belgium, showed extraordinary finesse in enamel work. The Moretti-Caselli Studio of Perugia founded by Francesco Moretti (d. 1917) exemplifies the level of quality. As in Belgium, the technique could be used for portraiture, especially for the nobility, among whom a conservative image of meticulous detail was prized. The technique allows exquisite rendering of fabrics, as in the satin and lace dress of Queen Marguerite of Savoy, commissioned in 1881 in a life-size format. The same meticulous detail was sometimes preferred for religious imagery, since it reproduced the tempera on panel and oil paintings of the fifteenth and sixteenth centuries, the glory of Italy's past. The ethereal grace of the possibilities of the technique is realized in the replica of the *Coronation of the Virgin* by Perugino exhibited at the International Exposition in Paris of 1867. Rosa and Cecilia Casselli, great-nieces of Moretti, took over direction of the studio and produced reproductions of oil paintings and leaded windows through the first half of the twentieth century. One of their most impressive works is the life-size reproduction of Leonardo da Vinci's *Last Supper*, executed between 1925 and 1930 for the mausoleum of Forest Lawn Memorial Park, Glendale, California.

In Spain, as in France, restoration of medieval windows moved into national prominence, in particular the campaign to restore the cathedral of León. In 1873 Rossell de Torres published a study of stained glass in Spain with particular attention to the new and old windows of León. The Mauméjean Studio was founded in Madrid in 1860 by Jules Mauméjean, a native of France and developed during this period of concern for restoration of historic glass. His sons Joseph and Henri signed their work J & H Mauméjean Frères and developed several subsidiaries, including one in Barcelona, and built a thriving enterprise which exported to France and to the United States. Their installations

BELOW *Copying of historic paintings was motivated by varying agendas, from admiration for the artist, to religious veneration, to simply a desire to commemorate a voyage with a souvenir. All classes commissioned such replicas—the more sophisticated the client, the more refined the copy, exemplified by the oil copy after Raphael acquired by Harriet Beecher Stowe, the author of* Uncle Tom's Cabin, *for her Hartford Connecticut home. The Moretti studio produced such works, exemplified by the* Coronation of the Virgin, *after Perugino, 1867.*

included the west rose of Burgos Cathedral, where windows were also installed by the Mayer and Zettler studios. A section of Mauméjean Frères' large composition depicting the work of industry, agriculture, and commerce defines their appeal. The window exhibits solid, illustrative draftsmanship. Restrained color, of gray and brown, increasing to gold, dominates a clearly defined composition with definition of both figure and recession in space. Spain's major contribution to the revival, however, took place with the Art Nouveau style (discussed in Chapter Nine).

In the face of the burgeoning complexity of social, technological, and demographic changes, the nineteenth century became deeply committed to a belief that, through analysis and commitment, it could bring all that was viable in its past to bear upon the needs of the present. Rather than presenting puzzling challenges to our modern concept of authenticity and originality as primary determinants of "art," these works incorporate a completely different set of priorities. They gain their legitimacy from what they evoke as images of social meaning. They may be termed, in a very challenging way, an art far more serious than the art of museums.

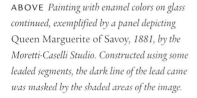

ABOVE *Painting with enamel colors on glass continued, exemplified by a panel depicting Queen Marguerite of Savoy, 1881, by the Moretti-Caselli Studio. Constructed using some leaded segments, the dark line of the lead came was masked by the shaded areas of the image.*

ABOVE RIGHT *Leonardo da Vinci's* Last Supper, *1495-98, for the dining area of monastery of Santa Maria delle Grazie in Milan may be the most imitated and reproduced work of the Renaissance. California's Forest Lawn Memorial Park, commissioned a stained glass*

replica from the Moretti-Caselli Studio. It is installed so that artificial light can be controlled to imitate the passage of light from dawn to dusk. The large sections of glass with their multiple enamel firings were fragile and sometimes cracked in the kiln.

OPPOSITE *Stained glass had become popular for windows in public installations. The Mauméjean Studio, Barcelona, designed a three-part window depicting industry, agriculture and commerce between 1904 and 1915. Industry is represented by smelting furnaces and ironwork.*

The Opalescent, Art Nouveau, and Arts and Crafts Movements

The period known as the "opalescent era" in the United States extended from about 1880 to 1920. Glass was produced in multicolored, marbleized sheets, often with an iridescent sheen. The windows designed with this glass demonstrate an entire gamut of quality and cost levels, from mass-produced window transoms for working-class dwellings to individually designed glass murals for the homes of leading industrialists such as William H. Vanderbilt and Frederick Lothrop Ames. The vast majority of American glass studios of the era provided windows in the opalescent style. The innovative concepts that began this process, however, can be attributed to the artistic impetus of John La Farge (1835–1910) and Louis Comfort Tiffany (1848–1933). The climate that supported such an intense interest in the decorative arts, and the embellishment of public and private space, was the economic and cultural coming of age of America as an industrial and commercial power. The windows tell of the aspirations of American educational and religious institutions as well as private individuals to demonstrate their belief that culture demands artistic expression.

ARTISTIC CLIMATE OF THE AMERICAN RENAISSANCE

Art at the turn of the century was greatly influenced by the social issue of newly acquired American wealth. Opalescent windows were commissioned in the United States during the first gilded age by fabulously wealthy people who sought to validate their newly found status through a conspicuous display of culture. The collection of antique glass, the inspiration of new figural glass in an eclectic but predominantly Italian Renaissance mode, and the installation of richly patterned decorative work were treated alike. Stanford White (1853–1906), a partner in the firm of McKim, Mead, and White, architects of the much-honored Public Library, Boston, Massachusetts, collected and commissioned stained glass for himself and his clients. The Payne Whitney House in New York City, the site of John La Farge's 1902 panel of *Autumn*, was once also decorated with medieval glass that White had purchased on his European trips. Charles Follen McKim (1847–1909), White's partner, installed medieval,

entered the domestic market. The abstracted, two-dimensional nature of Aesthetic design owed much to the influence of Christopher Dresser (1834–1904), lecturer on botany and botanical drawing at the Victoria and Albert Museum. He stipulated that, even when working from nature, the artist should redesign the image so that naturalistic elements of shading and perspective would be eliminated. His principles appear in the subtitle of his 1859 publication *Unity in Variety:* "As deducted from the vegetable kingdom; being an attempt at developing that oneness which is discoverable in the habits, mode of growth and principles of construction of all plants." The illustrations in Dresser's many texts developed hundreds of motifs abstracted from plant forms easily carried over into stained glass, as well as wallpaper, wall stencil pattern, or tile. His *Principles of Decorative Design*, 1873, contained a chapter dedicated to glass painting. Domestic uses of glass, which were then meshed with the overall interior furnishing, increased greatly.

Aesthetic-style windows are focal accents for the majestic staircase at Chateau-sur-Mer, Newport, designed by Richard Morris Hunt (1827–95) for George Peabody Wentmore, who served two terms as governor of Rhode Island and three terms in the United States Senate. The windows were designed by Donald MacDonald (1841–1916) and fabricated by W. J. McPherson and Company (1845–1900), Boston, which also provided windows for Harvard University's Memorial Hall. Organized in horizontal bands, the windows set squares of uncolored glass treated with silver stain linear plant forms against bold red bands of pot-metal glass. Most significant is the use of flattened and stylized floral motifs whose delicate geometric bands are silhouetted against the intense color.

These abstract patterns were used as well for religious edifices. Charleston, South

ABOVE *The Albert Cameron Burrage residence at 314 Commonwealth Avenue, Boston, designed by Charles Brigham in 1899, is typical of the luxurious homes that installed domestic stained glass at the turn of the century. The Back Bay structure incorporates faithful quotes from Loire valley châteaux, such as Chenonceaux.*

German, and Swiss Renaissance glass in the lavish library of financier and railroad tycoon J. Pierpont Morgan, constructed in New York City between 1902 and 1907 in a predominantly classical mode. Simply known to its visitors as the J. P. Morgan Library, it has been open to the public since 1924.

AESTHETIC STYLE: PRECURSOR

The Aesthetic Movement, in evidence in America during the 1870s and 1880s, continued the dependence on English styles discussed in Chapter Seven. Patterned non-figural glass popular in ecclesiastic work

Carolina, retains numerous houses of worship, such as the Unitarian Church, that show Aesthetic-style work. A window dedicated in 1882 in Grace Episcopal Church combines imagery such as lilies, cross and crown, and the lamb, with a scintillating combination of abstract designs in muted tones of tan and turquoise. Charleston's Kahal Kadosh Beth Elohim Synagogue, the birthplace of Reform Judaism in the United States, was constructed in 1840 in a classical revival style, and stained-glass windows were installed in 1886–87. Huge expanses of glass in various combinations of pastel ornament include simplified symbols such as the lamp burning in the sanctuary, grapes, or a dove over the waters. Without such symbols, or with a different set, such as a state seal or the scales of justice, these types of windows could function equally well in private homes and public institutions.

LEFT *Attuned to architectural principles, Aesthetic style windows show a structural clarity that carries well across interior space. They often appear in churches where the designs are coupled with religious symbols, as in the Hattie A. Bird memorial window, 1882, Grace Episcopal Church, Charleston. Alternatively the designs could frame a highly three-dimensional image.*

BELOW *Charleston experienced a devastating earthquake in 1886. During the rebuilding campaigns, many sites were also remodeled to bring them up to date. The Aesthetic style windows of Kahal Kadosh Beth Elohim Synagogue, 1886–87, date forty-six years after the construction of the building.*

227

GLASS IN A NEW FORM

Stained glass, whether inserted into a window, leaded into a lampshade, or used to make a skylight or window for a church or court, had become ubiquitous by the end of the nineteenth century. For the first time, large-scale American architectural installations were aesthetically and materially linked to a history of glass making. America had a very long tradition of quality production of the glass vessel, from the early days of the Sandwich Glass Company, Sandwich, Massachusetts, through the beveled and etched glass of the nineteenth century. It is significant that the Tiffany Glass and Decorating Company, the most prolific firm of this era, was as much at home with the production of glass objects, such as leaded lamp shades and molded and blown vases, as it was with the architectural installation of a window. The components of the glass were the same: richly variegated, sinuous forms and the unmistakable milky colors and pearly sheen of the surface. In the case of the windows, their actual three-dimensional quality likened them even more to the glass vessels and light fixtures displayed within the home. The density of color enhanced by the three-dimensional cast jewels created the solid weight of sculpture. The use of textured glass, even in manipulated folds, evoked techniques of bas-relief and fused the opalescent window with the carved reliefs in wood and stone of the buildings they adorned. Their colors and "glassiness" linked them with the glass objects set within those buildings, such as hanging lamps, vases, or paperweights.

The American development of variegated colors and surfaces within the material itself precipitated a discussion of the traditional role of paint on glass. Writers on stained glass began to question the usefulness of paint within this new style. Supporters of opalescent design argued against it, as in Roger Riordan's 1881 analysis of a "Window in Pure Mosaic" by John La Farge.

> In this sort of work the style should always be pure mosaic. There need be no lack of variety. Besides the endless combinations of geometrical forms, derivable from mediaeval designs, the Arabesque and Japanesque systems of abstract ornamentation are in practice drawn upon by all our designers. Mr. La Farge has led off with Renaissance designs in pure mosaic ... The simple shapes of the lower animals and plants are easily imitated in this manner. Their forms may be indicated by the leading alone, or may be rendered with an almost illusive naturalness by the choice of wrinkled, bulging, and concave pieces of glass, as is done by Mr. Tiffany ... Even in the case of the largest and most important work, the benefits conferred by enamel are, for the most part, obtainable also in mosaic. The partial opacity which it

BELOW *Tiffany Studios produced windows with cast and broken nuggets of glass, called jewels. The studio's many designers, such as Maitland Armstrong, responsible for the windows of St. Columba's Church, Middleton, Rhode Island, 1880s, often worked independently.*

gives, at some artistic cost, can be got in the glass itself without any loss of surface quality. (*American Art Review* 2/2 [1881]: pp. 61-62)

Riordan emphasized the role of pure glass and leadlines in the opalescent era against the traditional use of translucent colored glass on which the artist applied painted designs. The article was published in the same year that La Farge installed his first plated and opalescent window for Harvard University's Memorial Hall. The groundbreaking *Battle Window* is achieved predominantly with the colors and textures inherent in the glass—although paint was used in some areas to modulate brightness. The issue of the nature of "true principles" of glass design—structural material versus paint—is at the core of artistic choices in stained glass, and still hotly debated today.

Glass as material continued to attract admirers in the opalescent era. In 1898, a popular writer on the arts of the period, Cecilia Waern (1853–after 1920), wrote on Louis Comfort Tiffany's Favrile glass for *The International Studio*, a monthly arts magazine. She described in enthusiastic terms Tiffany's Corona glassworks (Jamaica, New York) with its stock of 200 to 300 tons of glass stored in cases and on numbered racks bringing order to the selection of 5,000 colors. The machine-rolled glass sheets appeared remarkable for their varieties of color.

A pane of dark blue and white, harsh and crude in reflected light, becomes suddenly glorious when seen in transmitted light, like a sunset all at once illuminating the sky in this land of rich effects ... Other pieces suggest priceless onyx or lovely marbles, when seen in reflected light, shot through with throbbing color when held up to the window. (*The International Studio* 5 [1898]: pp. 17–18)

Waern also described the handmade glass that retained varying thicknesses, bubbles, and imperfections from the process of the throwing:

As many as seven different colours out of different ladles or spoons have been thrown together in this way ... The throwing of certain masses and colour can be regulated, of course, and a definite

ABOVE *Although Tiffany had designed light fixtures since 1885, only in 1899 did the firm begin production of table lamps with bulbs under glowing colored shades. The Dragonfly lamp, after 1902, has both base and lamp identified with a specific model number and the location, Tiffany Studios New York.*

design is often employed with a view to providing the glazier with "useful" glass for obtaining certain effects of drapery, modeling or backgrounds ... The famous Tiffany glass is made by manipulating the sheet while still hot, as one would do with pastry (with iron hooks, the hands cased in asbestos gloves) and pushing it together until it falls into folds. (Ibid)

Tiffany's glass has been much discussed but rarely in the context of the wide popularity of opalescent glass and the many sources of opalescent glass production of the time. Publication of a portion of the archival information concerning Arthur J. Nash and Leslie Nash, both of whom directed production of opalescent glass at the Corona glassworks for Louis Tiffany, needs to be evaluated to profile the nature of collaboration in this field. Before engaging Nash, Tiffany had experimented with glass in 1875 at Thill's Glasshouse, Brooklyn. Between 1880 and 1893 he used glass made expressly for him by the Heidt Glasshouse, also in Brooklyn. In 1892 he hired Arthur J. Nash (1849–1934), who had learned glassmaking in the Dennis Glass Works, near Stourbridge, England, and built his own glass furnaces in Corona, Jamaica, New York. In 1894 Tiffany registered the Favrile trademark. At that time, however, opalescent glass was already being produced elsewhere, the most significant producer being Kokomo Opalescent Glass, Kokomo, Indiana.

Kokomo Opalescent Glass was incorporated in 1888 and was managed by three partners, R. E. Hoss, president; J. W. Learner, secretary; and W. E. Blacklidge. The company's economic advantage rested on what was once a huge pocket of gas. Discovered in the 1850s, the deposit extended from Ohio to Howard County, Indiana, and included most of the town of Kokomo. This resource provided ideal fuel for glass furnaces. The flourishing American

market for glassware encouraged the founding of over ninety glass factories producing mostly vessels such as glasses, pitchers, vases, and bowls. Kokomo Opalescent Glass, then known simply as "The Opalescent Glass Works," specialized in one-of-a-kind sheets of art glass. They sold not only to the burgeoning studio clientele, but to Tiffany as well. In 1893, even while the Corona factory was open, Tiffany purchased from Kokomo Opalescent Glass; one invoice lists almost 10,000 pounds of glass to "The Tiffany Glass Decorating Co." When the gas source dried up a few years later, smaller companies in the town closed, but Kokomo Opalescent survived. Today the company has the ability to manufacture over 22,000 different color/density/texture combinations, an indication of the variety that was available at the height of the opalescent era.

NEW ARTISTS FOR AN OLD MEDIUM

The opalescent era encouraged academically trained artists to design for glass. We also find the phenomenon of the out-of-house designer, as well as the studio with designers working exclusively in a team of glass cutters, painters, and fabricators. La Farge, Tiffany, and David Maitland Armstrong (1836–1918), painters and later designers of stained glass, never actually touched the window. They may have provided designs and supervised execution, but they were not the artists who cut or painted the glass or assembled the window into its frame. John La Farge is arguably one of the great innovators in the art of stained glass. Born in New York, he was the son of John Frederick La Farge and Louisa Binsse de Saint-Victor, French émigrés. His early education was bilingual and emphasized literature and art. His Roman

Catholic background encouraged a Catholic-affiliated schooling and he matriculated at Mount Saint Mary's College, Maryland, receiving a Master's degree in 1855. Following this he studied law in New York while continuing to mingle in artistic circles. From 1856 to the fall of 1857 La Farge traveled in Europe, predominantly France and Belgium, familiarizing himself with the European painting tradition that would be so characteristic of his work.

La Farge was a believer—in traditional art and in established religion—and he would write about the art he admired with an almost evangelical conviction. One of his most cherished models was Eugène Delacroix (1798–1863) whom he described as one who "saw further than the outside of beautiful objects; he saw men themselves with their anxieties and their delights and to each one he gave a colour and shape" (*The Gospel Story in Art*, New York, 1913). In the preface to this posthumously published book, his editor, Mary Caldwalder Jones, wrote that La Farge had long cherished the subject of the book. She explained that La Farge was, "Born and educated in the older faith of Christendom," and he revered the subject to which he brought a life-long study of the history of works of art and "classical writings of the Western and the older Eastern world."

La Farge's intense admiration for the monuments of the past and his commitment to innovation of the present encouraged his experimentation with opalescent glass. The material evoked an older, tactile adornment of early Christian stone inlay and mosaic. La Farge later described his combining selected stained glass in a variety of tones and a new material, an opalescent type of commercial glass previously used mainly as a porcelain substitute in toiletries such as brushes and mirrors. He applied for a patent for these techniques in November 1879. The

application makes it clear that he did not claim to have invented the milky glass of variegated color we now call opalescent. Rather, he claimed a patent for its use in plated stained-glass windows where areas of the window are comprised of several layers of glass stacked one on top of the other and leaded together. Plating adds depth to the play of color and light in the composition. With such work, La Farge was seen as a designer of promise, and in 1880 Herter Brothers, a decorating firm in New York, hired him to provide windows for the homes of American millionaires, including Cyrus W. Field, Darius Ogden Mills, and J. Pierpont Morgan in New York. One of his first successful figural commissions in glass was for the William H. Vanderbilt House in New York in 1881: *The Fruits of Commerce, and Hospitality/ Prosperity* (now in Biltmore House, Ashville, North Carolina).

An image of *St. John the Evangelist* (Charles Evans and Martha Scriven Evans Memorial) from the Judson Memorial Church, New York City, glazed between 1895 and 1910, exemplifies La Farge's spatial composition. The window is framed, setting up a transition between the three-dimensional picture of the subject and the flatness of the wall into which the window is set. The possibilities of opalescent glass can been seen in the variegated colors of the green robe, and russets, grays, and green of the architectural setting, which evoke the multicolored stone of Roman revetment, as used for the interior of the Pantheon. La Farge looked toward early Christian sources of inspiration, particularly mosaic decorations of places such as Ravenna and Rome. He owned a plaster model of the famous early Christian ivory plaque showing the archangel Michael, in the British Museum, London. The thin, scooped folds of the ivory undoubtedly inspired his depiction of drapery with multiple small segments of glass.

All of La Farge's windows of major importance are plated, for example *Wisdom Enthroned* of 1901, in Unity Church, North Easton, Massachusetts. The complex window evokes Renaissance prototypes with the female image of Wisdom under a classical baldachino flanked by Youth and Old Age, and is a memorial for Oaks Ames, investor in real estate, and his two sons. Plating is most visible in lighter colors, as exemplified in the *Resurrection* installed in 1894 in the First Congregational United Church of Christ, Methuen, Massachusetts. Methuen at the time was a wealthy suburb to the north of Boston, and the window and the chancel renovation are memorials to Colonel Henry Coffin Nevins. A pale section of glass is laid over a pattern of smaller segments leaded together. This technique serves to tone down the precision of the came, allowing La Farge to play with a variety of strengths of line in a manner similar to the modulation possible in a drawing. The combination of plating of several sections of glass, variegated color of the segments, and the textured surfaces served to mesh both hue and transparency, allowing the artist to modulate the "painting" in glass as if with a brush loaded with pigment. Such sensitive and elaborate plating is the hallmark of La Farge's most intricate work. Where the Tiffany Studios might use a molded segment of drapery glass, La Farge invariably employed extremely delicate irregular cuts and multiple plates to suggest the folds of drapery.

Like La Farge, D. Maitland Armstrong was a painter in the first half of his life, producing carefully crafted landscapes of the Hudson River region and of Italy. He was an intellectual, holding a law degree and an appointment as United States consul to the Papal States, or consul-general to Rome. In 1872 he returned to the United States to pursue painting but soon developed a stronger interest in the applied arts. He was associated with Tiffany Studios from at least

1881 to 1887, after which he designed independently. While working with Tiffany he designed the richly worked program for St. Columba's Chapel, Middletown, Rhode Island. Shortly before 1893 he formed his own firm of Armstrong and Company. His daughter, Helen Maitland Armstrong (1869–1948), began designing windows as early as 1894 and later became his partner in the firm. Armstrong, unlike La Farge, typically associated with other designers, first with the Associated Artists organized by Tiffany, discussed below, and then with his daughter. Armstrong's profile allows us to see how the expanded clientele for stained glass translated into a vastly expanded number of studios and artists designing for glass. In New York City, one of Armstrong's most impressive commissions is the Italian Renaissance-style decorative schema for the dome and windows of the Appellate Court Building.

J. & R. Lamb Studios was founded in 1857 by English-born Joseph Lamb (1833–98) and his brother Richard (1832–1909). Located in New York City for eighty years, J. & R. Lamb Studios is considered the first American firm to specialize in all facets of ecclesiastical design. At midcentury, the dominant style was the Gothic, particularly for many Episcopalians. The Church of England had since the 1830s embraced a return to a more liturgically enriched worship, linked to the Middle Ages, and Episcopal churches in the United States followed suit. In the Northeast, the English-born architect and Gothicist Richard Upjohn (1802–78), a devoted Episcopalian, dominated ecclesiastic design. J. & R. Lamb's early work concentrated on wood, stone, and textiles in the medieval revival mode. In 1876 an older son, Charles Rollinson Lamb (1860–1942), began designing and the firm expanded to include more variety in its styles, secular commissions, and work in stained glass, mosaics, and stone

monuments. In 1885, Frederick Stymetz Lamb (1863–1928), Charles's younger brother, completed his artistic studies at the Académie Julien in Paris, and after returning to New York continued to paint in association with progressive artists such as George Inness (1825–94), known for his landscape paintings. He also became aware of the opalescent experimentation of John La Farge, whose fabricating studios were in proximity to the Lamb Studios. Influenced by La Farge's work, Frederick Lamb took his family's firm in the new direction. His career

BELOW *Pious tradition elaborated the biblical reference that Pilate's wife had been troubled in a dream about the "just man" her husband was about to condemn (Matt. 27:19). She was thought to have heard Christians through the centuries repeating the Apostles' Creed with its phrase "suffered under Pontius Pilate." Gustave Doré's print showed the woman surrounded by ghostly faces and was used by the J. & R. Lamb studio for Stanford University's Chapel.*

BELOW *Tiffany Studios pioneered the landscape window. These works actually drew praise from Modernists such as Frank Lloyd Wright, who stated "The magnificent window-painting and plating of the windows of the religious edifice is quite another matter. There the window becomes primarily a gorgeous painting—painting with light itself." Typical is* At Evening Time it Shall be Light, *1901 in the First Presbyterian Church, Brooklyn Heights, New York.*

demonstrates the complexity of the schools at that time, since he associated with people who could be categorized as part of two movements: Arts and Crafts, and American Renaissance. Lamb executed work with the British designer Walter Crane (1845–1915) and the American furniture maker Gustav Stickley (1858–1942), and

wrote a number of articles for Stickley's magazine, *The Craftsman*. He was also highly active in numerous organizations dedicated to the arts and their place in civic design. Opalescent glass was, indeed, the hallmark product of artists' studios at this time, seen in thousands of installations throughout the United States.

One of J. & R. Lamb's major commissions was for over sixty windows installed between 1899 and 1903 in the Memorial Chapel of Stanford University, California. Jane Stanford, wife of the governor and the project's patron, planned the designs modeled on time-honored paintings of the life of Christ. Prints by Bernhard Plockhorst (1825–1907), Heinrich Hofmann (1824–1911), Holman Hunt, and Gustave Doré, among others were executed by the studio as complex, opalescent windows. Doré's (1832–83) *Dream of Pilate's Wife*, for example, was greatly enhanced by the opalescent gloom of spectral faces behind the angel's robes. Lamb's own design is seen in *Religion Enthroned* of 1899, a large composition, now in the Brooklyn Museum. In the allegorical composition, Religion is seated on a Gothic throne flanked by the archangels Michael and Gabriel representing the Church Militant, clad in armor, and the Church Triumphant, in robes.

The best-documented artist in the field, undoubtedly, is Louis Comfort Tiffany, the son of Charles Louis Tiffany, founder of the jewelry company Tiffany & Company of New York. His first association was with three other designers in 1881, Samuel Colman (1832–1920), Lockwood de Forest III (1869–1949), and Candace Wheeler (1827–1923), in the firm of Associated Artists. In 1881–82 the firm designed the interior of Mark Twain's sumptuous residence in Hartford, Connecticut, and the Fifth Avenue mansions of Ogden Goelet and Cornelius Vanderbilt II in New York. Eclectic combinations of Japanese, Chinese, Moorish, and East Indian elements with

the Italian Renaissance became an early signature of the firm. Throughout his career Tiffany remained highly sensitive to the total environment and to blown glass as well as the window. The three-dimensionality of the cast and chiseled nuggets of glass that made up some of the most scintillating of the studio's work seemed connected to the blown vessels and the lamps also produced by the studio. The drapery glass, pulled and twisted before it cooled, paralleled the surface of sculptured reliefs. Tiffany introduced the landscape window, for example in the First Presbyterian Church of Brooklyn Heights, New York, installed in 1901, as a major ecclesiastic statement. The light penetrating the window's opalescent colors seems to bathe the depicted world in spiritual light.

In the second decade of the twentieth century the taste for opalescent glass began to wane, as simpler forms of Arts and Crafts and Art Deco began their ascendancy. The Second Gothic Revival, which began in the United States about 1910, championed medieval inspiration as the only appropriate style of windows. It challenged the appropriateness of the "picture window," a window done in the style of a painterly composition, for a religious edifice, and Tiffany Studios began a gradual decline. In 1932 it filed for bankruptcy and the following year Tiffany died at the age of eighty-four.

At the height of the studio's popularity, Tiffany oversaw a huge enterprise and willingly worked with other artists and designers. The firm executed three windows for Harvard University's Memorial Hall, Cambridge, Massachusetts, designed by painters: *Aristides and Themistocles*, 1892 by Edward Emerson Simmons (1852–1931), and *Student and Soldier* and *General Joseph Warren and Reverend John Eliot*, both 1889, by Francis Davis Millet (1846–1912). Tiffany also frankly acknowledged his adaptation of well-known paintings as the basis for

stained-glass designs, for example his *Seven Gifts of the Holy Spirit* after Botticelli's *Virgin and Child Attended by Seven Angels* and *Christ Leaving the Praetorium* by Gustave Doré. In 1884 Tiffany entered into an agreement with Siegfried Bing, a Parisian art dealer, to fabricate windows after designs by French artists, including Bonnard, Maurice Denis, Toulouse-Lautrec, and Félix Vallotton, which Bing exhibited at his gallery, the Salon de l'Art Nouveau, in 1885. Many of the designers working for Tiffany, including Edward Peck Sperry (1850–1925), Rosina Emmett Sherwood (1854–1948), Jakob Adolf Holzer (1858–1938), and Agnes Northrop (1857–1953), later worked independently. The studio's most characteristic figural work, however, was indebted to Frederick Wilson (1858–1932), an Englishman who went to New York in the 1890s and stayed for over thirty years. Wilson's work is visible in the elegant Pre-Raphaelite style of facial types, with long, slender noses, broad foreheads, high cheekbones, and invariably reddish tonality to hair and beard. His windows of the *Beatitudes*, based on Christ's Sermon on the Mount (Matt: 5:1–12), Arlington Street Church, Boston, made in about 1904, show many of the Tiffany Studios' cherished forms and techniques.

There was an enormous output of opalescent glazing around the turn of the century, and this brief overview can give only a hint. The extent of the trend to embellish can be seen in the attraction of the opalescent figural window for congregations formerly opposed to imagery. In 1896 Henry Landon Parkhurst (1867–1921), an artist and instructor in Art and Architecture at Cooper Union, New York City, designed the brilliantly executed *Angel of Praise* for the Union Congregational Church, Worcester, Massachusetts, reinstalled in 1992 in Pakachoag Church, Auburn, Massachusetts. The window exploits the mauve, turquoise, ocher, and

ABOVE *Frederick Wilson was the Tiffany Studios' most widely employed designer. He showed a delicacy of draftsmanship in the production of facial types that seemed appropriately ethereal. The* Personification of Virtue, *about 1910, for Calvary Baptist Church, Providence, Rhode Island is an excellent example of his style.*

emerald possible with the opalescent process. Congregation Sherith Israel, San Francisco, built in 1904, installed large expanses of opalescent glass. Great half-circle scenes illuminate the balconies—on one side the *Story of the Good Woman*, on the other *Moses*. Miriam commands another window; below a dancing figure with tambourine, an inscription reads: *"Miriam Said Sing to the Lord for He Has Triumphed Gloriously."* The streaky segments of glass showing several colors are used to evoke

the patterned weave of a brilliant sash, the shading on the inner side of a cloak, the shifting blues of a sky with clouds, or the patches of grass, stone, and earth on a path. Likewise, American Baptists could be found with important opalescent windows such as the multilight standing figures with details of landscapes made by the Gorham Company out of New York City, which employed some of the same designers, such as Edward Peck Sperry and Frederick Wilson, as the Tiffany Studios. Many American studios produced highly original works in the American mural art tradition, such as the *Pilgrim's Progress* window by Frederick Crowninshield (1845–1918) for Emmanuel Church, Boston. Against a vast landscape of "the Delectable Mount," female virtues flank Christian.

Until the second decade of the twentieth century, glass was so ubiquitous as an architectural element that it was impossible for an architect to design a building without considering the leaded window. Sometimes beveled and made of simple etched or frosted glass, or even unworked segments of machine-rolled glass, the idea of glass in the decorative scheme of an architectural structure was a reality. The Boston home

LEFT *The Gorham Company, known for silver work, listed stained glass in its 1888 annual catalogue and described the company as an agent for the London firm of Heaton, Butler & Bayne. By 1904, Gorham's catalogue noted offerings of American opalescent glass, listing Edward Peck Sperry as its designer-in-chief. The opalescent head of* Isaiah, *Calvary Baptist Church, Providence, Rhode Island, is one of the early works of the firm, possibly by the designer T. W. Bladen.*

FAR LEFT *The opalescent window of* Miriam *1904, for Congregation Sherith Israel, San Francisco depicts the jubilation of the Israelites after God had parted the sea for their passage and had then destroyed Pharaoh's army. Miriam, the prophetess, the sister of Aaron "took a timbrel in her hand: and all the women went forth after her with timbrels and with dances" (Exodus 15:20).*

OPPOSITE *Wilson's compositions for Tiffany successfully organized full windows. The window* Blessed are the Meek, *about 1904, for Arlington Street Church, Boston, displays subtle color harmonies and extensive use of drapery glass. Similar designs were projected for the ten openings of the balcony. Over several decades, only six were eventually fabricated, the most recent abandoning the costly use of drapery glass.*

Frederic Crowninshield, Harvard '66, studied painting in Europe 1867–78. On his return to Boston he taught at the Museum of Fine Arts for seven years and was prominent in New York art organizations where he resided after 1885. His stained glass shows the three-dimensional and monumental parameters inspired by the Italian Renaissance. The personification of Charity is a detail of Pilgrim's Progress, *1898, in Emmanuel Church, Boston, Massachusetts.*

of financier William Powell Mason, Jr., designed in 1883 by the firm of Rotch and Tilden, Boston, in a rich Queen Anne style, exemplifies the seemingly universal use of stained glass in a domestic interior. Rotch, a graduate of Harvard College and the architectural school of Massachusetts Institute of Technology, also collected ancient stained glass, and three fifteenth-century panels from Milan Cathedral from his collection are now in the Massachusetts

Institute of Technology's collection. In Mason's home, the great mahogany staircase includes a curving bay illuminated by predominantly uncolored glass with borders and accents of opalescent hues. The uncolored glass is a ripple design, but highly variegated so that no adjacent areas appear cut from the same section.

Just as in the Middle Ages, the construction of patterned windows of a variety of formats was an essential part of glazing programs. One of La Farge's first compositions was in 1881 for the decoration of the United Congregational Church, Newport, Rhode Island. The windows, inscribed with a diamond stylus with the 1879 date of his opalescent patent, are uncolored glass combined with a simple, deep blue-green geometric band. In the same vein, train stations, banks, courthouses, libraries, and public auditoriums were constructed to include stained glass in nonfigural systems. Virtually any city in the United States at the turn of the century could furnish examples of architectural installations of stained glass in commercial and domestic buildings; among them are the City Hall, Sheraton Palace Hotel, and Olympic Club of San Francisco, Cypress Lawn Cemetery, Colma California, St. Louis's Union Station, and Pittsburgh's Lake Erie Railroad Terminal. Nonfigural glass was popular on all levels of production. A hall area of the First Presbyterian Church of Newport shows opalescent windows with cast "bottle bottom" borders, equally suitable for secular use. Details of this opalescent

material even in simple windows available through builder's catalogues show that the texture of the glass and the changes in the opalescent color create extraordinary effects in fluctuating light.

LEFT *Virtually all American studios had become adept at working with this new opalescent aesthetic. The sophistication of an installation restricted to uncolored glass and border accents is demonstrated by the stairwell glazing in the mansion of William Powell Mason. 211 Commonwealth Avenue, Boston. The panels, about 1900, display the irregular cuts of a hand-work design.*

BELOW *In the period following the great San Francisco earthquake and fire of 1906, many buildings were constructed in the Renaissance Revival mode. One of the city's most prolific stained glass studios at that time was the United Art Glass Company, owned by Harry and Bert Hopps, whose grandfather had established the firm in 1850, then called Hopps & Sons. The lavish Garden Court of the Sheraton Palace Hotel exemplifies the firm's work.*

ABOVE *The United Art Glass Company of San Francisco installed the majority of the glass domes and ceilings of the cemetery buildings of Cypress Lawn, Colma, a short distance from San Francisco.*

RIGHT *The inherent quality of glass developed during the Opalescent Decades imbued even the simplest windows with the capacity to capture light in exciting ways. Across the United States, innumerable homes received transom, stairwell, or sidelight windows, many set in as "catalogue" purchases when the homes were built.*

EUROPEAN ART NOUVEAU

The attraction of the new American glass was integrated into the movement of Art Nouveau in Europe. A phenomenon of great cities, notably Brussels, Barcelona, Milan, London, Paris, Nancy, and Prague, the style emphasized organic forms, sinuous contour, and reliance on inspiration from plant motifs. The international expositions that had begun in midcentury were particularly efficacious for spreading the influence of the movement. The decorative arts developed broad markets, as discussed above, for glass in entranceways or breakfast nooks, and transom lights in middle-class homes as well as in public institutions such as banks, theaters, railroad stations, and courthouses. In Brussels, Victor Horta (1862–1947) used glass extensively, for example in the stairwell glazing for his own home at 23–25 rue Américaine, built in 1898, and for the home of E. van Eetvelde. His public commission, the Maison du Peuple, 1896–99, brought the style to international attention and emulation across Europe. In Paris, the Samaritaine department store, 1905, used glass extensively, and three years later the Galeries Lafayette installed an art glass dome designed by Jacques Gruber (1871–1936) of Nancy. This was the era of the architect Hector Guimard (1867–1942), whose work transformed many areas of Paris, leaving a lasting popular impression through the design of subway entrances. Artists were producing glass on a more intimate scale as well. Eugène Grasset (1841–1917) designed *Spring*, 1894, fabricated by Félix Gaudin (1851–1901) in a style that paralleled the poster art made popular by Toulouse-Lautrec and Alphonse Mucha (1860–1939). In 1931, Mucha designed a window for the cathedral of Prague, showing his characteristic sinuous line and brilliant color to achieve a highly legible multiple-figure image.

In the United Kingdom, London's Liberty Store promulgated the new style primarily in decorative arts and furniture, but in Glasgow stained glass reached unusual prominence in the Art Nouveau environment. The name synonymous with this era is that of the architect and designer

BELOW *Art Nouveau, as pioneered by the architect Victor Horta conceived of the entire environment as a flowing, organic whole. Horta's own home, now the Horta Museum in Brussels contains a staircase whose flowing design links wall, lighting, balustrade and glass.*

ABOVE *Art Nouveau architecture quickly arrived in progressive urban centers such as Barcelona. Domènech i Montaner's Hospital de Sant Pau Barcelona, designed in 1902, shows a vast interplay of pavilions where pattern and structure become indissoluble. Window, ceiling, and wall function as intersecting planes of decoration.*

RIGHT *The house of Baron van Eetvelde of 1895–97, another Brussels residence, boasts an extraordinary salon. A circle of slender iron columns supports a dome of glass. Here Horta reveals his study of the projects of the French architect Viollet-le-Duc, that encouraged him to use iron, glass, and masonry in new and expressive ways.*

OPPOSITE *Alphonse Mucha designed a window honoring Saints Cyrl and Methodius, Apostles to the Slavs in the Cathedral of St. Vitus, Prague. Installed in 1931, the window's brilliant color, bold contours, and two-dimensional schematization of the figure reflects Mucha's renowned poster art at the turn of the century.*

Charles Rennie Mackintosh (1868–1928), who designed the Glasgow School of Art in 1897 and a series of restaurants, "Miss Cranston's tea rooms," 1897–98, the Willow Tea Rooms, 1903, as well as private houses in an extraordinary symbiosis of elegant line and natural materials. Under the direction of Francis H. Newbery (1853–1946), the Glasgow School of Art was transformed to emphasize the decorative arts. The school of stained glass, established in 1893, incorporated the new directions, including the use of the new American opalescent material. A 1902 composition depicting Tristan and Isolde still installed near the entrance to the Glasgow School of Art, by Dorothy Carlton Smyth (1880–1933), School of Art staff and book illustrator, demonstrates the principles that animated these artists.

In Italy Art Nouveau was called Liberty Style. The exuberance of the production in Milan is exemplified by windows installed in 1914 by Beltrami and Company in the main staircase of the Banca d'Italia in Milan. Personifications of Abundance and Temperance as kneeling women in flowing draperies flank an image of Hermes in flight.

In Spain the center was Barcelona. Powerful figural work was designed by the architect Antoni Gaudí (1852–1926), for the royal chapel of the cathedral of Majorca, 1904, as well as nonfigural windows for his church of the Holy Family (Sagrada Familia) of Barcelona and for the crypt of Santa María de Cervello, the chapel of the Güell colony in Barcelona, 1898–1914. Two other architects, Josep Puig i Cadafalch (1867–1956) and Lluis Domènech i Montaner (1849–1923), also designed buildings that integrate sculpture, architecture, surface decoration, and stained glass. A section of a window in the house of the Punxes, designed by Puig i Cadafalch in 1905 functions as a screen allowing glimpses of the exterior to mesh with the geometricized floral patterns.

Planned in 1902 and under construction until 1930, Domènech i Montaner's Hospital de Sant Pau is a vast complex of patterned pavilions. The entrance building is dominated by a great vaulted ceiling, glazed cupolas, and open and blind clerestories, creating large open spaces set against narrow corridors. The windows incorporate both clear panes and leaded elements of translucent organic form whose patterns reflect those of the painted walls and the ceramic inlays. Similarly, Montaner's Palace of Catalan Music, built between 1905 and 1908, combines extensive use of stained glass, including a huge inverted cupola in the auditorium and leaded wall dividers and screens throughout. Light both penetrates and is diffused by the glass and the polychrome ceramic mosaic of the exterior and interior.

Figural work in stained glass for churches was also produced in the Art Nouveau style. In Austria, where the style was associated with the Sezession group, Koloman Moser (1868–1918) designed windows in 1904 for the church of St. Leopold at Amsteinhof.

RIGHT *Puig i Cadafalch designed for the total space visible to the inhabitant. In this house of the Punxes, 1905, Barcelona, the architect mixes clear and semi-transparent elements in windows to link exterior and interior.*

FAR RIGHT *Although he is most known for his brilliant organic abstraction in architecture and decoration, Antoni Gaudí also created figural work such as the powerful* St. Valerian, *1904, for the royal chapel of the cathedral of Palma, Majorca.*

Moser, a painter, was one of the founders of the Wiener Werkstätte, a Viennese crafts association that promoted a unity among design, craft, and architecture, and he exploited the angularity of geometric systems with his use of leadlines as contours. In Switzerland, the studio of Kirsch & Flechner (1884–1938) of Friburg produced meticulously drafted figural work, including the series of windows designed by Fortuné Bovard for the parish church of Cugy (canton of Fribourg) in 1907.

An original American interpretation of Arts and Crafts and the Art Nouveau style can be found in the work of Thomas Augustin O'Shaughnessy (1870–1956). Beginning in 1912, he installed over eighty new windows for Old St. Patrick's Church, Chicago, built between 1852 and 1856 and now the oldest religious building in the city. Ornamental panels frame the images of Irish saints in the nave windows. O'Shaughnessey's inspiration for the ornament was the Celtic designs exhibited at the 1893 World's Columbian Exposition in Chicago, Lady Aberdeen's Irish Village, and his study in Dublin of manuscripts such as the ninth-century Book of Kells. In 1921 O'Shaughnessy installed three balcony windows on the theme of the theological virtues of Faith, Hope, and Charity, relying even more on Art Nouveau for inspiration, J. & R. Lamb Studios made opalescent windows in an Irish-inspired design for Lakewood Mausoleum, Minneapolis, Minnesota. Installed in 1908, the windows show the extraordinary richness of opalescent glass and its ability to achieve impact by exploiting only color and leadline.

Other artists in the United States began to turn away from the opalescent. Chief among them were New York's Otto Heinigke (1850–1915) and Boston's Harry Eldredge Goodhue (1873–1918). Harry, the brother of architect Bertram G. Goodhue , was a partner in the architectural firm of Cram, Goodhue and Ferguson, Boston. Heinigke and H. E. Goodhue's art stressed the two-dimensional nature of the window and strong surface graphic, distinguishing themselves from the Victorian realism and sentimentality so characteristic of the opalescent windows produced at the time. For example, Heinigke's designs, as evident in the angels and apostles in Philadelphia's First Baptist Church (1900), are elegantly attenuated through flat segments of intense color. As Heinigke's work evolved, it moved closer to the aesthetics of continental Symbolist movements, and in some instances quite parallel to the Austrian painter Gustave Klimt (1862–1918) or of Koloman Moser, mentioned above. H. E. Goodhue's two windows dating to 1905, for the east aisle of All Saints, Massachusetts, contrast male and female figures from Scripture: Joshua, the Archangel Michael, and Gideon, and Mary Magdalene, Mary the Mother of Jesus, and St. Elizabeth. The clarity of color and abstraction of the modeling enhance the sweeping drama of the gestures.

ABOVE *The United States is a land of great ethnic diversity. Irish, Polish, or German Catholics often wanted church designs to reflect their specific traditions. Encouraged by Irish nationalism, Irish patrons felt that they had choices in styles, as at St. Patrick's. Chicago. Thomas O'Shaughnessy was able to offer stained glass unabashedly patterned after early Irish manuscripts and metalwork.*

LEFT *The J. & R. Lamb Studios, created an entire interior for the Lakewood Mausoleum, in Minneapolis. An extraordinary program of mosaics, windows, and even carpet design link all elements of the centrally planned building. The opalescent glass almost seems to mimic the alabaster slabs used in Early Christian buildings, clearly the inspiration for the design.*

This period also witnessed a distinct and highly fruitful effort to continue figural work inspired by late medieval traditions, led by Christopher Whall (1849–1924). Whall began his career working as a designer for major London firms of the Victorian era but became dissatisfied with the impersonal division of labor in many studios, since specialists either designed, cut glass, or assembled the window. Even among the glass painters themselves, divisions frequently existed between the painters of flesh, drapery, or decorative elements. Whall, as he explained later in his book *Stained Glass Work*, believed that for a window to be successful, the studio system must be altered to allow greater communication about all aspects of a window's fabrication. He encouraged the studio owner to "keep his hand of mastery over the whole work personally at all stages."

The development of "Early English" glass by the firm of Britten & Gilson for the architect E. S. Prior in 1889 provided a new material exactly suited to Whall's needs. The new glass was unusually thick and uneven, encouraging emphasis on color and texture and discouraging over-fussy paint manipulation. Whall and his circle, especially his daughter Veronica Whall (1887–1967), who became a co-owner of his firm, transformed figural work in Great Britain and the United States in the movement known as Arts and Crafts. The artists in this circle included Louis Davis (1861–1941), Reginald Hallward (1858–1948), Mary Lowndes (1857–1929), David Gauld (1865–1936), Selwyn Image (1849–1930), John Gordon Guthrie (1874–1961), and Robert Anning Bell (1863–1933), who executed the decorative friezes designed by Rennie Mackintosh for Miss Cranston's Buchanan Street tea room in Glasgow.

ABOVE *Harry Eldridge Goodhue produced the dramatic image of* Mary Magdalene, *a detail from the* Biblical Heroines *window, in 1905 for All Saints Church, Brookline, Massachusetts.*

OPPOSITE *The Honan Chapel of University College, Cork, was designed with Celtic inspiration as a core theme. Ernest Child's* Risen Christ, *1916, demonstrates the lasting inspiration of Whall's approach to the material of glass, corresponding well with the simplicity of the chapel.*

Whall's masterpiece, which he produced in cooperation with his daughter Veronica, is generally accepted to be the windows of the Lady Chapel and chapter house of Gloucester Cathedral, 1899–1909. The Lady Chapel is one of the largest in England, and was built between 1460–90 in the attenuated Perpendicular Gothic style. Originally richly decorated, it became dilapidated, and Whall was commissioned to reglaze the building. The project shows Whall's great strength: his ability to evoke the reciprocal functions of glass and decorative tracery in fourteenth-century England. His use of large areas of uncolored glass juxtaposed with intense, streaky red and blue evokes the great east

window of the cathedral. The entire plan, suggested by Whall, narrates the transformation of human nature as depicted through the Incarnation of Christ and the Virgin Mary.

The young American Charles Connick (1875–1945), who viewed windows made by Whall for All Saints Church, Ashmont, Massachusetts, in 1905, and the Church of the Advent, Boston, in 1910, before they were placed in the building, was deeply impressed by Whall's clarity of materials and the dignity of his figures. Connick emphasized both characteristics in his own window of *Saints Stephen, Paul, Peter, and James*, in All Saints Church, Brookline, Massachusetts, 1910. The intense graphic power of the design equalizes the surface tension among colored and white glass. An equally eloquent tribute to Whall is Connick's *Holy Grail* window of 1919 for Cram and Ferguson's Proctor Hall, Princeton University. Original plans for the commission had accepted a design by Florence and Walter Camm, English artists working within the Whall circle, but the advent of World War I prevented execution.

In Ireland, the Arts and Crafts influence coincided with a revival of nationalism and a reverence for the decorative arts that are the glory of the Celtic tradition from the eighth to the tenth centuries. The change began in 1901 when Edwin Martyn, co-founder of the Irish Literary (later Abbey) Theatre and a fervent supporter of the Irish cultural movement, asked Whall to help develop a school of progressive stained-glass design. Whall visited Ireland but was not then free to accept the charge. He sent over in his stead his chief assistant, Alfred Ernest Child (1875–1939), who was appointed in September 1901 as instructor in stained glass at the Dublin Metropolitan School of Art.

LEFT *The George Hobron Champlin Memorial Window, 1910, All Saints, Brookline, was Charles J. Connick's opportunity to install a window in a building designed by the most influential architect in America's twentieth-century Gothic Revival. Ralph Adams Cram became one of Connick's great supporters and ally in the effort to turn the tide away from opalescent glass in houses of worship.*

Behind the success of the Irish stained-glass revival was the financial and spiritual leadership of the painter Sarah Purser (1848–1943). In cooperation with Child, she established in January of 1903 *An Túr Gloine* (Tower of Glass), a cooperative stained-glass workshop that brought creative artists together under quality working conditions. The ethos of *An Túr Gloine* was emphatically artistic: "each window should be in all its artistic parts the work of one individual artist, the glass chosen and painted by the same mind and hand that made the design and drew the cartoon; in fact a bit of stained glass should be a work of free art as much as any painting or picture" (*Anniversary Booklet*, p. 9).

Almost all significant Irish artists in stained glass were at some time associated with the workshop. Michael Healy (1873–1941), whose early work displayed humanistic modeling and intensity of expression, produced windows from 1904 to 1940 for Loughrea Cathedral, Galway, Ireland. Wilhelmina Geddes' (1887–1955) window of the *Crucifixion*, 1922, appears in the east window of St. Luke's, Wallsend-on-Tyne, Northumberland, and communicates great spiritual power through the monumentality and sobriety of her style. One of the most distinctive of the *An Túr Gloine* artists was Harry Clarke (1889–1931), whose work is characterized by meticulous craftsmanship and allusion to the continental artists such as the French Symbolist Gustave Moreau, the Russian stage designer Léon Bakst, and the English illustrator Aubrey Beardsley. The Honan Chapel of St. Finbarr, University College, Cork, contains a series of Irish saints, the depiction of which were executed in 1915–17 by artists of *An Túr Gloine*, primarily Harry Clarke and Ernest Child. Clarke also completed a large series of Apostles with images of the Stations of the Cross for St. Patrick's Purgatory, Lough Derg, County Donegal, 1928–29. His *Geneva Window*, now held at the Wolfsonian Foundation, Florida, was commissioned by the Irish Free State in 1926 for the League of Nations in Geneva, Switzerland. Clarke's decision to illustrate fifteen contemporary Irish writers, many with controversial explicit sexual imagery, caused the window to be withdrawn.

Many of these styles were to continue well into the twentieth century. Others, however, such as the opalescent, fell out of favor as the leaner lines of Art Deco and the Modern came to the fore in the 1920s. The twentieth century brought greater complexity to the leaded and painted window by introducing many new techniques as well as profound social and architectural changes.

The Glass of the Twentieth Century

THE EARLY YEARS

The early years of the twentieth century witnessed a large number of simultaneous expressions: Art Nouveau, Arts and Crafts, Munich School, opalescent, and academic traditions. The Art Nouveau interior had deeply impressed European and American sensibilities, especially its design concepts that could link furniture, architecture, and windows in a coordinated whole. Frank Lloyd Wright's (1859–1967) work was conceptually linked to these ideals, although highly individual in form. He designed windows as an integral part of a finely conceived spatial aesthetic, inherited from his six years working under Louis Sullivan (1856–1924) at the Chicago architectural firm of Adler and Sullivan. Sullivan's work involved extensive design of stained glass in many buildings, exemplified by Chicago's Auditorium Hotel and Theater (now Roosevelt University), in 1889. Sullivan's inspiration was curvilinear; Wright's, as seen in his famous Prairie-style houses, was rectilinear, inspired by the low horizontal lines of the prairie on which they sat. Their long rows of casement windows under low-pitched roofs further emphasized the horizontal theme.

Wright's inspiration led other Chicago architects to work in what has often been referred to as the "Prairie School" manner. Ecclesiastic buildings were rare in Wright's work, although his own father had been a Unitarian minister. One notable exception was the Unity Temple, Oak Park, Illinois, built between 1906 and 1909. The twenty clerestory windows form a horizontal band around the upper portion of the building, allowing the skylight segments to repeat the geometric plan of the building itself. Wright was concerned that the window be functional, allowing light and, when opened, air to circulate, as well as the object of attractive decorative materials. He said that "nothing is more annoying to me than any tendency toward realism of form in window glass, to get mixed up with the view outside. A window pattern should stay severely 'put'" (Wright, p. 201).

Wright's ability to develop an interaction between interior and exterior forms through a screen of glass is exemplified in his designs for all his homes, stairwell windows, entrance doors, living rooms, even to the

sprightly colors of the Coonley Playhouse windows. Patterns of quickly shifting small rectangles cluster at the lancet heads and appear again as a minor echo at the base. The tall, narrow lancets, whose verticality is emphasized by the thrust of the leadlines, "stay severely put" as architectural elements, repeating the vertical shapes of the house and the rectangular patterns of the interior furnishings.

GOTHIC REVIVAL IN THE UNITED STATES

Under the aegis of architects such as Ralph Adams Cram (1863–1942), the United States experienced a twentieth-century Gothic Revival of a historicism and direction very different from the early Modernism of Wright. Cram thought opalescent windows inappropriate for a spiritual atmosphere and gave explicit directions to studios to avoid them. His disdain for opalescent glass appears to have been associated with its ubiquity— from lampshades to row-house stairwells— from which he deduced its inappropriateness for a church. Cram's

efforts began the twentieth-century polarization that generally relegated the stained-glass window in America to church decoration, a situation that lasted until the 1960s when a rebirth of stained glass became again linked to contemporaneous work in the fine arts. Cram was also explicit in his criticism of Munich-style windows. Writing in the journal *Stained Glass* in 1931 (vol. 26:224), he stated that they were "too terrible to contemplate" and argued that it had become a question of "how to get rid of them without impiety. There was and is but one way. Go they must." Cram called for replacement windows of the same subject "but made by real artists," flattering the stained-glass trade perhaps in an attempt to realize his agenda.

Like Pugin, Cram was a writer, organizer, and scholar; he was one of the founding members of the Medieval Academy of America. Given the importance of the architect in the selection of a stained-glass studio, American studios quickly espoused the style, until it became almost universal. Nicola D'Ascenzo (1871–1854) of Philadelphia worked in a variety of styles but is best remembered for windows inspired by the Middle Ages such as those

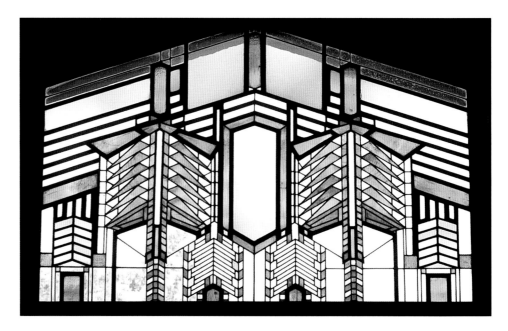

in the cathedral of St. John the Divine, New York City. Another Philadelphia studio that was early patronized by Cram was William Willet (1969–1921), responsible for the *Seven Liberal Arts* window, 1913, for Proctor Hall, Princeton University, and also windows for the chapel. Cram explicitly advised Willet to model the Proctor Hall windows after those of the clerestory of Chartres. The English-born Clement Heaton (1861–1940), who went to the United States in 1914 at Cram's behest, was a versatile artist who had designed Art

Nouveau work around 1905. In the United States, he produced French-inspired Gothic Revival, as seen in the west rose of the church of the Blessed Sacrament in New York as well as English style in St. Philip's Church, Charleston, South Carolina.

Boston saw the rise of large and influential studios working in a Gothic-Revival style, such as those of Wilbur Herbert Burnham (1887–1974) and Reynolds, Francis & Rohnstock (Joshua G. Reynolds, 1886–1972), both with significant windows in the National

ABOVE RIGHT *In 1925, Clement Heaton's All Saints chancel window was set in the mother church of the Episcopal diocese of South Carolina, St. Philip in Charleston whose foundation dates to 1670. After a fire, the present building, finished in 1838, was constructed in a neoclassical style inspired by London's St. Martin-in-the-Fields. Heaton respected the context by including classical columns as organizing principles and favoring a light palette.*

Charles Connick's
Coronation of the Virgin, 1927, one
of fifteen medallions of the Mysteries
of the Rosary made for St. Mary of
Redford, Detroit, was inspired by twelfth
and thirteenth century French art.
The dominant color of the windows is
blue; the red of the background, warmer
towards the center, is shaded with
short strokes that remove the mat paint.
In keeping with the medieval figural
aesthetic, modeling on Christ and the
Virgin's faces is limited to several tonal
values and dark trace outlines, as was
recommended in the twelfth-century
treatise of Theophilus.

Cathedral, Washington, D.C., George C. Ball, Earl Edward Sanborn (1890–1937), Harry Wright Goodhue (1905–1931), and Margaret Redmond (1867–1948) with work in Trinity Church, Boston. Charles J. Connick (1875–1945) was the movement's chief polemicist, and headed possibly its most prolific studio. His window of the *Holy Grail* for Proctor Hall, in an Arts and Crafts mode inspired by Christopher Whall, is consonant with the restructuring of medieval religion to refer to modern goals of education. By the late 1920s, as demonstrated by his circular medallion of the *Coronation of the Virgin*, he was drawing inspiration from the twelfth-century Romanesque style typified by Le Mans cathedral and the thirteenth-century

Gothic style exemplified by the windows in the Sainte-Chapelle, Paris. Connick's method of painting should be compared to details of medieval application of mat and trace.

Carefully crafted windows that closely emulated medieval precedents were possible because the American Gothic-Revival studios, like their European predecessors, could rely on publications by restorers of stained glass. Many restorers published books with lavish reproductions and tracings or other detailed restoration drawings. Westlake's *History of Design in Stained Glass*, for instance, was an essential reference for American studios; translations of Viollet-le-Duc's section on stained glass from his *Dictionnaire* were also available.

Indeed, many of the illustrations that Connick used for his own *Adventures in Light and Color*, 1937, were borrowed from the books of Westlake and Viollet-le-Duc. Like their books, Hugh Arnold (1872–1915) and Lawrence Saint's (1885–1916) *Stained Glass of the Middle Ages in England and France* (London, 1913) was cherished by glass studios for its clear overview of what had become the canon of great medieval windows: Le Mans, Poitiers, Canterbury, Chartres, York, through Rouen and Fairford of the fifteenth century. That medieval windows were valued above all other glass, however, had everything to do with the taste of collectors and writers.

The popularity of Gothic Revival architectural styles in America coincided with the growth in size and in prestige of American colleges and universities. Associated with the English precedents of the universities of Oxford and Cambridge, the Gothic mode found fertile ground in the American university expansion.

Princeton, Yale, Boston College, and the Universities of Chicago and Michigan were among the many schools engaged in complex building programs in the 1920s. Yale's Harkness Tower, chapel, and Sterling Memorial Library are Neo-Gothic. The glazing of most of Yale's buildings between 1921 and 1932 was supplied by Owen Bonawit (1891–1971), director of a New York studio. The "secular" Gothic Revival window system retained more of the Arts and Crafts structure of windows. A great deal of white glass was simply accented with small medallions in the mode of post-High Gothic glazing such as the grisaille and panel windows of Saint-Urbain of Troyes. Bonawit produced his medallions from an extremely heterogeneous group of sources having the theme of illustrated books as the only common link. The small size of the panels and their placement within the latticework of the leading system of white glass achieved a visual coherence within which diversity could operate.

RIGHT *Heinrick Campendonk's work was derived from early German Expressionism, with which he was associated. The simplicity of the image takes its strength from the study of both children's art and that of pre-industrialized cultures. The window of St. Michael, 1953, standing in triumph over Satan in Essen Cathedral has both the awe of an iconic image and the charm of a child-like experiment with blocks of color.*

EARLY MODERNIST WORK
AND ART DECO

In Germany, however, considerable
progressive work was developing, some of
it inspired by the impact of Frank Lloyd
Wright's architectural glass. The movement
had broad roots, one of them being the
De Stijl movement, which originated in
Holland, pioneered by Theo van Doesburg
(1883–1931). Himself influenced by the
work of the abstract painter Piet Mondrian,
van Doesburg propagated his principles
of abstraction through the magazine *De
Stijl*. Precocious work such as Bruno Taut's
Glass House in the German *"Werkbund"*
exhibition, Cologne, 1914–15, an
extraordinary juxtaposition of a fountain,
polychrome glass mosaics, and projected
polychrome light, incorporated designs
by Germany's most progressive artists, such
as the Expressionist painter Max Pechstein
(1881–1955). Artists and architects shared
a common goal of nothing less than the
radical transformation of all art and
industrialized production.

Jan Thorn-Prikker (1868–1932) arrived
in Germany from his native Holland in
1904. He executed ten large windows in
the chancel and passages of the church
of the Three Queens in Neuss, 1911–12.
Influenced by the philosophies of German
Expressionist groups such as the Blue Rider,
by 1921 he was committed to avoidance
of subject matter superbly exemplified
in a 1931 panel, *Orange*. His influential
career included over thirty years of
consistent stained-glass production. His
pupil Heinrick Campendonk (1889–1957)
associated with the painters Franz Marc
and Wassily Kandinsky and became a
member of the Blue Rider in 1911. In 1926
Campendonk was appointed an instructor
at the prestigious Düsseldorf Academy, but
in 1933 he was dismissed as a "degenerate"
artist during efforts by the Nazi party
to attack Modernist tendencies; he later

taught at the Amsterdam Academy.
Campendonk's work in glass is figural
abstraction drenched with powerful color.
Another pupil of Thorn-Prikker, Anton
Wendling (1891–1965), produced work
that included the choir of the cathedral
of Aachen, 1949–51, where shimmering
patterns of colored light of circular and
cruciform motifs enhance the historic
Gothic architectural frame. Wendling's
figural work is equally inspired, evident in
the baptismal window for the St. Sebastian
church, Aachen, 1954. The ancient symbol
for Christ is represented by a fish transfixed
by a cross, swirling through animated water
and leading others together in his wake.

The Bauhaus movement was founded
to promote work in all media, and
therefore glass as well. In 1919 Walter
Gropius assumed the position of head
of a new school, calling it *Das Bauhaus*,
an allusion to the medieval building
associations, *Bauhütten*, which grouped all
of the craftspersons—masons, carvers,
metalworkers, glass workers. The course
of instruction bore out these principles,
since for the preparatory levels all students
followed the same curriculum. Initially,
under the leadership of Johannes Itten,
beginning students were challenged to
confront the nature of different materials
such as paper, tin, and cotton, and
their impact on form. This emphasis
was inspired by Wassily Kandinsky's *On
the Spiritual in Art*, a seminal work on
Modernism of 1912, as well as his Bauhaus
book *Point and Line to Plane* of 1926.
Under the subsequent direction of Joseph
Albers (1881–1976), the course took on a
functionalist direction, and a grounding
in the elaboration of elemental, rational
forms that was extremely important for the
course of twentieth-century architecture.
After heading the Bauhaus's department
of stained glass, Albers taught at Black
Mountain College, North Carolina, from
1933 to 1948, then at Yale University from

ABOVE *The Mexican muralist, Diego
Rivera, (1886–1957), also designed
stained glass. A series of stairwell
windows of 1929 for the Secretariat of
Health, Mexico City, shows occupations
including mining, farming, fishing, and
heavy industry. The characteristic
abstraction of Rivera's style is well
suited to the broad expanse of densely
colored glass.*

1950. Theo van Doesburg, Sophie Taeuber-Arp (1889–1943), Paul Klee (1879–1940), and László Moholy-Nagy (1895–1946) all designed in stained glass. Bauhaus and other artists were, like Campendonk, suppressed during the National Socialist campaign to purify Germany from all foreign influence. Adamantly opposed to all forms of abstraction, which it labeled "degenerate" and linked to both racial impurity and mental illness, the movement culminated in the infamous exhibition "*Entartete Kunst*" of 1937 in Munich displaying 650 confiscated works of art from thirty-two German museums. From 1933 onward, the artists' departure to other countries carried Modernism across the world.

Art Deco also made its mark in stained-glass design on an international scale. The term derives from the 1925 Paris "*Exposition Internationale des Arts Décoratifs Industriels et Modernes*," which focused on contemporary design in both fine arts and everyday life. Joep Nicolas (1897–1971) exerted enormous influence on stained glass in Europe with the design of the *St. Martin* window for the *Exposition*. Art Deco objects generally share characteristics of geometry and simplicity, often combined with clear shapes and vibrant colors. Stained glass, with its linear patterns and brilliant hues, was particularly suited to the Art Deco aesthetic. Madrid exemplifies the urban popularity of the style for installations in both commercial and private buildings. Often windows were commissioned for staircases where light was important but they were also a way of masking the exterior. Often traditional pot-metal glass carried stylized designs of a wide variety of natural forms. When the glass is uncolored, the black of the leadline and the cast shadows created by the textured glasses form an integrated linear pattern admirably Art Deco in its elegance. Established firms such as Mauméjean of

Madrid and Barcelona sought out these new opportunities and embraced a variety of different design trends.

Although of a highly individualist expression, the stained glass of Marguerite Huré (1896–1967) echoes the progressive sensibilities of Art Deco. Her work at Notre-Dame du Raincy (1924–27) is constructed of segments of glass that earned the building the epithet "the Sainte-Chapelle of reinforced concrete." The architect Auguste Perret (1874–1954) designed a vast open space reminiscent of a medieval "hall church" with the side aisles of the same height as the nave, in which the windows present as grilles of light and color. Huré saw the window integrated with the architecture, stating that "the window is only color and light."

WORLD WAR II CHANGES IN GERMANY

Germany suffered massive material loss as a result of World War II, which paradoxically promoted a surge of creativity. In the *Wirtschafswunder* (economic miracle) of recovery, concerted efforts to rebuild and rededicate churches increased opportunities for artists working with glass. Anton Wendling was an early inspiration. Georg Meistermann (1911–), motivated by religious faith, sought to infuse abstract painting with a symbolic imagery, ultimately creating an emblematic art that found great success in the design of monumental stained-glass windows. He pioneered a renewed sense of architectural scale, rejecting the geometric abstraction prevalent among many of his colleagues. Organic flow and movement are dominant qualities of his aesthetic. One of his most important works is a series of windows fabricated by the Oitdmann Studios, Linnich, for St. Mary's Church in Cologne-Kalk, 1965.

Meistermann influenced a number of slightly younger artists through his work and his academic appointments, including those at the academies of art in Düsseldorf and Karlsruhe. Ludwig Schaffrath (1924–) early installed a series of windows filling the triple-light cloister windows of Cologne Cathedral, 1962–65. The abstracted forms evoked the position of the body of Christ as remembered in the Stations of the Cross. The glass is colorless, evoking Cistercian sobriety, with pattern defined by the lead system telling with graphic energy from the exterior as well as from the interior. His work became synonymous with the new spirit of German work in glass, appearing widely in all the new venues, schools, town halls, train stations, galleries, swimming complexes, united to the architectural structure of the building. Maria Katzgrau, like Schaffrath, was an assistant to Wendling in Aachen before the war and from 1947 to 1954. Katzgrau executed many works, showing a great strength in the integration of figural reference and abstract pattern. She often used traditional paint as in the windows depicting *St. Sebastian* and *St. Barbara*, 1958, in the church of St. Ursula, Düroslar, and a 1979 series on the theme of St. Francis' hymn to the sun for the cloister of the church of St. Elizabeth, Aachen. Her work also shows formal geometric abstraction, as in the nave windows of *St. Elizabeth*.

ABOVE *Highly progressive in her commitment to abstraction, Marguerite Huré was able to create energized windows calibrated to their architectural setting. Her definition of the window as "a translucent wall of color, destined to give light at the same time as ornament to architecture," can be seen in her windows at Notre-Dame du Raincy of 1924–27. The subtle shift in dominance of colors and careful variation among the circles, squares and triangles reinforce the geometric simplicity of the building all the while giving a sense of mystery and brilliance.*

A large number of creative artists found support in the building of new churches and renovation of old ones. Windows by Johannes Schreiter (1930–) show a strong graphic sensibility. Schreiter, who was a vital part of international glass art conferences such as Portcon in Palo Alto, California, pioneered the use of lead as a design graphic. Rather than functioning simply as a connective element and divider between colors, the lead lines become an independent graphic intersecting the fields created by the expanses of color. Jochem Poensgen (1931–) is completely self-taught and his works exhibit an uncanny ability to incorporate the sense of architectural structure in the window itself. Wilhelm Buschulte's (1923–) work shows a delight in the planar surface, grouping areas of color within designs dominated by a classical sense of vertical and horizontal balance.

NEW DEVELOPMENTS IN FRANCE

Germany was not alone. France, in the years after World War I, under an impetus of liturgical renewal had encouraged art closely tied to the Christian spirituality of the artist. Alliances such as the Ateliers de l'Art Sacré founded in 1919 by Maurice Denis (1870–1943) and Georges Desvallières (1861–1950); the Arche; and the Artisans de l'Autel supported work in stained glass. Great studios like that of Jacques Simon (1890–1974), who was in charge of restoring the windows of Saint-Rémi and the cathedral of Reims after the bombardments of World War I, also executed contemporary windows. In the late 1930s, ecclesiastic patrons began to consider more intensely the inherent spiritual potential in the art of all artists of quality. One of the first patrons to seek the Modern painters was the Dominican father Marie-Alain Couturier

(1897–1954) of Notre-Dame-de-Toute-Grâce at Plateau d'Assy, where Marguerite Huré had executed windows in the crypt in 1938. Georges Rouault (1871–1958), Jean Bazaine (1904–80), and Marc Chagall (1887–1958), among other painters, designed windows at Assy. Rouault, whose art seems so innately linked to the color and isolation of leads known in windows of the Middle Ages, worked in a stained-glass studio but never made glass himself. Paul Bony (1911–) translated the artist's work (as well as that of Matisse, Braque, and Chagall) into glass using plating, etching, paint, and enamel colors. Despite the nature of the individual works, critics have regarded Assy as containing too great a difference among styles for the windows to coalesce into a coherent environment.

Environment, however, was very much the goal of the work of subsequent installations. One of the most memorable

environments of the 1950s is the Rosary Chapel at Vence designed by the eighty-one-year-old Henri Matisse (1869–1954). He planned both the altar of St. Dominic and the windows, 1947–51, stating that he set himself the task "to take an enclosed space of reduced proportions and to give infinite dimensions through the play of colors and lines alone" (*Vitrail français*, p. 306).

Similarly committed to environmental impact, the painter Alfred Manessier (1911–) designed a series of eight deeply saturated dalle-de-verre windows in 1959 for the crypt of Essen Cathedral. In 1948–52 he produced seven leaded windows of the church of Les Bréseux (Doubs), a small rural church dating from the late eighteenth century. Manessier's nonobjective panels, the first in France for a religious building, present a web of intense color, several concentrating cooler blue to the center and warmer reds to the edges.

ABOVE LEFT *Jochem Poensgen has been able to combine reference to historic work such as the depiction of the winding sheet of the* Resurrection, *an exhibition window of 1982, in Renaissance crosshatch modeling.*

ABOVE RIGHT *Wilhelm Buschulte produced a series of window on the Mysteries of the Rosary for St. Heribert in Cologne, 1977/78. The bold colors and block-like construction of the figures and decorative surround recall building stones of a church.*

part of the architectural structure of the wall itself. Gabriel Loire (1904–96), head of a large French studio near Chartres, was one of the major proponents of dalle-de-verre. His works are international—Chile, Morocco, Egypt, Scotland, Japan, and, in the United Kingdom, five windows in the apse of Salisbury Cathedral, 1979. In his Kaiser Wilhelm Memorial Church, Berlin, 1959, the interior is dominated by a double wall of blue squares set in a cement lattice. His seminal work for the United States is the First Presbyterian Church, Stamford, Connecticut, built 1956–57. When the French artists Robert Pinart (1927–) and Jean-Jacques Duval (1930–) emigrated to the United States, they took the technique of dalle-de-verre with them. Other artists followed. For example, Georgy Kepes (1906–2001), professor of visual arts at the Massachusetts Institute of Technology, began to design in dalle-de-verre glass, including a mural for KLM airline's ticket office in New York City and a similar installation at the Harvard Square transit station, Cambridge, Massachusetts. His best-known ecclesiastical commission is the towering windows in dalle-de-verre symbolizing the four elements, for St. Mary's Cathedral, San Francisco, installed in 1970.

THE ARTS UNITED

Contemporary expression in fine arts now found a solid place in glass design. Concepts of the entire environment became common in gallery work. Similarly, the stained-glass artist became less and less focused on the design of "a window," as John Piper put it, and "more and more in the simultaneous creation of a light-filled architectural unit" (Piper, p. 60). Stylistically, the stained-glass designer moved more closely into relationship with artists working in modes of color field, abstract expressionism, and minimalism.

ABOVE *Gabriel Loire's work with dalle-de-verre glass for the First Presbyterian Church, Stamford, Connecticut, 1956–57, demonstrates the seamless integration of structural and decorative elements into a single architectural environment.*

Windows by Manessier in the cathedral of Friboug, Switzerland, between 1976 and 1988 calibrate vastly different color harmonies to correspond to window form and placement within the cathedral.

This era brought new materials and processes. One of the first new techniques was dalle-de-verre, an innovation pioneered by French commissions, such as Manessier's crypt at Essen. Chunks of glass, frequently chipped at the edges to enhance light refraction, are set in a concrete or epoxy matrix. The result is that the glass is

The tendency to abstract imagery in stained glass since the 1950s was also part of the general direction of contemporary art. Parallels are evoked by Frank Stella's (1936–) protractor series of brilliant color and texture, Robert Motherwell's (1915–91) large floating forms, and Bridget Riley's (1931–) abstracted colored light shifting focus through the optical play of pattern and hue. Al Held's (1928–) subdued interactions parallel David Wilson's marvelous play of geometry and subtle shift of intensity through texture of uncolored glass, as discussed below. Held restricts the canvas to black and white; the few thin lines (which could almost be leads) intersect, yet create the impression of immensely complicated space.

Scale increased in painting, particularly with color-field works where their power was connected to their size. The work is thus able to create an architectural presence, a "field" that exerts a corporal force on the spectator. Probably one of the purest examples is the Rothko Chapel, part of the Menil collection in Houston, Texas. Opened in 1971, the chapel was conceived as three elements, an octagonal brick church, Marc Rothko's (1903–1970) paintings, and Barnett Newman's (1905–1970) *Broken Obelisk* set in a reflecting pool facing the chapel (the obelisk was later dedicated to the memory of Martin Luther King, Jr.). The chapel is a most uncompromising sacred space, stressing meditation. Rigorously aniconic, the paintings' message is developed by the spatial presence of deep color set within subtly varied rectangles. The chapel operates in a manner similar to installations of glass where the light, with or without recognizable image, permeates an interior. Modern glazing often produces a sensation of depth in pulsating color that advances and recedes and seems to hover in space according to the intensity of the light.

As in France in the 1940s, a heightened direction of the 1980s was the recruitment

ABOVE *Yaakov Agam's windows of* The Twelve Tribes of Israel *were installed in 1981 in the Synagogue at Hebrew Union College, New York City. The windows' three-dimensional structure presents a different façade as the viewer changes position, thus demonstrating to the spectator that sacred space is dependent on the worshipper's own involvement. Agam also designed the Torah Arc, Eternal Light and the Torah mantle.*

of artists in other media and the transformation of older studios to work with these new designers. Martin Harrison prophetically announced in 1979 that although craftsmanship in the medium is essential "it is simply that the great designer and the great craftsman are usually psychologically and temperamentally different characters, and it is self defeating to insist that they must be one and the same person" (Clarke, p. 69). Clients and patrons became confident that the technical expertise was available to allow collaboration of the most creative kind among designers and fabricators. This direction parallels similar collaborative work of contemporary artists and "fabricating" printmaking studios such as that of Tatyana Grosman's Universal Limited Art Editions (ULAE) studio in West Islip, New York, from 1957, which

collaborated with Robert Rauschenberg (1925–), among many others, in pioneering the modern print revival. A notable example of an artist from other media working in glass is the Israeli Yaakov Agam (1928–). His work in glass follows the direction of his kinetic paintings, sculpture, and architectural projects that emphasize change and movement, their images shifting as the viewer's viewpoint changes.

Stained glass also began to see collaboration across national boundaries, and artists began moving among countries to study and apprentice. The Pilchuck School, Washington, has welcomed international artists to the United States. The school was founded in 1971 to foster creative exchange among practicing artists and aspiring students in hot and flat glass. It has become one of the key resources for developing progressive work in the last quarter of the twentieth century. Schaffrath, Albinas Elskus, Patrick Reyntiens, and Linda Lichtman taught courses at the school.

German studios, in particular, have developed sophisticated techniques of production ranging from kiln-formed and laminated glass, to traditional leaded glass, with applied imagery using silkscreen, photographic transfer, painting with enamel colors, sandblasting, etching, and engraving. The fabrication facilities at Mayer of Munich and Heinrich Oidtmann Studios, Linnich, serve an international group of artists.

In Europe, artists of modern stained glass often associated with scholars dedicated to historical research, and with restorers. The relationships were varied, but invariably linked to a shared admiration that saw in the principles of historic windows inspiration for the present. Barcelona, a city with a rich legacy of turn-of-the-century glass, actively supported cooperative exchange among restorers, contemporary creators, and historians, exemplified by the Institut del Vitrall. Joan Vila-Grau (1932–), both artist and art historian, and an author in the Corpus Vitrearum series, executed windows for the Conselleria Economia I Finances in Barcelona. He did not want to install a false copy of a historic style but designed a free flow of colored and clear glass in organic forms to achieve the spirit of the Art Nouveau, yet still retain modern authenticity. Barcelona's José Fernándes Castrillo explains that his works in glass are influenced by parallel aesthetic developments in painting and sculpture, yet they achieve the architectural import. He, like Vila-Grau, has executed independent panels and new installations such as the *Alpha–Omega* sculpture in glass for a funerary chapel of Sabcho de Avila, Barcelona. He has also installed windows in historic buildings, such as Barcelona's church of Santa Maria del Mar, which contains intensely colored Gothic figural windows. The modern window uses small incised glass slabs laminated to large sheets of colored glass.

ABSTRACTION AND GEOMETRIC PATTERN

The formal graphics pioneered by the German Modernists in the 1950s reverberated in the United Kingdom and the United States. The American Robert Sowers (1923–90) was a key figure. Admired as both practitioner and theorist, he was a catalyst for bringing the Modern German school to the attention of American artists. He was awarded a Fulbright Fellowship in 1950 for travel to Europe, primarily England, and published *The Lost Art* in 1954. He subtitled it *A Survey of One Thousand Years of Stained Glass* and asked the distinguished art historian and museum curator Sir Herbert Read to write an introduction, perhaps in an effort to secure validation for his field from the academy. Read had written his own work

on stained glass in 1926 entitled *English Stained Glass*. About twenty pages of Sowers's work are devoted to historic periods, then about fifty pages to contemporary glass, interspersed with selective comparisons with medieval examples to define what he saw as issues of architecture and light. Despite its brevity, *The Lost Art* is a comprehensive call for the "rediscovery of plastic essentials" and for the collaborative work of designing wall treatment as a vital part of an architectural ensemble. Sowers's own work such as the American Airlines Terminal at Kennedy International Airport, New York, 1959, testifies to his principles. His panel *Red One* was included in an exhibition of New Talent at the Museum of Modern Art, New York City, in 1954 and illustrated in his 1965 book *Stained Glass: An Architectural Art*, which promoted the aesthetics of the German artists.

Brian Clarke (1953–), visiting Germany in 1972, was among the vigorous young voices calling for a "new constructivism" and committed to the integration of the arts. In his *Architectural Stained Glass*, 1979, which included essays by leading German and British critics and artists, he extolled the "complete building [as] the final aim of the visual arts ... Architects, painters, and sculptors must recognize anew the composite character of the building as an entity. Only then will their work be imbued with the architectonic spirit it has lost as a 'salon art'" (Clarke, p. 14). He stated that "collaboration at its highest level is when the artist ceases to be a decorator and becomes, alongside the architect, a joint manipulator of architectural space" (Clarke, p. 18). His work is characterized by a passion for color contained within geometric forms of considerable variety. The color is given texture through his selection of glass. In his large-scale work, such as the shopping centers in Oldham, 1993, and Leeds, England; Norte Shopping center, Rio de Janeiro; and the Corning Museum of Glass,

ABOVE *Joan Vila-Grau's career includes a fifteen-panel window of the Resurrection in Gaudí's church of the Holy Family, Barcelona. In one of the lower panels, the warm tonalities of the earth give way to the increasing clarity of ethereal blue.*

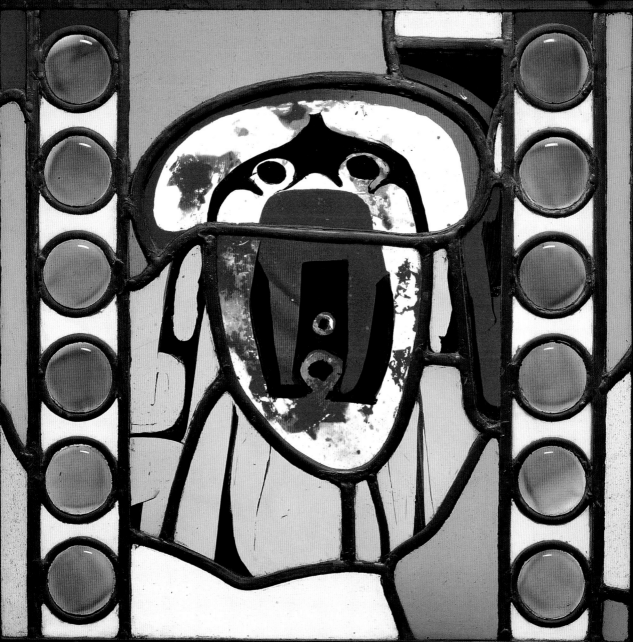

the installations often evoke sensations of landscape, trees against a sky, falling leaves, or birds in flight. The strength of the color and insistent geometry negates any sense of illusionism. Selection of contrasting blue and orange, complementary colors, add to the push and pull of spatially active color.

David Wilson (1941–) became familiar with Robert Sowers's ideas through *The Lost Art* while at the Middlesbrough College of Art, United Kingdom. Later, in New York City, while he was working for Rambusch Studios in 1963, he and Sowers became friends. Wilson's many collaborations with architects on large-scale works for both public and private buildings, consider not only the window, but also the patterns of structured light that bathe the interior space. He uses a carefully selected gamut of glass finely calibrated to carry out his graphic systems. Like much art in the Modernist tradition, the slightest miscalculation of proportion or density can rupture the harmony. Recently, Wilson has incorporated dichroic glass into many compositions with mouth-blown antique French and German glass and beveled glass. His glass selection frequently creates a play between blocking and allowing the exterior image, and the image

transformed through the fragmented prisms of the glass. He retains the technique of leaded glass yet pushes it to brave new possibilities, as in the boardroom of Corning Incorporated, New York City, 1991, repositioned in 2000. Wilson is as responsive to houses of worship as to public, institutional, and corporate installations, and his award-winning commissions range from the Beth David Reform Congregation, Gladwyne, Pennsylvania, 1996, to the NEC monorail station, Newark Airport, New Jersey, 2002.

PAINTERLY EXPRESSION

In France, artists often favored visible evidence of the brush. Jean-Dominique Fleury (1946–) of Toulouse developed great sensitivity to the complex issue of installation of modern windows in historic settings. For several commissions for churches in southern France with medieval wall paintings, such as Notre-Dame-de-Saux (Tarn-et-Garonne), he provided low-key grid and border patterns varied by a painterly application of grisaille and neutral tonal washes in 1985. For more independent installations he allows the

ABOVE *The* Glass Wall *by Brian Clarke was first exhibited in 1998. It was subsequently purchased by the Corning Museum of Glass, Corning, New York where it is on permanent display. The work plays with juxtaposition of scale and relationship of spectator to environment where he or she is bathed in an intense sense of color and confrontation of forms usually within grasp but now outsized and overwhelming.*

OPPOSITE *The* Red One, *1952, Corning Museum of Glass, reflects Robert Sowers' study of medieval glass, in particular the design of large clerestory figures of prophets and apostles, where the segment of the eyes and forehead is treated as one leaded unit and the lower portion of the face another.*

graphic strength of his expression to become more dominant. Didier Quentin shows a strong formal geometry in his handling of paint. Often a freely applied stroke is intersected by a precisely parallel linear motif lifted off the painted surface. Sylvie Gaudin (1950–94) took over the management of the Gaudin studio, Paris, at the death of her father. Her work demonstrates the contemporary acceptance of many techniques. She speaks of painting from the "emotion born from the density of values, from light gray to transparent black, as they mount through the application of grisaille, a powder that becomes a paste, a sort of liquid glass." She prints, stencils, and uses photographic transfer and as well as manipulating the paint while wet and dry. In addition to her installations that include windows in the cathedrals of Rouen and Beauvais, she continued the studio's impressive record of historic restoration typified by windows in the Sainte-Chapelle, Chartres Cathedral, and the abbey of Saint-Ouen, Rouen.

Ellen Mandelbaum (1938–) holds a Master of Fine Arts (MFA) degree in painting from Indiana University, Bloomington, and studied painting on glass at the Pilchuck School, Washington, in 1983 and 1984. She explains that

"traditionally artists divide glass painting into matting and tracing, first putting down a general tone, and then creating a thin line. I do them together, which is a little more like regular painting in a way. I love to put down a tone and blend using a wide brush: then I scratch through and release the light." Her brushwork is richly gestural and the window combines both the spontaneity and the solidity of architectural forms. The windows for the Adath Jeshurun Synagogue,1995, in Minnetonka, Minnesota, were awarded a Religious Art Award from the American Institute of Architects. The windows create brilliant intersections of representation and reality, allowing clear glass to bring the view of the natural landscape into the image. In 2000 she created windows for the South Carolina Aquarium, Charleston.

Linda Lichtman (1941–) was early influenced by Patrick Reyntiens, with whom she studied. She received an MFA in Architectural Stained Glass in 1976 from the School of the Museum of Fine Arts, Boston. Her work for the Charter Oak State College, New Britain, Connecticut, demonstrates her ability to conceive both form and symbol within an architectural setting. The panels work as a wall, but also evoke the growth of a tree, as the

BELOW *The windows representing the Minyan (ten worshippers needed for prayer) by Ellen Mandelbaum for the Adath Jeshurun Synagogue progress, each one larger than the last. The reamy glass, showing a characteristic fluid, watery texture supports the design which flows from left to right in a manner suggests the flow of water that is so often evoked in the Psalms.*

spontaneity of Lichtman's gesture suggests the spontaneity of the movement of leaves, her choice of colors suggest the change of seasons. Painterly imagery inspired by nature provides a human connection and environment for the viewer. In the *Light Garden* for the Dana Farber Cancer Institute in Boston, Lichtman positioned stained glass throughout the two clinics as "glowing windows of light." The glass provides a ubiquitous theme, from raised coves in elevator lobbies and waiting areas, to wayfinding markers at hallway corners, to sidelights at conference and procedure room doorways. *Light Garden* is based on the concept that the physical environment is a material expression— re-statement—of the caring given by Dana Farber to its patients.

ABOVE *Linda Lichtman's installation in the Dana Farber Cancer Institute, Boston, of 1998 creates an inviting, patient-friendly environment in a sub-basement, devoid of natural light. Lichtman creates using a variety of techniques: acid etching, engraving, lamination, and enamel as well as vitreous painted segments.*

LEFT *In the Dana Farber Cancer Institute, glass inserts into partition screens around waiting areas create colorful patterns with a reflective glint, to engage waiting patients. Each site has its own program and conditions to which the glass responds.*

CAST, FUSED, AND SCULPTURAL INSTALLATIONS

Contemporary architectural glass has also been influenced by the rise of interest in glass as a sculptural material. The growth of the "hot glass" movement has encouraged experimentation with materials and effects that have been incorporated in the "flat" (window) movement. James Carpenter (1949–) graduated from the Rhode Island School of Design in 1972 and is the founder of James Carpenter Design Associates, New York, a collaborative studio dedicated to exploring new and emerging glass technologies. His commissions are international and include London, Berlin, and Genoa, as well as San Francisco and Portland. Carpenter's work is at the intersection of sculpture and architecture,

for example his *Dichroic Light Field* of 1995, set on a building façade at Columbus Avenue and 68th Street, New York City.

Ed Carpenter (1946–) studied stained glass design and technique with Patrick Reyntiens in England in 1973 and large architectural glass design with Ludwig Schaffrath in Germany in 1976. Based in Portland, Oregon, he has received numerous public and corporate commissions. During the 1970s and 1980s he produced windows such as the 48-foot-long lounge glazing for the Cell Biology Building of the University of Oregon, Eugene. Much of his recent work has been sculptural projects often involving dichroic glass, such as the installation for the Pavillion of the Hokkaido Sports Center, Sapporo, Japan, 1999, and the *Light Veil*, a 60-by-25-foot sculpture for the Memphis

BELOW *In James Carpenter's* Dichroic Light Field *of 1995, the changing light of the day strikes the fins of dichroic glass with different saturation and at different angles. The result is a constant shift of color and density, acting as a foil to and reflection of the colors of the sky.*

Public Library, Memphis Tennessee, in 2001. In 1997, for St. Mark's Cathedral in Seattle, Washington, Carpenter worked with Olson-Sundberg Architects to create a major window and reredos behind the altar. The kiln-formed panels surrounding the rose were fabricated by Douglas J. Hansen (1949–) of Seattle.

Stephan Knapp (1947–) graduated from Hamilton College with a liberal arts degree in 1969 and entered a career in photography. By 1979 his relationship with a number of progressive interior designers and architects encouraged him to begin designing large-scale site-specific photographic installations, such as ceramic murals for USAA Federal Savings Bank in San Antonio, 1985. He speaks of Robert Rauschenberg and Isamu Noguchi as perhaps his biggest influences. Having experimented with new processes as a photographer, in his large-scale work Knapp explored techniques for etching metals and the application of porcelain enamel to steel. His recent work includes walls and door elements exemplified by the 44-foot wall for Harnischfeger Industries, Milwaukee, Wisconsin in 1996. His dichroic glass light sculpture has been installed in the University of Massachusetts Medical Center, Worcester, Massachusetts, among other sites.

LAMINATION AND FLOAT GLASS

In much modern work an inexpensive type
of glass, "float glass," is used as a base
for artistic manipulation. Introduced in
the 1950s by Sir Alastair Pilkington of the
British firm Pilkington Glass, float glass
is now the standard process used for
producing quality sheet glass with uniform
clarity and flat fire-polished sides. A ribbon
of hot glass is floated on a bath of heated
liquid, usually tin.

Lutz Haufschild (1943–), born in
Germany, established himself as a glass
artist in Vancouver in 1969. Working in
almost every type of technical process

available, he has become one of the
most respected figures in contemporary
glass in the United States and Canada.
For the Potter residence, Ottawa, his *Light
in Equipoise* uses tiny segments of beveled
glass laminated on half-inch float glass
to separate the foyer from the living
areas of the home. The screens are
suspended so that they can open to the
side when guests are being entertained,
creating an environment of prismatic
light. Conceptually simple, the result is
architecturally transformative. For *The
Great Wave*, 1996, in the Vancouver
international airport, Haufschild also used
float glass in evocative ways: the massive

OPPOSITE *Marc Chagall described his canvasses as "painted arrangements of inner images that obsess me." Loyal to the realm of representation, his juxtaposed images seem to have been arranged through a kaleidoscope of memory. A window in Reims Cathedral of 1975 shows Old Testament events, such as Jacob's Ladder, prefiguring the advent of Christ.*

BELOW *John Piper's windows of 1955 for Oundle School Chapel, Northamptonshire depict* Nine Aspects of Christ. *In three windows of three lights each the subjects are (left to right) the Way, the Truth, and the Life; the True Vine, the Living Bread, and the Water of Life; and Christ the Judge, the Teacher, and the Good Shepherd. Evoking, not imitating medieval forms, the haunting images set a row of mysterious figures glowing in deeply saturated colors relieved by hits of light.*

seascape appears to roll out to sea, complementing the bronze sculpture of a Native American canoe, *The Spirit of the Haida Gwai* by Bill Reid, coming in to shore.

FIGURAL TRADITION

The figural tradition was never lost, even under the dominance of Modernist abstraction. For many faith communities and other institutions, explicit reference to imagery was a priority for defining aspects of tradition and ritual. Katherine Lamb Tait (1895–1981) was born into the family of J. & R. Lamb Studios, founded by her grandfather Joseph Lamb and his brother Richard in 1857. Capable of designing in a variety of modes, Tait created the *Spirituals* window, 1933, for the Tuskegee Institute, Alabama, in a linearity redolent of Art Deco. For the Marine Corps chapel at Camp Lejeune in North Carolina, she worked in a conservative English style using a realistic drafting technique and extensive silver stain. The ten stained-glass windows installed in 1948 depict Old Testament archangels above illustrations of major events in Marine Corps history. In the borders of each window are scenes from wartime photographs taken by Marines. Helen Carew Hickman (1925–), who was the chief designer for the Conrad Schmitt Studio, New Berlin, Wisconsin, showed similar versatility with studio commissions. In 1978, she became the first woman president of the Stained Glass Association of America. Her *Pietà*, an exhibition panel of 1952, Corning Museum of Glass, evokes the power of medieval abstraction even as it speaks a language of modernity.

More overtly Modernist tendencies in figural work came through the association of independent painters with glass design. With the sculptor Henry Moore and the painter Graham Sutherland, John Piper (1903–92) was one of the major figures

in the British School, deeply admired for
both spiritual depth and flexibility. He
collaborated with the composer Benjamin
Britten as the designer of several of the
latter's operas. Piper has also been
influential as a writer and critic, and
with Myfanwy Evans, he edited the avant-
garde journal *AXIS*. Piper's windows, such
as the *Adoration of the Magi*, 1980, for
Robinson College, Cambridge, and
Coventry Cathedral's baptistery window,
1959–62, are as vital for their expressive
color as for the applied graphic of the
image. His windows were produced in
collaboration with Patrick Reyntiens
(1925–), who has frequently led
workshops on glass painting. Like many
of the artists of the twentieth century,
Reyntiens showed variety in his
approaches. Many windows for religious
spaces show restricted paint intervention,
exploiting glass selection; others such as
Ulysses, 1992, exhibit a painterly approach.

Marc Chagall, in a long collaboration
with the craftsman Charles Marq, was one
of the most beloved artists in glass. His
works convey deep emotion, nostalgia,
and values of family endurance, delight,
and wonder at the world. His windows for
the Synagogue of the Hadassah-Hebrew
University Medical Center were executed
in 1960–62. They depict the twelve sons
of the patriarch Jacob, from whom
descended the twelve tribes of Israel. Like
Chagall's canvases, the windows contain
floating figures of animals, flowers, and
fish, as well as Jewish symbols that
represent each tribe. When he worked
in stained glass, Chagall invariably used
deeply saturated color, most often
designing each window in an analogous
tonal harmony that he then alternated
from window to window. The Jerusalem
windows were exhibited in New York and
Paris before their installation. In 1966
Chagall designed for the United Nations
a window entitled *Peace* in memory of

Dag Hamarskjöld. In 1975 windows of the *Life of Christ* in the east chapel of Reims Cathedral were installed and in 1976 the *American Windows* in honor of the Bicentenary commissioned by the Art Institute of Chicago.

The Dutch artist Joep Nicolas moved with his family to New York City in 1939; there he did freelance work for the Rambusch Decorating Company and mingled with progressive young artists. In 1954 his daughter Sylvia Nicolas (1928–) embarked on a thirteen-year apprenticeship with her father, who five years later returned to Holland. Her work includes windows for the church of the Annunciation in Washington, D.C., the church of St. Pancratius in Tubbergen, the Netherlands, and the Chapel of St. Dominic, Providence College, Rhode Island, 2000. The sixty-one stained-glass panels for Providence College reflect a family tradition of fluid draftsmanship, meshing the figure, through both graphic and color, with the background.

Benoit Gilsoul (1914–2000) moved to the United States from Belgium. He distinguished himself in painting and drawing as well as mosaics and murals in Europe with over fifty solo shows in Belgium, France, and Luxembourg. In 1960 he had his first solo show in New York City, where he began working more with stained glass, in leaded and dalle-de-verre, showing breadth of scope and an ability to combine figurative ideals and Modern abstraction. He spoke of his art as an effort to "separate the visible from the invisible to give that dimension a tangible form." His many works are well represented in metropolitan New York: United Nations Interfaith Chapel (1963); St. John the Evangelist Church at 55th Street (1972); Emmanuel Lutheran Church, 88th Street; St. John's Friary, Capuchin Center; and, in New Jersey, Supreme Court Chambers, Trenton, and the Temple Shalom Somerville.

Artists like Albinus Elskus (1926–), author of *The Art of Painting on Glass* (New York, 1980), have worked in a photo-realist style highly compatible with glass. Elskus studied art and architecture in Lithuania, Germany, and France before moving to the United States, where he became acquainted with the early Arts and Crafts designers such as John Gordon Guthrie (1874–1961). In his numerous commissions he has always been able to blend his extraordinary gifts of draftsmanship with the architectural requirements of the leaded window. His influence on other artists has operated through his personality and work, but also through his many workshops, including those at the Parson's School of Design, New York, and the Pilchuck School of Glass where he was an artist-in-residence. In New Jersey his work is found at the Chapel-Mausoleum, Gate of Heaven Cemetery, East Hanover, as well as at the Mausoleum of the Good Shepherd, St. Gertrude's Cemetery, Colonia.

Very different approaches to the figure are visible today. Hans von Stockhausen (1920–) has produced a steady stream of figural work in Europe and the United States, containing both image and structural pattern sensitively coordinated with the architectural structure. Judith Schaechter (1961–) has used glass primarily in autonomous panels. Since graduating from the Rhode Island School

OPPOSITE ABOVE *In 1990 Benoit Gilsoul designed a series of window for St. Christopher's church, Parsippany, New Jersey that include the Seven Days of Creation and the Corporal Works of Mercy. For the Second Day and the separation of the waters, the hand of God traces a circle symbolizing the universe. The simplicity of the forms enhances the contemplation of the luminous quality of the glass.*

OPPOSITE BELOW *Albinus Elskus is one of the most influential proponents of figural imagery and his works show a deep sensitivity to a broad tradition. In an autonomous panel of 1983 using vitreous paint and enamels,* Homage to Pontormo, *Elskus honors a master of the Renaissance, Jacopo Pontormo (1494–1557) renowned for his vivid but enigmatic presentation of the body. The play on the oval in the egg in the upper border accentuates the abstract oval of the face and points to the basic geometry behind all natural forms.*

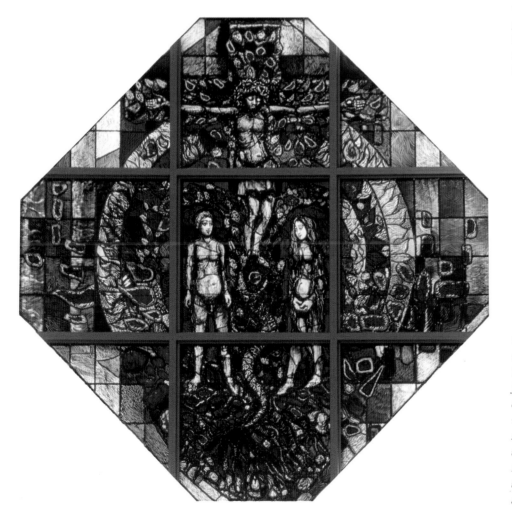

LEFT *Hans Gottfried von Stockhausen's window of* Christ the Redeemer, *1991, for the chapel of St. Joseph, Saint Joseph's University, Philadelphia, is characteristic of his work. The traditional medieval harmonies of red and blue support a densely pictorial image. Christ, the New Adam, is show upon the Tree of Knowledge from the Garden of Paradise, the serpent vanquished below and Adam and Eve on either side.*

of Design's glass program in 1983, she has exhibited widely in galleries, including the 2002 Whitney Biennial. Her vigorous figural style in the German Expressionist tradition has earned her inclusion in the Philadelphia Museum of Art, the Corning Museum of Glass, the Renwick Gallery of the Smithsonian Institution, and the Metropolitan Museum of Art, among others. She works with the color within the glass itself, using flashed glass that she models through sandblasting and engraving, adding detail with vitreous paint. Her work often features small, doll-like figures, evoking associations of size, such as the boxes of surrealist-inspired Joseph Cornell (1903-72). Using layers of glass and framing devices of pattern and color contrast she also creates strong shifts in spatial association. Narcissus Quagliata is another artist whose work is in prestigious collections, including the Victoria and Albert Museum and the Corning Museum of Glass. Paul Marioni (1941-) and Peter Mollica (1941-) continue to develop the field and teach new generations of artists.

The contemporary world is witnessing a return of figural imagery. Rauschenberg continues to produce compelling works mixing the realism of the photograph and the intense experience of gestural brushstroke that emphasizes the picture plane. David Hockney moves easily among poster-like hard edge and a more gestural form. Recently Arthur Stern (1950-) Studios developed a series of *Stations of the Cross* windows for St. Mary's parish church in Lakeport, California, combining geometric lattice and realistic black and white "snapshots" of Christ's journey drawn by Randy Dixon, an architect and religious illustrator. In the history of glass, there have been as many different kinds of windows as there have been art movements—some monumental, some intimate in scale. The success of the

window is always the ability of the designer to understand the materials and to respond to the context.

The artist in stained glass must be attuned not only to his or her own creative integrity but also to that of the architect and the users of the building. This is the method of creation that has made the art of the cathedrals retain its attraction for the modern viewer. The modern world is far more complex in its construction and financing than was the medieval era with its nobility and powerful clerics, or even the Renaissance with its elite circles of educated connoisseurs and cultivated artists. As architecture has again emerged as one of the dominant forms of artistic expression, we have seen art movements seek to eliminate the hierarchy that had crept into modern thinking between art and craft. The Bauhaus movement in Germany was founded with the presumption that all artifacts could be designed so that the aesthetic would be integral to use. Frank Lloyd Wright's direction was similar, taking his mentor Louis Sullivan's dictum "Form follows function" a step further to declare that "Form and function are one." As architecture has become more flexible and attuned to sensuality and even overt symbolism, the place of glass will continue to expand. Artists, as always, will look back to historic times when structure, adornment, and feeling united. In this survey of stained glass from its origins to the present, the author has tried to speak to the living function of the window as an element of architectural space.

OPPOSITE *Judith Schaechter's* Ship on her Shoulder, *2002, evokes various levels of associations through image and composition. Her harlequin-dressed female pirate appears to be hijacking a ship—yet she also evokes the mythological concept of the ocean filed with sea nymphs that aid transport, as well as Renaissance pageants and works of art featuring the personification of the four elements—earth, air, fire and water. Water is invariably depicted as a costumed woman wearing a headdress adorned with a ship. To add to the associations, the ship is a photo transfer from historic print, and the border of the panel inspired by Victorian advertisements.*

Glossary

Derived from The Corpus Vitrearum, United States of America.

Abrade (abrasion): to selectively remove the colored surface layer of FLASHED GLASSES to reveal the uncolored base glass, by scratching or grinding it away using an iron point, file, wheel, or bit.

Acid etching: the selective removal of the colored layer of glass from FLASHED GLASS by the application of hydrofluoric acid (cf. Abrasion). This technique seemed to have been used sporadically since the late fifteenth century, but it was not widely practiced until the nineteenth century.

Antique glass: a term used after the revival of stained glass in the nineteenth century to indicate hand-blown (also referred to as "mouth-blown") glasses manufactured to resemble medieval ones.

Cartoon: a full size rendering of the sketch for windows or panels. Generally, the leadlines, the details to be painted on the glass, and the colors of the glass are indicated on the cartoon.

Cold paint: unfired paint found on a stained glass window. Most glass paints are fired for permanence.

Copper foil (copper foiling): a technique of joining pieces of glass in a stained glass panel in which thin strips of copper are wrapped around the edges of the pieces of glass which are then joined together by applying solder to the exposed upper and lower surfaces of the copper foil. This technique was used extensively in the creation of stained glass windows in the US in the late nineteenth and throughout the twentieth centuries, as well as in the restoration of older stained glass.

Drapery glass: a technique normally associated with opalescent glass in the US from the 1880s though the 1930s. A ladle of glass was thrown on a metal table and, before it cooled, manipulated with rollers and tongs until it formed ridges and folds.

Enamel: vitreous colorant fired on the glass. Enamel is a vitreous material consisting of a base of ground glass with metallic oxide(s) and suspended in an organic medium for application to the glass; it could be spread like paint. Upon firing, the medium burns off and the enamel fuses with the glass substrate. Enamels were not commonly used on window glass until the sixteenth century, although there are a few known examples in Austria and Germany in the early fifteenth century.

Flashed glass: by the fourteenth century the most common technique for making red glass. A molten gather (a glob of glass adhering to a blowpipe) of one color is coated with a thicker gather of a different color, usually clear, or a tint of green, yellow, etc. This layered gather is then blown into a sheet. More than one colored layer is possible.

Glazier: artisan working in stained glass (and, today, sheet glass).

Glazing: assembling the glass and lead on the bench.

Grisaille: a window or panel or ornamental (geometric or floral) designs, composed almost exclusively of uncolored glass in which the designs are created by the leads alone, called blank glazing, or with the addition of PAINT and SILVER STAIN.

Grozing: a method of shaping a piece of glass by using a grozing iron, or notched iron bar, to nibble the edges of the glass. Today grozing pliers are used.

Lead came: a strip of lead, H-shaped in section, which provides the structural network that holds the glass pieces together. The cross bar of the "H" which separates the two edges (the flanges) is called the heart of the lead.

Mat (matting): an evenly applied wash of PAINT, usually providing half-tone shading. It is manipulated with brushes to attain different textures, from smooth to stippled and was normally applied before the TRACE.

Opalescent glass: a glass introduced in windows in the 1880's with the work of John La Farge and Louis Comfort Tiffany. The glass varied from a translucent to a semi-translucent milky glass. It is often streaky, with a mixture of different colors.

Paint: the paint used on glass in all periods was normally vitreous. It consisted of a mixture of finely ground glass, iron or copper oxide, and flux, applied to the glass with a brush and fired.

Pot-metal glass: glass which is colored by metallic oxides in the glass composition.

Refractive index: the amount a ray of light is bent when traveling from air into a solid. By matching the refractive index of a particular glass (it varies depending on the composition of the glass) and conservation adhesive, it is possible to achieve a less noticeable repair.

Score: a deep scratch made on the glass to guide a break.

Silver stain: a transparent yellow stain produced from the early fourteenth century on containing a compound of silver. It is applied to the glass surface and fired. During the firing, silver ions migrate into the glass and are suspended within the glass network, rather than fused onto the surface.

Solder: an alloy of lead and tin which has a lower melting point than lead and can, therefore, be used in its molten form to join LEAD CAMES in a stained glass panel.

Stopgap: a piece of old glass (not necessarily contemporary with the panel) used in restoration to fill a loss.

Trace: a dark, usually opaque paint line typically used for the contours. It is often applied over the MAT.

Waxed-up: individual pieces of glass are temporarily adhered to a larger sheet of plate glass using a mixture of beeswax and rosin to facilitate glass selection and painting.

General Bibliography

See also Chapter Bibliography

Stained Glass, published by the Stained Glass Association of America.

Journal of Glass Studies, published by the Corning Museum of Glass.

Journal of Stained Glass published by the British Society of Master Glass Painters.

Series publications: CVMA: Corpus Vitrearum Medii Aevi.

Art, Technique et Science: La creation du vitrail de 1830 à 1930. International Colloquium, Liège, 11–13 May 2000. Dossier de la Commission Royale des Monuments, Sites, et Fouilles de la Région wallone, Liège, 7: Liège, 2000.

Brown, Sarah. *Stained Glass: An Illustrated History.* New York, Crescent Books, 1992.

Caviness, Madeline H. assist. by Evelyn Staudinger. *Stained Glass before 1540: An Annotated Bibliography,* Boston: G. K. Hall, 1983.

Brady, Darlene and William Serban. *Stained Glass: A Guide to Information Sources,* Detroit: Gale Research Co, 1980.

Brisac, Catherine. *A Thousand Years of Stained Glass.* Doubleday & Co.: New York, 1986.

Lévy, Edmond. *Histoire de la peinture sur verre en Europe et particulièrement en Belgique,* Brussels: Tircher, 1860.

Representations architecturales dans les vitraux, International Colloquium of the Corpus Vitrearum, Brussels, 22–27 August 2002. Dossier de la Commission Royale des Monuments, Sites, et Fouilles de la Région wallone, Liège, 9: 2002.

Morris, Elizabeth. *Stained and Decorative Glass,* New York, 1988.

Sturm, James L. *Stained Glass from Medieval Times to the Present: Treasures to be Seen in New York,* New York: E. P. Dutton, Inc., 1982.

Westlake, Nathanial J. *A History of Design in Painted Glass* (four vols.) London: James Parker, 1881–94.

AUSTRIA CVMA
I. Frodl-Kraft, Eva. *Die mittelalterlichen Glasgemälde in Wien,* Vienna, 1962.

II.1. Frodl-Kraft, Eva, *Die mittelalterlichen Glasgemälde in Niederösterreich, I: Albrechtsberg-Klosterneuburg,* Vienna, 1972.

III.1. Bacher, Ernst, *Die mittelalterlichen Glasgemälde in der Steiermark. I. Graz und Strassengel,* Vienna, 1979.

BELGIUM
Grieten, Stephaan, Marc Mees, Jan Van Damme and Linda Van Langendonck. *Een Venster op de Hemel: De Glasramen van de Onze-Lieve-Vrouwekathedraal van Antwerpen,* Antwerp, 1996.

Vanden Bemden, Yvette, Jost Caen, Warner Berckmans, Anne Malliet, and Lode Lambrechts, *Glas in Lood,* Brussels: Ministerie van de Vlaamse Gemeenschap, Bestuur Monumenten en Landschappen, 1992.

CZECH REPUBLIC CVMA
Matous, Frantisek, *Mittelalterliche Glasmalerei in der Tschechoslowakei,* Prague, 1975.

FRANCE
Aubert, Marcel, et al. *Le Vitrail français,* Paris: Editions Deux Mondes, 1958.

CVMA France Recensement Series
I. *Les vitraux de Paris, de la Région parisienne, de la Picardie et du Nord-Pas-de-Calais,* Paris, 1978.

II. *Les vitraux du Centre et des Pays de la Loire,* Paris, 1981.

III. *Les vitraux de Bourgogne, Franche-Comté et Rhône-Alpes,* Paris, 1986.

IV. *Les vitraux de Champagne-Ardenne,* Paris, 1992.

V. Herold, Michel and Gatouillat, Françoise. *Les vitraux de Lorraine et d'Alsace,* Paris, 1994.

VI. Id. M. Callias Bey, V. Chaussé. *Les vitraux de Haute-Normandie,* Paris, 2001.

GERMANY
Oidtmann, Heinrich. *Die rheinischen Glasmalereien vom 12. bis zum 16. Jahrhundert,* Vols. 1–2, Düsseldorf: L. Schwann, 1912, 1929.

Wentzel, Hans. *Meisterwerke der Glasmalerei,* Berlin, Deutscher Verein für Kunstwissenschaft, 1954.

Beeh-Lustenberger, Suzanne. *Glasmalerei um 800–1900 im Hessischen Landesmuseum in Darmstadt,* plate vol., Frankfurt am Main, 1967; text vol., Hanau, 1973.

Lymant, Brigitte. *Die Glasmalereien des Schnütgen Museums, Bestandskatalog,* Cologne, 1982

CVMA Germany Catalogue Series
I.1. Wentzel, Hans. *Die Glasmalereien in Schaben von 1200–1350,* Berlin, 1958.

I.2. Becksmann, Rüdiger. *Die mittelalterlichen Glasmalereien in Schwaben von 1350–1530 (ohne Ulm),* Berlin, 1986.

I.3. Scholz, Hartmut. *Die mittelalterlichen Glasmalereien in Ulm,* Berlin, 1994.

II.1. Becksmann, Rüdiger. *Die mittelalterlichen Glasmalereien in Baden und der Plafz (ohne Freiburg),* Berlin, 1979.

III.2. Hess, Daniel. *Die mittelalterlichen Glasmalereien in Frankfurt und im Rhein-Main-Gebiet,* Berlin, 1999.

IV.1. Rode, Herbert. *Die mittelalterlichen Glasmalereien des Kölner Domes,* Berlin, 1974.

VII.2. Becksmann, Rüdiger, and Ulf-Dietrich Korn. *Die mittelalterlichen Glasmalereien in Lüneburg und den Heideklöstern,* Berlin, 1992.

XIII.1. Fritzche, Gabriela. *Die mittelalterlichen Glasmalereien im Regensburger Dom,* 2 vol., Berlin, 1987.

XV.1. Drachenberg, Erhard, Karl-Joachim Maercker and Christa Schmidt. *Die mittelalterliche Glasmalerei in den Ordenskirchen und im Angermuseum zu Erfurt,* Berlin, 1976 (DDR 1,1).

XV.2. Drachenberg, Erhard. *Die mittelalterliche Glasmalerei im Erfurter Dom,* Berlin, 1980 and 1983 (DDR 1,2).

XVI. Richter, Christa. *Die mittelalterlichen Glasmalereien in Mülhausen Thüringen,* Berlin, 1992.

XVIII.1. Maercker, Karl-Joachim. *Die mittelalterlichen Glasmalereien im Stendaler Dom,* Berlin, 1988 (DDR 5,1).

XVIII.2. Maercker, Karl-Joachim. *Die mittelalterliche Glasmalerei in der Stendaler Jacobikirche,* Berlin, 1995.

GREAT BRITAIN
Read, Sir Herbert. *English Stained Glass.* London: G. B Putnams, 1926.

Marks, Richard. *Stained Glass in England during the Middle Ages,* Toronto: University of Toronto Press, 1993.

CVMA Great Britain, Summary Catalogue Series
3. Hebgin-Barnes, Penny. *The Medieval Stained Glass of the County of Lincolnshire,* London, 1996.

4. Marks, Richard. *The Medieval Stained Glass of the County of Hamptonshire,* London, 1998.

CVMA Great Britain, Catalogues
I. Newton, Peter, with the collaboration of Jill Kerr. *The County of Oxford. A Catalogue of Medieval Stained Glass* London, 1979.

II. Caviness, Madeline A. *The Windows of Christ Church Cathedral, Canterbury,* London, 1971.

III.1. French, Thomas, David O'Connor. *The Medieval Painted Glass of York Minster, fasc. I., The West Windows of the Nave,* London 1987

ITALY
Marchini, Giuseppe. *Italian Stained Glass Windows,* New York, 1956.

PORTUGAL CVMA
Vitorino Da Silva Barros, Carlos. *O vitral em Portugal,* Lisbon, 1983.

SCANDINAVIA (NORWAY, SWEDEN, FINLAND) CVMA
Andersson, Aaron, Sigrid Christie, Carl A. Nordman, Aage Roussel. *Die mittelalterlichen Glasmalereien Skandinaviens,* Stockholm, 1964.

SPAIN
Nieto Alcaide, Victor, et al. *La Vidriera Española del gùtico al siglo XXI* [exh. cat. Fundaciùn Santander Central Hispano] Madrid, 2001.

CVMA Catalogues
VI. Catalonia I. Ainaud I De Lasarte, Joan, Joan Vila-Grau, and M. Assumpta Escudero I Ribot. *Els Vitralls Medievals de l'Esglesia de Santa Maria del Mar a Barcelona,* Barcelona, 1985.

VII. Catalonia II. Ainaud I De Lasarte, Joan, Joan Vila-Grau, M. Assumpta Escudero I Ribot, Antoni Vila I Delclos, Jaume Marques, Gabriel Roura, and Josep M. Marques. *Els Vitralls de la catedral de Girona,* Barcelona, 1987.

VIII. Catalonia III. Ainaud I De Lasarte, Joan, Joan Vila-Grau, and Antoni Vila I Delclos. *Els Vitralls del monestir de Santes Creus i de la catedral de Tarragona,* Barcelona, 1992.

IX. Catalonia IV. Ainaud I De Lasarte, Joan, Joan Vila-Grau, and Antoni Vila I Delclos. *Les vitralls de la catedral de Barcelona I del Monastir de Pedralbes,* Barcelona, 1997.

SWITZERLAND CVMA CATALOGUES
I. Beer, Ellen J. *Die Glasmalereien der Schweiz vom 12. bis zum Beginn des 14. Jahrhunderts,* Basle, 1956.

III. Beer, Ellen J. *Die Glasmalereien der Schweiz aus dem 14. und 15. Jahrhundert, ohne Königsfelden und Berner Münsterchor,* Basle, 1965.

UNITED STATES OF AMERICA CVMA
Checklist Series
I. Caviness, Madeline H., ed. *Stained Glass before 1700 in American Collections: New England and New York States* (Studies in the History of Art, 15) Washington D.C., 1985.

II. Caviness, Madeline H., ed. *Stained Glass before 1700 in American Collections: Mid-Atlantic and Southeastern Seabord States* (Studies in the History of Art, 23) Washington D.C., 1987.

III. Caviness, Madeline H., and Michael N. Cothren, eds. *Stained Glass before 1700 in American Collections: Midwestern and Western States* (Studies in the History of Art, 28) Washington D.C., 1989.

IV. Husband, Timothy B. *Stained Glass before 1700 in American Collections: Silver-stained Roundels and Unipartite Panels* (Studies in the History of Art, 39) Washington D.C.,1991.

Occasional Papers
I. Caviness, Madeline H. and Timothy B. Husband, eds. *Studies in Medieval Stained Glass: Selected Papers from the XIth International Colloquium of the Corpus Vitrearum, New York, 1–6 June 1982,* New York, 1985

Catalogues
VIII/2. Raguin, Virginia and Helen Zakin with contributions by Elizabeth Pastan. *Stained Glass before 1700 in the Collections of the Midwest States* [Illinois, Indiana, Ohio, Michigan], London: Harvey Miller Publishers, 2001.

Chapter Bibliography

See also General Bibliography

1 SYMBOL AND STORY: THE ART OF STAINED GLASS

Durandus: Guillaume Durand de Mende. *Manuel pour comprendre la signification symbolique des cathédrales et des églises*, Le Pin de Luquet: La Maison de Vie, 1996.

Hammond, Mason, "The Stained Glass Windows of Memorial Hall, Harvard University," typescript, Cambridge, Massachusetts, 1978.

Hearn, Millard F. "Canterbury Cathedral and the Cult of Thomas Becket," *Art Bulletin* 76 (1994): 19–52.

Hillgarth, J. N., ed. *Christianity and Paganism, 350–750*, Philadelphia: University of Pennsylvania Press, 1986.

Hirshler, Erica E. *A Studio of Her Own: Women Artists in Boston 1870–1940*, Boston: Museum of Fine Arts, 2001.

Lasko, Peter. *Ars Sacra: 800–1200*, Harmondsworth: Penguin Books, 1972.

Luneau, Jean. *Monuments, Sites, et Fouilles de la Région wallone*, Liège, 7: Liège, 2000, 129–38.

Raguin, Virginia, Kathryn Brush and Peter Draper, eds. *Artistic Integration in Gothic Buildings*, Toronto: Toronto University Press, 1995.

Id. "The Living Museum of the American City: Reflections on Stained Glass In Buildings and Museum," *Journal of the Walters Art Gallery* 52/53 (1994/95): 49–60.

Id. "Memorial Hall Windows Designed by Sarah Wyman Whitman," *Harvard Library Bulletin*, new series 11/1 (2000): 29–53.

Panofsky, Erwin, ed. *Abbot Suger on the Abbey Church of St. Denis and its Art Treasures*, 1946, second ed., Gerda Panofsky-Soergel, Princeton, 1979.

Smith, Betty S. "Inside SPNEA: Sarah de St. Prix Wyman Whitman," *Old-Time New England* 77/266 (1999): 46–64.

Vasiliu, Anca. "Le mot et le verre: une définition médiévale du 'diaphane,'" *Journal des Savants* (Jan.-June 1994): 135–63.

Voelkle, William. *The Stavelot Triptych: Mosan Art and the Legend of the True Cross*, New York: The Pierpont Morgan Library, 1980.

Weis, Helene. "Those Old Familiar Faces," *Stained Glass* 86/3 (1991): 204–7, 216–18.

Wolff, Arnold. *Der kölner Dom*, Cologne: Vista Point Verlag, 1995.

2 ORIGINS, MATERIALS, AND THE GLAZIER'S ART

Bray, Charles. *Dictionary of Glass: Materials and Techniques*, Philadelphia: University of Pennsylvania Press, 1995.

Brill, Robert H. *Chemical Analyses of Early Glasses*, 2 vols., Corning: Corning Museum of Glass, 1999.

Brown, Sarah and David O'Connor. *Medieval Craftsmen: Glass-Painters*, Toronto: University of Toronto Press, 1991.

Caviness, Madeline H. *Stained Glass Windows* (*Typologie des sources du moyen âge occidental*, 75), Turnhout, Belgium: Brepols, 1996.

Carboni, Stefano and David Whitehouse with contributions from Robert H. Brill and William Gudenrath. *Glass of the Sultans*, New Haven: Yale University Press, 2001.

Down, Jane L. "The Yellowing of Epoxy Resin Adhesives: Report of High-Intensity Aging," *Studies in Conservation* 31 (1986): 159–70.

Duthie, Arthur Louis. *Decorative Glass Processes*, 1911; repr. New York: Dover Publications, 1982.

Elskus, Albinas. *The Art of Painting on Glass: Techniques and Designs for Stained Glass*, New York: Charles Scribners Sons, 1980.

Grisaille, Jaune d'Argent, Sanguine, Email, et Peinture à Froid: Techniques et Conservation, International Forum for the Conservation and Restoration of Stained Glass, Liège, 19–22 June 1996. Dossier de la Commission Royale des Monuments, Sites, et Fouilles de la Région wallone, Liège, 3: Liège, 1996.

Higgins, Mary Clerkin. "Harry Clarke and his Geneva Window," *Stained Glass* 88 (Spring 1993): 17–25.

Hammesfahr, James E. and Claire L. Strong, *Creative Glass Blowing*, New York: W. H. Freeman, 1968.

Merrifield, Mary P. *Medieval and Renaissance Treatises on the Arts of Painting, Original Texts with English Translations*, London: J. Murray, 1849; repr. Mineola, New York: Dover Publications, 1999.

Newton, Roy G. *The Deterioration and Conservation of Painted Glass: A Critical Bibliography and Three Research Papers*, CVMA Great Britain, Occasional Papers I. London, 1974.

Id. *The Deterioration and Conservation of Painted Glass: A Critical Bibliography*, CVMA Great Britain, Occasional Papers II. London, 1982.

Newton, Roy G. and Sandra Davidson. *Conservation of Glass*, Oxford: Butlerworth Heinemann, 1996.

Reyntiens, Patrick, *The Technique of Stained Glass*, London: Batsford, 1967.

Stained Glass Association of America. *Reference and Technical Manual: A Comprehensive Guide to Stained Glass*, 2nd Edition. Lee's Summit: The Stained Glass Association of America, 1992.

Royce Roll, Donald. "The Colors of Romanesque Stained Glass," *Journal of Glass Studies* 36 (1994): 71–80

Tennent, N. and J. Townsend, "The Significance of the Refractive Index of Adhesives for Glass Repair," *Adhesives and Consolidants* (1984): 205–212.

Theophilus: John G. Hawthorne and Cyril Stanley Smith, eds. *Theophilus On Divers Arts: The Foremost Medieval Treatise on Painting, Glassmaking, and Metalwork*, New York: Dover Publications, 1979.

3 THE REVIVAL OF MONUMENTAL ARCHITECTURE AND THE PLACE OF GLASS

Bernard of Clairvaux – see below Rudolf, Conrad.

Beyer, Victor, Christiane Wild-Block, and Fridtjof Zschokke, with the collaboration of Claudine Lautier. *Les vitraux de la cathédrale Notre-Dame de Strasbourg*, CVMA France IX.1, Paris, 1986.

Caviness, Madeline H. *The Early Stained Glass of Canterbury Cathedral: circa 1175–1220*, Princeton: Princeton University Press, 1977.

Id. *Sumptuous Arts at the Royal Abbeys in Reims and Braine: Ornatus Elegantiae, Varietate Stupendes*, Princeton: Princeton University Press, 1990.

Id. *Paintings on Glass: Studies in Romanesque and Gothic Monumental Art*, Aldershot, Hampshire: Valorium, 1997, which includes "Bible Stories in Windows: Were They Bibles for the Poor?" entry XII.

Cothren, Michael. "Suger's Stained Glass Masters and their Workshop at Saint-Denis," in *Paris: Center of Artistic Enlightenment, Papers in the History of Art from the Pennsylvania State University*, IV (1988): 46–75.

Drachenberg, Erhard, Karl-Joachim Maercker and Christa Schmidt. *Die mittelalterliche Glasmalerei in den Ordenskirchen und im Angermuseum zu Erfurt*, CVMA Germany, XV.1, Berlin, 1976.

Frank, Jacqueline. "The Moses Window from the Abbey Church of Saint-Denis: Text and Image in Twelfth-Century Art," *Gazette des Beaux-Arts* 128 (1996): 179–94.

Gerson, Paula Lieber. *Abbot Suger and Saint-Denis: A Symposium*, New York: Metropolitan Museum of Art, 1986.

Grodecki, Louis. *Les vitraux de Saint-Denis: Étude sur le vitrail au XIIᵉ siècle, I. Histoire et restitution*, CVMA France, Studies Series I, Paris, 1976.

Id. *Études sur les vitraux de Suger à Saint-Denis (XIIᵉ siècle)*, CVMA France, Studies Series I.2, Paris, 1995.

Grodecki, Louis with Catherine Brisac and Claudine Lautier. *Le Vitrail roman*, Fribourg: Office du Livre, 1977.

Martin, Frank. *Die Glasmalereien von San Francesco in Assisi*, Regensburg: Schnell und Steiner, 1997.

Panofsky, Erwin, ed. *Abbot Suger on the Abbey Church of St.-Denis and its Art Treasures*, 1946, second ed, Gerda Panofsky-Soergel, Princeton, 1979.

Rudolf, Conrad. *The "Things of Greater Importance": Bernard of Clairvaux's Apologia and the Medieval Attitude Towards Art*, Philadelphia: University of Philadelphia Press, 1990.

Zakin, Helen Jackson. *French Cistercian Grisaille Glass*, New York, 1979.

4 THE AGE OF GREAT CATHEDRALS: THIRTEENTH TO FIFTEENTH CENTURIES

Arnold, Hugh, and Lawrence B. Saint. *Stained Glass in England and France*, 1913; repr. New York: The Macmillan Company, 1955.

Aubert, Marcel, Louis Grodecki, Jean Lafond, and Jean Verrier. *Les vitraux de Notre-Dame et de la Sainte-Chapelle de Paris*, CVMA France I.1, Paris, 1959.

Bierschenk, Monika. *Glasmalereien der Elisabethkirche in Marburg*, Berlin: Deutscher Verlag für Kunstwissenschaft, 1991.

Grodecki, Louis and Catherine Brisac. *Le Vitrail gothique 1200–1300*, Fribourg: Office du Livre, 1984; trans. *Gothic Stained Glass*, Ithaca: Cornell University Press, 1985.

Kemp, Wolfgang. *The Narratives of Gothic Stained Glass*, Cambridge: Cambridge University Press, 1997.

Jordan, Alyce A. *Visualizing Kingship in the Windows of the Sainte-Chapelle*, Turnout, Belgium, Brepols, 2002.

Lafond, Jean, with the collaboration of Paul Popesco and Françoise Perrot. *Les vitraux de l'église Saint-Ouen de Rouen, I, Les vitraux du choeur*, CVMA France IV.2, Paris, 1970.

Lillich, Meredith, *The Stained Glass of Saint-Père de Chartres*, Middletown Conn.: Wesleyan University Press, 1978.

Id. *Rainbow Like an Emerald: Stained Glass in Lorraine in the Thirteenth and Early Fourteenth Centuries*, University Park: The Pennsylvania State University Press, 1991.

Id. *Armor of Light: Stained Glass in Western France 1250–1325*, Berkeley: University of California Press, 1994.

Manhes-Deremble, Colette, with the collaboration of Jean-Paul Deremble. *Les vitraux narratifs de la cathédrale de Chartres*, CVMA France, Studies Series II, Paris, 1993.

Papanicolau, Linda. "The Other Tours Genesis Window," *Gesta* 37/2 (1998): 225–31.

Raguin, Virginia. *Stained Glass in Thirteenth-Century Burgundy*, Princeton: Princeton University Press, 1982.

Ritter, Georges. *Les Vitraux de la cathédrale de Rouen*, Cognac, 1926.

Schubert, Ernst. *Der Naumburger Dom*, Halle an der Saale: Verlag Janos Stekovics, 1996.

Westermann-Angerhausen, Hiltrud, with Carola Hagnau, Claudia Schumacher, et al. *Himmelslicht: Europäische Glasmalerei im Jahrhundert des kölner Dombaus (1248–1349)* [exh. cat., Schnütgen-Museum] Cologne, 1998.

William, Jane Welch. *Bread Wine & Money. The Windows of the Trades at Chartres Cathedral*, Chicago: University of Chicago Press, 1993.

5 FIFTEENTH- AND SIXTEENTH-CENTURY TRANSFORMATION OF THE NARRATIVE

Anderes, Bernhard. *Glasmalerei im Kreuzgang Muri, Kabinettscheiben der Renaissance*, Bern: Hallwag, 1974

Boesch, Paul. *Die alten Glasmaler von Winterthur und ihr Werk: 286 Neujahrsblatt der Stadtbibliothek Winterthur*, Winterthur, 1955.

Id. *Die schweizer Glasmalerei*, Basel: Birkhäuser, 1955.

Id. *Die alte Glasmalerei in St. Gallen: 96. Neujahrsblatt der Historischen Verein des Kantons St. Gallen*, St. Gallen, 1956.

Butts, Barbara, and Lee Hendrix, with essays by Hartmut Scholz, Barbara Giesieke. *Painting on Light* [exh. cat., The J. Paul Getty Museum] Los Angeles, 2000.

Cole, William. *A Catalogue of Netherlandish and North European Roundels in Britain*, CVMA Great Britain, Summary Catalogue Series 1, London, 1993.

French, Thomas. *York Minster: The Great East Window*, CVMA Great Britain, Summary Catalogue Series 2, Oxford, 1995.

Gothic and Renaissance Art in Nuremberg, 1300–1550 [exh. cat., Metropolitan Museum of Art] New York, 1986.

Husband, Timothy B. *The Luminous Image: Painted Glass Roundels in the Lowlands, 1480–1560* [exh. cat. The Metropolitan Museum of Art] New York, 1995.

Knowles, John A. *The York School of Glass Painting*, New York: The Macmillan Company, 1936.

Lehmann, Hans. *Geschichte der luzerner Glasmalerei von der Anfängen bis zu Beginn des 18. Jahrhunderts*, Lucern, Keller & Co. 1942.

Raguin, Virginia. *Northern Renaissance Stained Glass: Continuity and Transformations* [exh. cat., Iris & B. Gerald Cantor Art Gallery, College of the Holy Cross] Worcester, Mass., 1987.

Rushforth, Gordon McNeil. *Medieval Christian Imagery as Illustrated by the Painted Windows of Great Malvern Priory Church, Worcestershire, Together with a Descriptions and Explanation of All the Ancient Glass in the Church*, Oxford: Clarendon, 1936.

Schneider, Jenny. *Glasgemälde: Katalog der Sammlung des Schweizerischen Landesmuseums, Zürich*, 2 vols., Stafa: Th. Gut, 1970

Scholz, Hartmut. *Entwurf und Ausführung: Werkstattpraxis in der Nürnberger Glasmalerei der Dürerzeit*, CVMA Germany, Studies Series 1, Berlin, 1991.

Woodforde, Christopher. *The Norwich School of Glass-Painting in the Fifteenth Century*, London: Oxford University Press, 1950.

6 LARGE-SCALE RENAISSANCE STAINED GLASS

Belgium

Lévy, Edmond. *Histoire de la peinture sur verre en Europe et particulièrement en Belgique*, Brussels: Tircher, 1860.

Helbig, Jean. *Les vitraux de la première moitié du XVIe siècle conservés en Belgique. Anvers et Flandres*, CVMA Belgium II, Brussels, 1968.

Helbig, Jean and Yvette Vanden Bemden. *Les vitraux de la première moitié du XVIe siècle conservés en Belgique. Brabant et Limbourg*, CVMA Belgium III, Ghent/Ledeberg, 1974.

Vanden Bemden, Yvette. *Les vitraux de la première moitié du XVIe siècle conservés en Belgique. Liège, Luxembourg et Namur*, CVMA Belgium IV, Ghent/Ledeberg, 1981.

Vanden Bemden, Yvette. *Les vitraux de la première moitié du XVIe siècle conservés en Belgique. Province de Hainaut, fascicule 1. La Collégiale Sainte-Waudru de Mons*, CVMA Belgium V, Namur, 2000.

Vanden Bemden, Yvette, Chantal Fontaine-Hodiamont and Arnout Balis. *Cartons de vitraux du XVIIe siècle. La cathédrale Saint-Michel, Bruxelles*, CVMA Belgium, Studies Series I, Brussels, 1994.

France

Herold, Michel. *Les vitraux de Saint-Nicolas-de-Port*, CVMA France VIII.1, Paris, 1993.

Leproux, Guy-Michel. *Recherches sur les peintres-verriers parisiens de la Renaissance (1540–1620)*, Paris, 1988.

Leproux, Guy-Michel, et al., *Vitraux parisiens de la Renaissance* [exh. cat., Rotonde de la Villette] Paris, 1993.

Mémoire de verre: vitraux champenois de la Renaissance, Châlons-sur-Marne: Inventaire de Champagne-Ardenne, 1990.

Great Britain

Brown, Sarah and Lindsay MacDonald, eds. *Life, Death, and Art: The Medieval Stained Glass of Fairford Parish Church*, Phoenix Mill, Gloucestershire: Sutton Publishing: Cheltenham and Gloucestershire College of Higher Education, 1997.

Wayment, Hilary. *The Windows of King's College Chapel, Cambridge*, CVMA Great Britain, Supplemental Volume I, London, 1972.

Italy

Burnham, Renée. *Le Vetrate del Duomo di Pisa*, CVMA Italy II, Pisa, 2003.

Luchs, Alison. "Stained Glass above Renaissance Altars: Figural Windows in Italian Church Architecture from Brunelleschi to Bramante," *Zeitschrift für Kunstgeschichte* 48 (1958): 177–211.

Marchini, Giuseppe. *Le vetrate dell'Umbria*, Rome: DeLuca, 1973.

Id. *Italian Stained Glass Windows*, London: Thames and Hudson, 1957.

Pirina, Caterina. *Le vetrate del Duomo di Milano (1400–1530)*, CVMA Italy 1. Milan, 1986.

The Netherlands

Van Harten-Boers, Henny and Zsuzsanna Van Ruyven-Zeman with the collaboration of Christiane E. Coebergh-Surie and Herman Janse. *The Stained Glass Windows in the Sint Janskerk at Gouda. The Glazing of the Clerestory of the Choir and of the former Monastic Church of the Regulars*, CVMA The Netherlands I, Amsterdam, 1997.

Van Ruyven-Zeman, Zsuzsanna, *The Stained Glass Windows in the Sint Janskerk at Gouda 1556–1604*, CVMA The Netherlands III, Amsterdam, 2000.

Spain and Portugal

Nieto Alcaide, Victor. *Las vidrieras de la catedral de Sevilla*, CVMA Spain I. Madrid, 1969.

Nieto Alcaide, Victor with the collaboration of Carlos Munoz De Pablo, CVMA Spain II. *Las vidrieras de la catedral de Granada*, Granada, 1973.

Vitorino Da Silva Barros, Carlos. *O vitral em Portugal*, CVMA Portugal, Lisbon, 1983.

Switzerland

Kurmann-Schwarz, Brigitte, *Die Glasmalereien des 15. bis 18. Jahrhunderts in Berner Münster*, CVMA Switzerland IV, Berlin, 1998.

7 THE REVIVAL OF STAINED GLASS IN THE UNITED KINGDOM AND THE UNITED STATES

Bayne, S. M. B. *Heaton, Butler & Bayne, A Hundred Years of the Art of Stained Glass*, Lausanne: Imprimerie Marendaz, 1986.

Clark, Willene. *The Stained Glass Art of William Jay Bolton* Syracuse: Syracuse University Press, 1992.

Cormack, Peter. *Henry Holiday 1839–1927* [exh. cat. William Morris Gallery] London, 1989.

Day, Lewis F. *Windows: A Book about Stained and Painted Glass*, London: Batsford, 1897.

Drake, Maurice. *The Costessey Collection of Stained Glass, Formerly in the Possession of George William Jerningham, 8th Baron Stafford of Costessey in the County of Norfolk*, intro. Aymer Vallance, Exeter: W. Pollard & Co, 1920.

Farnsworth, Jean. "The Stained Glass of New Orleans," *Stained Glass* 85/4 (Fall 1990): 282–90.

Farnsworth, Jean. *see* Chapter 8.

Frueh, Erne R. and Florence. *Chicago Stained Glass*. Chicago: Loyola University Press, 1983.

Fowler, William. *Colored Engraving of Roman Pavements, also of the Stained Glass windows of the Cathedrals of York, Lincoln, etc.* Vols. I–IV. Winterton, Yorkshire, 1796–1829.

Hampp: *Ancient Flemish Glass* [sale cat. Christies, 7 May] London, 1816.

Harrison, Martin. *Victorian Stained Glass*. London: Barrie and Jenkins, 1980.

Haward, Birkin. *Nineteenth Century Suffolk Stained Glass*, Norwich, England: Geo Books, 1984.

Haward, Birkin. *Nineteenth Century Norfolk Stained Glass*, Norwich, England: Geo Books, 1984.

Howe, Katherine S. and David B. Warren. *The Gothic Revival Style in America 1830–1870* [exh. cat. Museum of Fine Arts, Houston] Houston, 1976.

Lafond, Jean. "Le commerce des vitraux étrangers anciens en Angleterre au XVIIIe et au XIXe siècles," *Revue des Sociétés Savants de Haute-Normandie* 10 (1960): 5–15.

Marks, Richard. "The Reception and Display of Northern European Roundels in England," *Gesta* 37/2 (1998): 217–24.

Morris, William. *Society for the Protection of Ancient Buildings, Annual Reports* 7 (1884): 49–76; text reprinted as "The Mediaeval and the Modern Craftsman," *Merry England* 3 (October, 1884): 361–77.

Quellet-Soguel, Nicole and Walter Tschopp. *Clement Heaton, 1861–1940 Londres – Neuchatel – New York*. Hauterive, Switzerland, Editions Gilles Attinger, 1996.

Rackham, Bernard. "English Importations of Foreign Stained Glass in the Early Nineteenth Century," *Journal of the British Society of Master Glass Painters* 2 (1927): 87–94.

Raguin, Virginia. "Antiquarianism, Publication, and Revival: Stained Glass in the Nineteenth Century," in Virginia Raguin and Mary Ann Powers, *Sacred Spaces: Building and Remembering Sites of Worship in the Nineteenth Century* [exh. cat., Iris & B. Gerald Cantor Art Gallery, College of the Holy Cross] Worcester, Mass., 2002, 27–46.

Id. "Revivals, Revivalists, and Architectural Stained Glass," *The Journal of the Society of Architectural Historians* 49 (1990): 110–139.

Sewter, A. Charles. *The Stained Glass of William Morris and His Circle, 2 vols. Study and Catalogue*, New Haven: Yale University Press, 1974–75.

Shepard, Mary B. "'Our Fine Gothic Magnificence': The Nineteenth-Century Chapel at Costessy Hall (Norfolk) and its Medieval Glazing," *Journal of the Society of Architectural Historians* 54 (1995): 186–207.

Shepherd, Stanley A. in Paul Atterbury and Clive Wainwright, eds., *Pugin: A Gothic Passion*, New Haven: Yale University Press, 1994, 195–206.

Sherry, Beverley. *Australia's Historic Stained Glass*. Sydney: Murray Child, 1991.

Smith, Elizabeth Bradford, Kathryn McClintock, R. Aaron Rottner, et al. *Medieval Art in America: Patterns of Collecting 1800–1940* [exh. cat., Palmer Museum of Art, The Pennsylvania State University] University Park, Pa., 1996.

Stavridi, Margaret. *Master of Glass. Charles Eamer Kempe 1837–1907*, Hatfield, Herts.: John Taylor Book Ventures, 1988.

Vanden Bemden, Yvette and Jill Kerr. "The Glass of Herkenrode Abbey," *Archaeologia* 108 (1986): 189–226.

Id., "A Group of 16th-century Panels from the Low Countries Now in British Churches, *The Journal of Stained Glass* 18/1 (1983–84): 32–39.

Waring, J. B. *Catalogue of Drawings from Ancient Glass Paintings by the Late Charles Winston Esq. of the Inner Temple* [exh. cat. The Arundel Society] London, 1865.

Warrington, William. *History of Stained Glass from the Earliest Period of the Art to the Present Time*, London, 1848.

Winston, Charles. *An Inquiry into the Difference of Style Observable in Ancient Glass Paintings, especially in England: with Hints on Glass Painting, by an Amateur*, Oxford: J. H. J. Parker, 1847.

Winston, Charles. *Mémoires Illustrative of the Art of Glass-Painting*. London: Murray, 1865.

Woodforde, Christopher. "Foreign Stained and Painted Glass in Norfolk," *Norfolk Archeology* 26 (1938): 73–84.

8 HISTORIC REVIVALS IN GERMANY, FRANCE, BELGIUM, AND ITALY

Germany

Bornschein, Falko, Ulrike Brinckmann and Ivo Rauch, intro. Rüdiger Becksmann. *Erfurt. Köln. Oppenheim. Quellen und Studien zur Restaurierungsgeschichte mittelalterlicher Farbverglasungen*, CVMA Germany, Studies Series 2, Berlin, 1996

Beresford Hope, A.J.B. *Copies of Paintings on Glass in Christ Church, County of Kent, executed by the Royal Establishment for Painting on Glass, Munich, by the order of A.J.B. Beresford Hope*, Munich, 1852.

Eggert, F. X. *Die Glasgemälde in der neuerbauten Mariahilf-Kirche in der Vorstadt Au, München. Ein Geschenk seiner Majestat des Königs Ludwigs I von Bayern*, Munich, 1845.

Farnsworth, Jean, Carmine R. Croce, and Joseph F. Chorpenning, O.S.F.S. *Stained Glass in Catholic Philadelphia*, Philadelphia: St. Joseph's University Press, 2002.

Fischer, Josef L. *Vierzig Jahre Glasmalkunst: Festschrift F. X. Zettler*, Munich: Georg Müller, 1910.

Geerling, Christian. *Sammlung von Ansichten alter enkaustischer Glasgemälde nebst erlauterndem Text*, Cologne, 1827.

Gierse, Ludwig, ed. *Religiöse Graphik der Düsseldorfer Nazarener* [exh. cat. Düsseldorfer Stadtwerke] Düsseldorf, 1982.

Glasmalerei des 19. Jahrhunderts in Deutschland [exh. cat. Anger Museum] Erfurt, 1993.

Parello, Daniel. *Von Helmle bis Geiges: ein Jahrhundert historistischer Glasmalerei in Freiburg*, Freiburg i. Br.: Archives of the City of Freiburg, 2000.

Walter Schulten, ed. *Religiöse Graphik aus der Zeit des Kölner Dombaus 1842–1880* [exh. cat., Diocesan Museum] Cologne, 1980.

Tiroler Glasmalerei. *Die Tiroler Glasmalerei, 1886–93: Bericht über die Thätigkeit des Hauses*, Innsbruck, 1894.

Schneider-Henn, Dietrich. "Die Tiroler Glasmalerei im Zeitalter der Weltausstellung," *Antiquitäten-Zeitung* No. 16 (1983): esp. XII–XV and IXX.

Vaughan, William. *German Romantic Painting*, New Haven: Yale University Press, 1980.

Vaassen, Elgin and Peter Van Treeck. "Das Görresfenster im Kölner Dom," *Kölner Domblatt* 46 (1981): 21–62.

Vaassen, Elgin. *Bilder auf Glas: Glasgemälde zwischen 1780 und 1870*. Munich: Deutscher Kunstverlag, 1997.

France

Alliou, Didier, et. al. *Le Vitrail au XIXe siècle et les ateliers manceaux* [exh. cat., Collègiale Saint-Pierre-la Cour] Le Mans, 1998, esp. Chantal Bouchon, "Un approche du vitrail," 21–37 and Isabelle Isnard, "Les archéologues et le vitrail," 81–101.

Brisac, Catherine and Chantal Bouchon. *Les Vitraux de la Basilique de Sainte-Clotilde à Paris*, Paris, 1987.

Id. "Le vitrail au XIXe siècle: état des travaux et bibliographie," *Revue de l'art* 17 (1986): 25–38.

Brisac, Catherine, Alain Erlande-Brandenburg, Jean-Michel Léniaud, et. al. *L'Achèvement de la cathédrale de Limoges au XIXe siècle* [exh. cat., Ministère de la Culture] Limoges, 1988.

Bouchon, Chantal, et al. *Ces Eglises du dix-neuvième siècle*, Amiens: Encrage, 1993.

Bourassé, Jean Jacques and Manceau (cannon). *Verrières du coeur de l' église metropolitaine de Tours*, Paris, 1849.

Didron, Adolph Napoléon (l'ainé). "Peinture sur Verre: Vitrail de la Vierge," *Annales archéologiques* 1 (1844): 147–153.

Foucart, Jacques. *Ingres: Les cartons de vitraux des collections du Louvre* [62 Exposition-dossier du département de Peintures] Paris: Reunion des Musées Nationaux, 2002.

Le Vieil, Pierre. *L'Art de la peinture sur verre et de la vitrerie*, Paris: L.-F. Delatour, 1774; repr. Geneva: Minkoff, 1973.

Raguin, Virginia. "Revivals, Revivalists, and Architectural Stained Glass." *Journal of the Society of Architectural Historians* 49/3 (1990): 310–329.

Thévenot, Etienne. *Recherches historiques sur la cathédrale suivies d'un plan de restauration de ses vitraux*, Clermont-Ferrand, 1836.

Thibaud, Emile. *Notions historiques sur les vitraux anciens et modernes et sur l'art de la peinture sur verre*, Clermont-Ferrand: Thibaud-Landriot, 1838.

Id., *Considerations historiques et critiques sur les vitraux anciens et modèrnes et sur la peinture sur verre*, Clermont-Ferrand: Thibaud-Landriot, 1842.

Lassus, Jean-Baptist. "Peinture sur verre," *Annales archéologiques* 1 (1844).

Taralon, Jean. "De la Révolution à 1920," in Aubert, Marcel, et al. *Le Vitrail français*, Paris: Editions Deux Mondes, 1958, 273–91.

Hucher, Eugène, *Calques des vitraux peints de la cathédrale du Mans*. Paris: Didron, 1864.

Id. *Vitraux peints de la cathédrale du Mans; ouvrage renfermant les réductions des plus belles verrières et la description complète de tous les vitraux de cette cathédrale*. Paris: Didron, 1865.

Verdier, Paul. "Le Service des Monuments Historiques, son histoire, organization, administration, législation (1830–1934)," *Centenaire du Service*, vol. 1 (Paris, 1934), 53–286.

Viollet-le-Duc, Eugène. "Vitrail," *Dictionnaire raisonné de l'architecture française*, 1869; repr. Paris: V. A. Morel, 1876, vol. 9, 374–462.

Belgium

Ladon, Gust, and Theo Merten. *Uit Licht Geboren: Gust Ladon (1863–1942) Hoogtepunt van Neogotische Glasschilderkunst*, Lommel, 1990, esp. 97–112.

Vanden Bemden, Yvette, Jost Caen, Warner Berckmans, Anne Malliet, and Lode Lambrechts. *Glas in Lood*, Brussels: Ministerie van de Vlaamse Gemeenschap, Bestuur Monumenten en Landschappen, 1992.

9 THE OPALESCENT, ART NOUVEAU, AND ARTS AND CRAFTS MOVEMENTS

Adams, David. "Frederick S. Lamb's Opalescent Vision of 'A Broader Art': The Reunion of Art and Craft in Public Murals," in Bert Denker, ed. *The Substance of Style: Perspectives on the American Arts and Crafts Movement*, Winterthur, Del.: Henry Francis Dupont Winterthur Museum, 1996, 317–40.

Adams, Henry, et al. *John La Farge*, New York: Abbyville Press, 1986.

Bowe, Nicola Gordon with David Caron and Michael Wynne. *Gazetteer of Irish Stained Glass*, Dublin: Irish Academic Press, 1988.

Bowe, Nicola Gordon. *The Life and Works of Harry Clarke*, Dublin: Irish Academic Press, 1989.

Id. *The Arts and Crafts Movements in Dublin & Edinburgh: 1885–1925*, Dublin: Irish Academic Press, 1998.

Burke Doreen Bolger, et al. *In Pursuit of Beauty* [exh. cat., Metropolitan Museum of Art] New York, 1986.

Cormack, Peter. "Christopher Whall," *Stained Glass* 76 (1981-82): 320–118.

Donnelly, Michael. *Glasgow Stained Glass: A Preliminary Study*, Glasgow: Glasgow Museums and Art Galleries, 1981.

Duncan, Alastair, Martin Eidelberg, and Neil Harris. *Masterworks of Louis Comfort Tiffany*, New York: Harry Abrams, 1989.

Eidelberg, Martin and Nancy A. McClelland. *Behind the Scenes of Tiffany Glassmaking: The Nash Notebooks*, New York: St. Martin's Press with Christie's Fine Arts Auctioneers, 2000.

Faude, Wilson H. "Associated Artists and the American Renaissance in the Decorative Arts," *Winterthur Portfolio* 10 (1975): 101–30.

Frelinghuysen, Alice Cooney. "Louis Comfort Tiffany at the Metropolitan Museum," *Bulletin of the Metropolitan Museum of Art* 56 (1998).

Jones, Robert O. "New York Appellate Court Building: Armstrong Windows of the 'American School'," *Stained Glass* (Summer 1991): 124–29.

Koch, Robert. *Louis C. Tiffany, Rebel in Glass*. New York: Crown Publishers, 1982?.

McKean Hugh F. *The Lost Treasures of Louis Comfort Tiffany*. New York: Doubleday & Company Inc. 1980.

Powell, Edith Hopps. *San Francisco's Heritage in Art Glass*. Seattle: Superior Publishing Company, 1976.

Raguin, Virginia C. *Glory in Glass: Stained Glass in the United States: Origins, Variety, and Preservation* [exh. cat. The Gallery at the American Bible Society] New York, 1998.

Id. "John La Farge, Louis Comfort Tiffany et 'le Verre Américain,'" in *Art, Technique et Science: La Création du Vitrail de 1830–1930*, Liège: Commission royale des Monuments, Sites et Fouilles de la Région wallonne, 2000: 43–55

Spilman, Jane Shadel and Susanne K. Franz. *Masterpieces of American Glass* [exh. cat. The Corning Museum of Glass] New York, 1990.

Vila-Grau, Joan and Francesc Rodon. "Vitralls modernists catalans," in *El Vitrall Modernista* [exh. cat. Fundacio Joan Miro] Barcelona, 1984, 21–38.

Waern, Cecilia. *John La Farge, Artist and Writer*, New York: The Macmillan Company, 1896.

Weinberg, H. Barbara. *The Decorative Work of John La Farge*, New York: Garland Publishing, 1977.

Weisberg, Gabriel P. *Art Nouveau Bing: Paris Style 1900* [Smithsonian Institution Traveling Exhibition Service] New York, 1986, esp. 44–79.

Whall, Christopher W. *Stained Glass Work: A Textbook for Students and Workers in Glass*, New York: D. Appleton, 1905; repr. 1920, London: Sir Isaac Pitman & Sons.

10 THE GLASS OF THE TWENTIETH CENTURY

1900–1950-America

Quellet-Soguel, Nicole, and Walter Tschopp, eds. *Clement Heaton, 1861–1940 Londres – Neuchatel – New York*, Hauterive, Switzerland: Editions Gilles Attinger, 1996.

Connick, Charles J. *Adventures in Light and Color*, New York: Random House, 1937.

Tutag, Nola. *Discovering Stained Glass in Detroit*, Detroit: Wayne State University Press, 1987.

Frueh, Erne R and Florence. *Chicago Stained Glass*, Chicago: Loyola University Press, 1983.

Stillwell, Richard. *The Chapel of Princeton University*, Princeton: Princeton University Press, 1971.

Modern

Bletter, Rosaemarie Haag. "The Interpretation of the Glass Dream - Expressionist Architecture and the History of the Crystal Metaphor," *Journal of the Society of Architectural Historians* 40 (March 1981): 20–43.

Clarke, Brian, ed. *Architectural Stained Glass*, New York: McGraw Hill, 1979.

Kitschen, Friedericke. "Josef Albers," in Jeannine Fiedler and Peter Feierabend, eds. *Bauhaus*, Cologne: Konemann Verlag, 1999, 308–19.

Mathey, François. "Tendances Modernes," in Aubert, Marcel, et al. *Le Vitrail français*, Paris: Editions Deux Mondes, 1958, 292–310.

Moor, Andrew. *Architectural Glass: A Guide for Design Professionals*, New York: Watson-Guptill, 1989.

Id. *Architectural Glass Art: Form and Technique in Contemporary Glass*, New York: Rizzoli, 1997

Nieto Alcaide, Víctor, Sagrario Aznar Almanzán and Victoria Soto Caba. *Vidrieras de Madrid del Modernismo al Art Deco*, Madrid: Dirección General de Patrimonio Cultural, 1996.

Oidtmann, F. and L. *Licht, Glas, Farbe*, Aachen: M. Brimberg, 1982.

Osborne, June. *John Piper and Stained Glass*, Thrupp, Stroud, Gloucestershire: Sutton Publishing, 1997.

Perrot, Françoise. *Le Vitrail français contemporain*, Lyon: La Manufacture, 1984.

Pfaff, Konrad. *Ludwig Schaffrath*, Krefeld: Scherpe Verlag, 1977.

Piper, John. *Stained Glass, Art or Anti-Art*, London: Studio Vista, 1968.

Id. "Art or Anti-Art," in Brian Clarke, above, 58–64.

Raguin, Virginia. *Reflections on Glass: 20th Century Stained Glass in American Art and Architecture* [exh. cat. The Gallery at the American Bible Society] New York, 2002.

Rigan, Otto B. *New Glass*, San Francisco: San Francisco Co., 1976.

Siry, Joseph M. *Unity Temple: Frank Lloyd Wright and Architecture for Liberal Religion* Cambridge: Cambridge University Press, 1996, esp. 166–69.

Sloan, Julie L. *Light Screens: The Complete Leaded-Glass Windows of Frank Lloyd Wright*, New York: Rizzoli International, 2001.

Sowers, Robert. *The Lost Art: A Survey of One Thousand Years of Stained Glass*, London: Lund Humphries, 1954.

Id. *Stained Glass, an Architectural Art*, New York: Universe Books, Inc, 1965.

Id. "New Stained Glass in Germany," *Craft Horizons* 29 (May-June, 1969): 14–21, 69.

Id. *The Language of Stained Glass*, Forest Gove, Oregon: Timber Press, 1981.

Id. *Rethinking the Forms of Visual Expression*, Berkley: University of California Press, 1990.

Wright, Frank Lloyd. "In the Cause of Architecture, VI, The Meaning of Materials, Glass," *The Architectural Record* (1928); reprinted, id., *In the Cause of Architecture*, ed. Frederick Gutheim, New York: Architectural Record, 1975, 197-202.

Index

Picture Credits